Web Hosting

FOR

DUMMIES®

A Wiley Brand

Web Hosting FOR DUMMIES

A Wiley Brand

by Peter Pollock

FOR DUMMIES

A Wiley Brand

Web Hosting For Dummies®

Published by
John Wiley & Sons, Inc.
111 River Street
Hoboken, NJ 07030-5774
www.wiley.com

About the Author

Peter Pollock is a long-time blogger at PeterPollock.com, a conference speaker, husband, stay-at-home dad, and, of course, author.

He's also a web hosting trainer and geek (he was so excited to get an iPad that he made up a song and dance about it).

British by birth, he currently lives in California's Central Valley with his wife and three children. He ran a web hosting business for nine years, and has been building websites for even longer than that. This has led him to fall in love (possibly a little TOO much in love) with WordPress, and he can't understand why anyone would use anything different to build a site.

Peter also writes children's books in his spare time, although "spare" time is a little difficult for him to find these days.

Ultimately, Peter's passion is to help others achieve their goals with their websites and blogs — and he believes that, with a little help, anyone can have an awesome site — without having to spend thousands of dollars to make it.

Dedication

To my wife, Debbie. Thank you for loving me, believing in me, and supporting me all these years. This is the culmination of so many years of late nights, hard work, and vacations spent with me on the computer a dozen times a day. I couldn't and wouldn't have done it without you. I love you.

Author's Acknowledgments

First and foremost, I want to thank God and His Son Jesus Christ for loving me even in my sin and being willing to give it all to save me.

I would also like to thank the following people:

My wife for her never-ending patience and support (and chocolate pastries); my kids for being my little cheerleaders; my mum and dad for believing in me and helping me edit — and for that day back in 1989 when you argued with my English teacher that I was capable of doing double-English in my GCSEs; Jennie Pollock, my amazing sister, for not taking ALL of the writing ability in the family; and Sarah, Rachel, Ruth, Charlotte, and Breann for watching the kids while I tried to write.

The team at Wiley, especially Amy for giving me this opportunity and being so helpful and supportive. Charlotte, Debbye, and John for taking what was sometimes akin to drivel that I churned out and editing it into a great book. This could never have come to completion without you.

I'd also like to thank the hundreds of people who have supported me as I went through this endeavor, friends old and new who took the time to drop me a word or two of encouragement on Facebook as I went through. I'd like to particularly thank Ellen Gerstein, Kelby Carr, and Deborah Ng for the opportunities they gave me that led to this book being started.

Finally, I cannot leave out Kathy "Katdish" Richards, Duane Scott, Michael Perkins, Michael Hyatt, Molly D. Campbell, and Lisette Brodey for their encouragement, friendship, advice, and positivity. And I thank Spam, Shamu, and Amber-Lynn for taking their turns babysitting while I hid out in the office staring blankly at the screen wondering whether the book would just write itself if I stared long enough at the screen.

The list could go on and on, and to all those who remain anonymous in this list, please know that this book couldn't have happened without your help, prayers, and encouragement.

They say it takes a village to raise a child. Well, it took a small army to get this book done — and I appreciate you all!

Publisher's Acknowledgments

We're proud of this book; please send us your comments at `http://dummies.custhelp.com`. For other comments, please contact our Customer Care Department within the U.S. at 877-762-2974, outside the U.S. at 317-572-3993, or fax 317-572-4002.

Some of the people who helped bring this book to market include the following:

Acquisitions and Editorial

Project Editor: Charlotte Kughen,
   The Wordsmithery LLC

Acquisitions Editor: Amy Fandrei

Copy Editor: Debbye Butler

Technical Editor: John Saddington

Editorial Manager: Jodi Jensen

Editorial Assistant: Anne Sullivan

Sr. Editorial Assistant: Cherie Case

Cover Photo: © Baris Simsek/iStockphoto

Composition Services

Project Coordinator: Katherine Crocker

Layout and Graphics: Carrie A. Cesavice,
   Joyce Haughey, Andrea Hornberger

Proofreaders: John Greenough,
   Glenn L McMullen

Indexer: Potomac Indexing, LLC

Publishing and Editorial for Technology Dummies

   Richard Swadley, Vice President and Executive Group Publisher

   Andy Cummings, Vice President and Publisher

   Mary Bednarek, Executive Acquisitions Director

   Mary C. Corder, Editorial Director

Publishing for Consumer Dummies

   Kathleen Nebenhaus, Vice President and Executive Publisher

Composition Services

   Debbie Stailey, Director of Composition Services

Contents at a Glance

Table of Contents

Introduction

It was 2003 when I first dipped my toes into the world of web hosting — and it wasn't a good experience. The service I received was great at first, but then it quickly vanished and I was left floundering as I tried to work out how to use what I had paid for and do what I needed to do.

Convinced I could do better, I started my own hosting business and set out to help anyone and everyone understand hosting and get the best possible experience from hosting their own websites.

It was hard, and after almost a decade doing it, I really wasn't getting anywhere. There had to be a way I could help more people without overloading myself and my family. Then, along came For Dummies, like a knight in shining armor, giving me the perfect way to reach more people and still keep my help affordable.

I've poured all my experience as a host and as a support system for the hundreds of people I've helped with their hosting into this book. You now have all the knowledge I have in the palm of your hands, and when you're done with this book you'll see that web hosting is easy when you know how to do it.

About This Book

Web Hosting For Dummies introduces you to web hosting and explains in simple language all of its functions and facilities. My screenshots focus on the cPanel web hosting system because it is the most widely used tool. The concepts and basic operations behind all web hosting are the same whomever you are hosted with, though. Regardless of who your host is, this book shows you how to get the most out of your hosting.

This book introduces you to and shows you how to use technologies like the following:

- ✔ Self-hosted e-mail
- ✔ FTP

- ✔ Databases
- ✔ PHP MyAdmin
- ✔ Log Files
- ✔ Security
- ✔ DNS (Domain Name System)

The software or system you use to build your website is only a small part of what hosting your own website enables you to do. In this book, I show you how to take full control of your site, your domain name, and the online brand associated with it.

Conventions Used in This Book

I've made this book as easy to read as possible by applying a few typographical conventions.

URLs (web addresses) always use monospaced font:

`www.dummies.com/go/webhostingfd.`

When I use a new term I think you might not be familiar with, I apply *italic* to it so that you know I'm defining it.

I use numbered lists to show you when I'm walking you through a process step by step.

How to Read This Book

Read what you want and leave the rest — or pass it on to a friend.

This book works in logical steps chapter by chapter, but it is not designed so that it has to be read cover to cover like a novel.

Each separate concept or facility has its own chapter and so, if you know what you need to do but don't know how to do it, you can use the table of contents or the index to jump straight to where you need to go.

If you are totally new to web hosting, Chapter 1 is essential because in it I explain, using a real-world illustration, what each hosting function does. If you already know the basics, though, you don't need to read Chapter 1 at all.

Foolish Assumptions

I'm not going to try to even guess what assumptions you've made about me at this point — the answer might scare me. Here are a few I've made about you:

- You have a computer, know how to turn it on, and have connected it to the Internet.
- You either have or are planning to have a website or blog.
- You aren't a computer genius who knows almost everything there is to know about hosting and wants to learn the deepest, darkest secrets normally kept only for the likes of Bill Gates. This book is aimed at first-timers and those with a little experience who want to get a stronger grasp on the concepts.
- You know what a browser is and where to type in a web address, and you know that on websites you generally only have to click once on a link or icon but on your desktop you have to click twice to run a program.

How This Book Is Organized

This book is broken into seven parts that help you understand and use web hosting from the very basics to some of the more advanced stuff. Each chapter is about one different aspect of your hosting. The book is split up as follows.

Part 1: Getting Started with Web Hosting

In Chapter 1, I explain the whole system of web hosting using an example from the real world. The example I use is that of a store, and I parallel each function of web hosting with something that is required to make a store run smoothly.

Chapter 2 then helps explain the difference between web hosts and the different technologies they offer for your hosting. By the end of Chapter 2, you will have a good understanding of what hosts are offering and will be able to make an informed choice about the host you want to use.

Part II: Getting to Know the Essential Services

There are five chapters in this part, each taking you through one of the four major functions you will use most from your hosting. Chapter 3 takes you through the reasons why you would want to use hosted e-mail and how to configure and use those e-mail addresses.

Chapter 4 explains how to upload and download files to and from your website. There are a few different ways to do it, and in this chapter I describe how to do each of them and explain their relative strengths and weaknesses.

Databases are the focus of Chapter 5. Here I explain how to not be scared of them. You find out how and when to use databases and how to use some essential tools to monitor, repair, and back them up.

Chapter 6 discusses the often-ignored logs that are available from your web host. Logs have the capability to help you speed your site, spot hackers, and monitor your traffic flow. In this chapter, I explain where to find the logs and how to read them to get the most out of them.

I wrap up this part with Chapter 7, which explains web scripts and applications. Unless you are a genius and can code a site from scratch, you'll probably use scripts or apps at some point. This chapter explains how to use them successfully and safely.

Part III: Managing Security and Access

Chapter 8 explains how and why you need to take command of website security. Although there isn't a foolproof method for defeating all hackers, there is a lot you can do to lock the doors and windows and not invite the bad guys in. I walk you through all the tools that your hosting gives you to secure your site and make it as secure as Fort Knox.

The Domain Name System (DNS), which manipulates domain names and where they point visitors, is the focus of Chapter 9. By the end of the chapter, you'll be a DNS ninja. From nameservers to MX records, I cover it all and show you how you can make your site more resilient and feature-rich.

Chapter 10 deals with some of the more advanced functions of your control panel. Specifically, I look at three functions common to most control panels that can help your site run more smoothly, professionally, and automatically.

Chapter 11 shows you how to manage your control panel from a mobile device. Using the control panel is a little more tricky on a small screen of a smartphone or other mobile device, but there are some tools you can use to make it easier and more straightforward.

Part IV: Knowing What to Do When Things Go Wrong

Yes, things go wrong occasionally. Don't worry, though. Chapter 12 walks you through some of the most common problems and explains how to fix them.

There are many reasons why you might want to change web hosts. Chapter 13 helps you decide if that's what you need to do and takes you step by step through the process of successfully moving.

Part V: Increasing Control with a Virtual Private Server or Dedicated Server

Whether you're a control freak or you just have a successful site that needs more resources, moving to a Virtual Private Server (VPS) or dedicated server might one day be necessary. Chapter 14 helps you choose which is right for you and explains how best to configure it.

Chapter 15 introduces you to a whole new world of behind-the-scenes facilities that come with a VPS or dedicated server and shows you how to use the management tools you are given without breaking anything.

For the real geeks among you, your web hosting may come with command-line access. If it does, Chapter 16 shows you how to connect using Secure SHell (SSH), and introduces you to some of the command-line functions you'll need.

Part VI: The Part of Tens

The part of tens is in every For Dummies book. In my Tens lists, I show you ten free apps you'll find invaluable, ten things your host won't help you with (unless you pay), and ten excellent online resources to help with your hosting and your site.

Part VII: Appendixes

Control panels vary by host, so in the appendixes I give you a quick tour around some of the major ones and show you where to find everything you need.

I also include a handy glossary. The extensive jargon and technical terms related to web hosting can get a little confusing, so I lay everything out for quick reference here.

Icons Used in This Book

Virtually every page of *Web Hosting For Dummies* includes icons. Here's a quick rundown of what they all mean:

The Remember icon reminds you of something important that you will need to be aware of when doing a certain task.

The Technical Stuff icon lets you know that what's coming is a little more geeky than most of the book. This icon is used for sections that go into a little more depth than most people need to know, but some people will find interesting and informative.

A Tip explains a shortcut, trick, or technique that will save you time and headaches.

You can do damage in the blink of an eye. Warnings let you know when there is something dangerous that you need to be aware of, so that you tread carefully and avoid pitfalls.

Where to Go from Here

If you're new to hosting, Chapter 1 is the next step, so you can find out what hosting is all about and start to understand the concepts and technologies involved. If you already know a little about hosting, look at the table of contents and jump right to the section you need. The book is not designed in a way that makes it necessary for you to read it from cover to cover. You'll be able to understand and glean information from it wherever you dive in.

Part I

Getting Started with Web Hosting

In this part . . .

- ✔ Understand what web hosting is and what its different facilities and functions do.
- ✔ Learn how to choose between hosts.
- ✔ Understand what your host does and does not provide.
- ✔ Read the fine-print to understand what your hosting contract really says.

Chapter 1

Explaining Web Hosting in Real-World Terms

In This Chapter

▶ Understanding what web hosting is

▶ Mastering the language

▶ Simplifying the different concepts and technologies

*W*eb hosting is a massive industry. With hundreds of millions of websites currently online, people all over the planet are finding themselves diving into a strange new world of technology that they've never explored before. It can be confusing and intimidating at first, and many people never quite grasp what hosting is all about, what it does for them, or how it affects them.

In this chapter, I explain the whole system of web hosting, paralleling every aspect of it with things that you already know and understand in the real world.

I start by getting some confusing terminology out of the way.

Many different terms can be used to describe web hosting, such as the following:

✔ Web hosting

✔ Website hosting

✔ Self hosting

✔ Blog hosting

✔ Hosted website or blog

The different names can be confusing at first. However, with the exception of "hosted website," they all mean that you have complete control of how your website is made available to the world.

In the case of a hosted website or blog, the hosting and all its related functions are done by another company. All you get is the facility to build your site, without any access to the powerful tools behind the scenes. This has its advantages and disadvantages. The biggest advantage is that you don't have to worry about any of the background functions behind your site; you just get to do all the fun stuff.

The disadvantage to a hosted website is that you are restricted in what you can do by the host in a multitude of ways.

If you start out with a hosted site, it's most likely that after a year or so you will find that the limits and restrictions imposed by your host make it too difficult for your site to expand the way you want it to. This is the time to move to self hosting.

Conceptualizing Web Hosting

For any website to be available for viewing on the World Wide Web, it has to be on a computer that is connected to the Internet. The computer your site is on is known as its *host*.

The host can be any computer at all, anywhere in the world. Your computer at home can host your website, if you want. You could also use a computer in your office, in a warehouse, or even in a shed. All you need for the host are

- ✔ Power
- ✔ An Internet connection
- ✔ A dedicated IP address

Each computer or device that connects to the Internet has an IP address. This address is unique and allows other computers on the Internet to find you. It's just as unique as the street address of your house. Most homes and even some businesses have a *dynamically allocated* IP address, which means that their Internet Service Provider (ISP) allocates the person or business an IP address each time a connection is made to the Internet. The IP address could be different for every connection.

For a site to be readily found online, it needs to always have the same IP address, which is called a *dedicated IP address*.

Think of it as a party. The person whose house the party is at is called the host. In the same way, the computer that your website resides on is the website host. That host has an address, which is how you can find the party. Likewise, your web host has an address, which is how the Internet finds your site.

The *IP* in the term *IP address* stands for *Internet Protocol.* The current version is Internet Protocol version 4 (IPv4), which has numeric addresses in the format xxx.xxx.xxx.xxx. There are approximately 4.29 billion possible combinations — and thus, 4.29 billion possible addresses. The problem with that, though, is that each device requires its own address. There are so many devices connected to the Internet that we're just about to run out of addresses. The solution is to move to IPv6, which has billions of times more addresses and is starting to be phased in now.

You could get your own dedicated IP address at home and host your site on your own computer, but what happens when the power goes out, your Internet connection goes down, or you need to reboot your computer? All of a sudden your website wouldn't be available for anyone to see, which would be bad.

Imagine each website you visit is in a house. Wouldn't it be annoying if you couldn't get to Google.com because the house it is in has a power outage? Or what if you couldn't open Amazon.com because it was on a computer in someone else's house and the phone lines went down?

The Internet would be terrible if that were the case. Sites would be up and down like yo-yos, and you would never be able to rely on a site to be up when you wanted to visit it.

The solution to this problem is web servers, which, as the name suggests, are dedicated machines that exist solely to serve websites to whomever wants to see them.

Servers are located in buildings called *data centers,* which are built specifically for housing web servers. Data centers have all manner of backup systems and generators to ensure everything keeps running smoothly. They have Internet connections coming in from multiple different companies so if one or more go down, there are always others to take the load. They have a whole host of other safety features — all with the aim of making your site available 24 hours a day, seven days a week.

Each server can host multiple websites, depending on the size of the sites. This is called *shared hosting.* Some servers, however, are dedicated just to one site or to a small number of sites belonging to one person or organization. These are called *dedicated servers.*

That's all that web hosting is. It's simply having space online to house your website and serve it to any visitors who come looking.

Now that you know what hosting *is,* I'm going to explain in simple terms what some of its main functions are and how they relate to your website.

Thinking about Your Site as a Store

To help you understand the different functions involved, I break hosting down for you with an analogy that you can easily understand. This will help you quickly and easily see which functions do what and when you will need them.

Even if you don't intend to use your website or blog to sell things, think of your site as a store and your visitors as customers to that store. The analogy works just as well whether you are selling something or not.

A blog is just a website designed to be easily updated with new posts. In this book, I mostly use the term *website* to mean blogs.

Imagine you are opening a new store. To open your store, you need

- ✔ A name
- ✔ A location
- ✔ Staff
- ✔ Products to sell

If any one of those essential items is missing, your store can't open, so you have to, at the very minimum, have all those things in place.

The same is true of a website. To start a website, you need the following:

- ✔ A name (the domain name)
- ✔ A location (a web server)
- ✔ Staff (someone to maintain and update your site — probably you)
- ✔ Products (something on the site for visitors to read/see/buy)

Without those four basic elements, you cannot get your website up and running.

In your hypothetical store, you might also want the following items:

- ✔ Security
- ✔ Advertising
- ✔ Decor
- ✔ An office
- ✔ Keys to get in
- ✔ Insurance
- ✔ An easy way to get new stock

These things are also available for your website. Security and advertising are self-explanatory, but the other items in a brick-and-mortar store translate to the following things on your website:

- ✔ Decor = the design of your site
- ✔ An office = your hosting control panel
- ✔ Keys to get in = your username and password
- ✔ Insurance = a good backup system
- ✔ A way to get stock = FTP

FTP stands for *File Transfer Protocol.* Most people don't realize that the http at the beginning of a web address stands for HyperText Transfer Protocol. The difference between the two is that when you specify http, the computer knows that you want to open the file and display whatever is inside it. When you use FTP, the computer knows you want to transfer the whole file to another location rather than displaying it.

Giving your store a name

When you open a store in the real world, the name is not the first thing you need. It helps to have the name first, but it isn't essential. In the hosting world, though, the site name, known as the domain name, is the first thing you need to decide on.

You can't buy hosting and start designing your site until you have decided on a name and have purchased the domain name. See Chapter 2 for an explanation of how to pick a name.

Finding the right location (and landlord)

As I explain earlier in this section, you should picture your website as a store regardless of whether you're actually selling anything.

Remember that in this analogy, your hosting is like a building that your store is in, and your website is the decor, products, and everything else that goes inside the store.

When you first open a store, you need to find a building you can lease in a good location at the right price.

You may want it in the local shopping mall, but that has its drawbacks because then you're restricted by the mall's opening hours and by its rules and regulations about what you can and can't do.

Alternatively, you may want to lease some property of your own or get some space in a strip mall. With the strip mall, you have more freedom but are still somewhat restricted; if you lease a piece of land, you're free to do whatever you like on it (providing the city council allows you).

Finding somewhere to host your website is the same. You can go for a hosted website as described earlier in the chapter, but a hosted site is like being in a mall. The plethora of restrictions might outweigh the benefits.

You can locate your site in the web-hosting equivalent of a strip mall — a shared server. There, you're fairly free to do what you want, but you're sharing the space with possibly hundreds of other sites, and some things you do might affect them (and vice versa).

The final option is to lease your own server. Like leasing your own plot of land, nobody can tell you what you can and can't do on your own server.

 Don't try to go too big too fast; your web hosting can grow with your website. Unless you know you will be getting thousands of visitors from the get-go, you don't need top-of-the-line hosting right from the start.

With a physical store, not only do you have to find the right location, but (unless you buy the land yourself) you need to make sure you have a landlord you can work with.

Your landlord leases you the building and is responsible for the physical building. It's his responsibility to make sure the walls are sound and the roof doesn't collapse, but beyond that, everything is up to you. If one of your racks or product display stands breaks, it isn't your landlord's responsibility. It's yours.

The same is true of your hosting. The web hosting company you buy hosting from is renting you space on a computer connected to the Internet. It's the web host's responsibility to make sure the computer keeps working and the Internet connection stays live, but beyond that, it's all up to you.

Most store owners only contact their landlords to pay the rent or to tell them when there is a problem with the building. Likewise, website owners only need to contact the web hosting company to pay the hosting charge or to report that the server seems not to be working correctly.

Ask around online to find out how good your chosen web host is as a landlord — in other words, how good the host's service, response time, and communication are.

Hiring the right staff

Before paying for hosting, think about who is going to keep the website updated. If you were opening a business, you'd have to think about what staff you are going to have in the store, whether you'll sell enough to pay them, and whether you'll ever get any sleep with all the work you'll have to do.

Keeping a website updated is very similar. Whether you're creating a site for your community group, a blog, or even an online store, who is going to keep it updated? It always sounds easy, but the challenge of writing every day or remembering to update the website with new events or even adding and deleting products can soon drive even the most patient person to insanity.

Stocking the shelves

It is not enough to open a store and stock the shelves once then never restock them. The stock on the shelves needs to be replenished regularly or people will have nothing to come back to buy.

Likewise, unless the content on your website changes regularly, there is nothing new for people to come back to your site for. Not all websites need to be updated daily, but regular new information gives your visitors a reason for continuing to return on a regular basis.

Your hosting plan and your website are not the same thing. Your hosting plan is the facility that gives you a location in which to house your website. The website itself is comprised of the files, databases, and pages that create something viewable to Internet users.

If you picture a store, you generally think of a building with products inside. What you're seeing, though, is two separate parts: a building and the decor/products. If you take the decorations, racks, products, and everything else out — and even take the sign off the front — the building is still there.

Hosting is the building. It's empty; it simply provides space for you to work in. Your website is everything that's inside the building. Delete your website and the computer it was hosted on still exists (and you'll still be charged for your hosting plan whether you're using it or not).

Every store needs an office. Somewhere where you can sit and relax without being in front of customers. Somewhere you can do all the background administration the store needs. For the hosting plan, that's called the control panel or the dashboard.

Your control panel is where you administer the hosting, set up passwords and e-mail accounts, and do all the back-end stuff that is related to the hosting but not specifically the site. With most hosting companies, you can run multiple sites under one control panel, like having a central office doing the administration for a chain of stores.

You need a lock and keys to keep your office safe, and that's your control panel's username and password that your host will have provided for you when you registered for hosting.

Stores need a way to get stock in and out, so where possible they have a loading bay. The loading bay is typically at the back so the customers don't see the deliveries being made and can't interfere with them.

FTP provides a loading bay for your website. Any time you need to update the site in any way, FTP is the tool you need to do that. It's like a delivery driver. You tell it which files you want delivered and where you want them delivered and the FTP does the rest.

Finally comes the part everyone hates — insurance. Nobody likes making insurance payments until something goes wrong, and then they're really glad to have insurance and wish they had paid a little more to get even better coverage.

Website owners face the same problem. Nobody wants to pay for daily backups — or even weekly or monthly ones — and many people choose not to, but then their website goes down and they *really* regret not having paid for the backup service.

Just as I would suggest that any company get insurance, I absolutely recommend that website owners get a good backup system.

Avoiding Misconceptions and Missteps

Building websites and purchasing web hosting are things that are still new concepts to most people. Knowing who does what and who is responsible for what does not come naturally.

A few things trip up many people . The next sections describe these things so you don't fall into the same mistakes.

Know what to expect from hosting support

Your web host will offer support in some manner. Some hosts offer phone support or an online chat option, whereas others might only offer support through an e-mail or ticket system. Either way, there are limits to what your host can do for you.

As I mention in the section "Finding the right location (and landlord)," your host's responsibility is to provide you with a computer connected to the Internet to host your website on.

Generally, the hosting support desk will work with you to ascertain whether the problem is with your site or the hosting plan. If it turns out to be your site that is causing the problem, most hosts will tell you to find someone to help you fix it, or they may offer to help fix it for an extra charge.

It would be unreasonable to assume that your host would be an expert in whatever language or script your site is hosted with and would have staff available to fix every problem you come across with the site you are creating.

Make sure that you identify in advance other ways to troubleshoot problems that arise with your site for those situations where your host cannot help. Knowing where to turn in an emergency can be a great comfort in itself.

Recognize that you're the owner and you're the responsible party

Whenever anything goes wrong at home, I always look for someone else to blame. My poor kids get the blame for everything!

The same is true online. Whenever something goes wrong, it's always someone else's fault. I never do anything wrong — at least, not that I'll admit.

The problem with that attitude, though, is that it gets me nowhere when something goes wrong with my website.

What I've learned, the hard way, is that a website is the owner's responsibility. You put a lot of time, work, effort, creativity, and money into creating the site, and, ultimately, if the worst happens and you lose it all then you're the only one who can re-create it. Re-creating it will take a long time.

You must take responsibility for your site and ensure that you have a good, recent backup of it at all times.

In case the server blows up or your host goes bankrupt or some teenager with nothing better to do on a Friday night hacks in and deletes everything you need, you must be sure you have a recovery plan.

Shouting at your host might feel good, and if the problem is the host's fault, suing the company might be successful, but neither of those actions will get your site back.

A website requires simply too much of your valuable time and talent for you to not do everything you can to ensure that you can recover it when disaster strikes.

Don't fall foul of your host's terms and conditions

Did you read the seemingly endless pages of your host's terms and conditions when you signed up?

I didn't think so — I never do either.

Web hosting terms and conditions make for interesting reading, though. You'd be amazed at what they say.

Every host's terms and conditions are slightly different, but here's the general gist of them:

"We've listed a thousand things that we could class as being unacceptable, and if we find you doing any one of them we will most likely suspend your account immediately and possibly even delete it without any notice."

Yes, seriously, your host is like a landlord, but there aren't many laws covering what it can and can't do. This means the host can, if it wants, change the locks right now and never give you access to your stuff again — for pretty much any reason.

Now, most hosts *won't* do that, but they generally give themselves the option should they need to.

Things that will normally get you in trouble with your host are pornography, illegal content, and phishing sites (where you mimic a bank or other website to try to steal people's login details).

If your site does get suspended, contact your host immediately. You'll probably have to do a little convincing that your site got hacked or you genuinely didn't realize that what you were doing was wrong, but most often your host will at least let you collect your files before deleting the account.

Don't delay in contacting your host, though, because delays can be seen as proof that you knew you were in the wrong and you're not going to fight to get your stuff back.

Don't fool yourself: Unlimited is NOT unlimited

Many hosts offer "unlimited" plans that seem almost too good to be true. You get an unlimited amount of web space and an unlimited amount of bandwidth to use every month.

You know what they say, though: If it seems too good to be true, it probably *is* too good to be true.

Web hosts work on an "average use" system. They know that for every site that has 10,000 visitors a month, there are 100 sites that have only 1 or 2 visitors. Because of this, the hosting companies play the odds. They know that while one site on the server may be using more than its fair share of space and bandwidth and is unprofitable to have as a client, there are dozens or even hundreds that have paid for hosting and are using very little or even none at all.

There are limits to that, though, and although some hosts do offer genuinely unlimited plans, most have a little clause in their terms and conditions that puts in limits. Look for something like, "Any website found to be using excessive amounts of server resources will be suspended immediately."

There's more to hosting than just space and bandwidth. The site is on a server, which is just a big computer. When people visit your site, the server has to do some thinking to deliver the web pages the visitors want to view. That takes processing time and memory space.

So what your unlimited plan gives you is unlimited storage space and unlimited bandwidth allowance, but a limited amount of processor time and memory use.

That's like saying you can have an unlimited number of cars and an unlimited number of parking spaces, but only a few gallons of gas between them.

Most websites will never use enough server resources for the limits to become a problem, but if your site is successful, you may find your host telling you that you need to "upgrade" your unlimited plan!

Chapter 2

Evaluating Web Hosting Technologies

....

....

You have a website and you need to find somewhere to host it. Sounds easy, right?

Then you start looking at web hosts and even though they try to make it as simple as possible, there are a dizzying array of options and different technologies.

In this chapter, you learn what all of the different options are and the advantages of each.

Understanding the Terms

Terms and names for the different aspects of web hosting and site building are thrown around freely by people in the industry. To newcomers, though, it's all jargon that can make you feel like you're on the outside of a club that's hard to join.

In this section, I explain some of the most important terms so you can see the difference between them and start talking like a web hosting master.

Domain names

A *domain name* is the name you type into your browser to view a particular website. For example, the website for the For Dummies books is found at dummies.com. That's its domain name. The domain name is also called the *website address* or *web address*.

Domain names are becoming a normal part of everyday life; you see them on commercials, posters, and flyers everywhere. Your domain name is important because it's what people have to remember and type in accurately to get to your website. The domain name differs, however, from the site name. Let me explain.

Let's say you own a store called Patti Percival's Cupcakes and you want to start a website.

When people visit your site, you want them to associate the site with your store, so you prominently display your store name and logo on the site. That's your *brand identity.*

When you're buying the domain name for the site, though, you want to choose a name that is as short as possible and has as little chance for spelling errors as you can manage.

In the case of the store used in the example, PattiPercivalsCupcakes.com is a fairly long name for people to type, and some people might have trouble remembering if it's Patti (with an *i*) or Patty (with a *y*). You might want to try a shorter domain name like PPCupcakes.com or even Cupcakes.com (if they're available).

All web hosts have a domain name-checking tool on their websites. You can check the availability of a name by going to your host's website and entering the name into the checker. On many sites, the checker even suggests alternatives if the name is not available.

Your website will still be called Patti Percival's Cupcakes, but its address will be PPCupcakes.com.

In Chapter 9, I explain how you can buy more than one domain name and have them all point at the same site. This means you could buy both PattiPercivalsCupcakes.com and PPCupcakes.com and have them both go to the Patti Percival's Cupcakes website. Sweet!

When many people say a website address, they preface it with www., the period inclusive. That is legitimate, and with most sites it gets you to where you want to go, but the www. is not necessary and is not part of the domain name. It's actually a subdomain (see Chapter 9 for more information on subdomains).

Hosting accounts

Hosting accounts (also called *hosting plans*) are very different from domain names. Your hosting account gives you space online to house your website. It's like leasing a building.

If you lease a building to use for your business, that building becomes your business address. You can move your business to another building, taking your name with you at any time. You aren't stuck in one building forever just because that's where you started.

You purchase a hosting account from a web host or hosting provider and, although it is often purchased in conjunction with a domain name, it is independent of the name. See Chapter 1 for an in-depth look at the concepts behind web hosting.

 The term *hosting plan* actually defines the specifications of your hosting account. The two terms, account and plan, are sometimes used interchangeably to mean the facilities and allowances you get with your account from your web host.

 The difference between a hosting account and a domain name is an important distinction to note. When it comes time to renew your name registration and hosting account, you must make sure you renew both. Just because you renew your hosting plan doesn't automatically mean you renew your name registration. In real-world terms, it's like saying that renewing your business license doesn't mean you have paid your rent.

Web scripts or platforms

There is often a lot of confusion between hosting accounts and platforms. A *platform,* or *web script,* is the software you install in your hosting account to build your website.

The platform is a group of files and maybe a database or two that work to give you a basic framework with which to design your site. The platform (the files and databases) can be moved from one hosting account to another and, like the domain name, is not tied to one particular web host.

When you talk about your site, you can say, "My domain name is xxxxx, it's built using yyyyy (the platform), and is hosted by zzzzz (the hosting company)."

For example, my site is `peterpollock.com` (xxxxx), it's built using WordPress (yyyyy), and it is hosted by my company, Day3 (zzzzz).

The three are completely separate and I can change any one of them at any time, but they come together to make my website viewable online for anyone who wants to see it.

Choosing between Servers

Linux hosting, Windows hosting, UNIX, cloud hosting, Virtual Private Servers (VPS), dedicated servers — the list of choices for your hosting is huge. So how do you choose which is best for you?

Start by defining your needs.

The most important consideration is what platform or program you are going to use to build your site. Some platforms and certain web technologies only work on certain types of hosting, so you need to know what you are going to use before you can pick a hosting plan. Are you planning on using a platform like WordPress or Joomla, or are you going to code the site yourself? If you are coding it yourself, which language will you use to write it? Knowing the answers to these questions gives you the starting point for choosing which server is best for your needs.

Any server needs an operating system and some web server software to be able to deliver websites to the Internet. The most commonly used are Windows/IIS and Linus/Apache.

Using Windows as a server

Windows servers are most commonly used by businesses that design their own sites and use Microsoft technology to build them with.

Windows servers run the Windows operating system (usually a version of Windows Server) and run Internet Information Services (IIS) to serve up web pages. The Windows server/IIS combination is great if you want to create a database for your website using Microsoft Access or if you want to use the ASP.Net framework. They are also capable of running PHP-based sites, but it is not their forte.

In my experience, Windows servers are fairly reliable and do the job well, but in general I would only recommend that you use Windows if you know you have a specific need for it. Most web technologies run better on UNIX and Linux.

Looking at the different flavors of UNIX and Linux

UNIX is an operating system originally developed by AT&T in the 1970s. Its purpose was to run the servers at large corporations and universities.

The way UNIX was licensed, the purchasers received a full copy of the source code (the code that makes up the operating system) so they could alter any and all parts of it to make it work on their particular computer hardware.

This resulted in different *flavors* or types of UNIX becoming available. Each flavor has its own strengths and is designed to work well on certain hardware. Today's UNIX flavors include

- AIX
- BSD
- SCO Unixware
- Solaris

Due to the cost of UNIX, in 1983 the GNU Project was started with the aim of providing a free UNIX-like operating system. This eventually spawned the Linux operating system, which is similar to UNIX but is freely available.

Like UNIX, Linux is being developed in a plethora of flavors (or distributions), the most popular of which are

- CentOS
- Debian
- Fedora
- FreeBSD
- OpenSUSE
- Red Hat
- Ubuntu

UNIX and Linux are robust, making them especially popular among web hosts. Linux is free, which keeps the host's costs to a minimum, so it is obviously the most popular.

Different hosts have their own preferences of which Linux flavor to use, depending on the particular hardware they have and their experience with each version.

The most popular flavor seems to be CentOS, which is built entirely on the Red Hat version of Linux, but to most website owners it doesn't seem to make too much difference which one is used.

Web hosting in the cloud

Cloud computing is all the rage these days and the hosting industry is no exception. The basic idea of cloud computing is that you join multiple computers together to provide faster, more reliable performance.

In terms of web hosting, that translates to meaning that websites get delivered faster and don't suffer from slowdowns. When one website receives a lot of traffic, the load is spread equally among multiple servers in the cloud.

Imagine it as a grocery store where, if the lines at the checkouts get long, shelf-stackers and other staff from around the store are summoned to temporarily open additional checkouts until the rush is over.

Cloud hosting has a couple of small drawbacks, but they affect only the most security-conscious users. Some users may be concerned about data security due to multiple websites floating around in the same cloud, and the potential exists for a hacker to break an entire cloud rather than one server, but for the majority of website owners, the advantages of the cloud far outweigh the drawbacks.

Virtual Private Servers

A VPS is the next step up from a standard shared server. With a shared server, all of the sites share all of the resources of the server, and if one site hogs the resources, all the other sites suffer. With a VPS, the server is divided into equal sections, and each site (or set of sites) is placed within its own section. These sections are called virtual private hosts because they act independently of each other and are like a set of mini web servers that all share the same hardware.

A VPS can be a good idea if your site has a fair amount of traffic because it guarantees a certain level of processor time and memory availability to you.

Dedicated Servers

A dedicated server is exactly what it says . . . a server dedicated to you. It is a physical server in a data center which is yours and yours alone. No one else shares it or even has access to it. This is the most expensive hosting option, but it is also the most powerful and gives you the most control over the environment in which your site is hosted.

All Hosts Are Not Equal

It's impossible to tell exactly how many web hosting companies there are in the world, but the number ranks in the hundreds of thousands if not millions.

Choosing among them can be tricky because they all make bold claims about their speed, reliability, and service. It sometimes can be nearly impossible to distinguish among them.

In this section, I explain a few things to look out for that might make the decision a little easier.

In the end, though, the best way to pick is by asking people you know which hosts they have used and which they would recommend. You can't believe everything you read online; personal recommendations trump just about every other way to select a web host company.

As reliable as Old Faithful

Most hosts claim to have a 99.9 percent uptime guarantee. That means that the server your site is on will be up and running and delivering pages to the web 99.9 percent of the time.

Let's break that down for a moment. There are 24 hours in a day, 365 days in a year. That's a total of 8,760 hours in a year.

If your web host claims the server will be up 99.9 percent of the time, that means it will be up for around 8,751½ hours every year, leaving a full eight and a half hours of downtime.

A server reboot takes maybe 20 minutes on a shared server. If the hosts are monitoring the servers, they should spot when those servers go down and be able to reboot them within 30 minutes.

So at 99.9 percent uptime, the server could go down once a month and be fixed by a simple reboot, which still leaves more than four hours of downtime for some other event. If the server you were on went down every month, even for just half an hour, you might think it was unreliable, but your host could still claim a 99.9 percent uptime.

The 99.9 percent uptime therefore doesn't really mean anything. Generally speaking, servers are reliable things, so comparing uptime claims is a waste of time.

It's simple. Servers are reliable. Occasionally, they hiccup and need a little work done on them. They might be down for a few hours at that time and, if it's serious, the downtime might extend to half a day or more. In general, however, whichever host you go with, the servers are made of the same parts, run the same software, and are as reliable as Old Faithful.

Expensive doesn't mean better

Prices vary wildly from host to host. Some offer hosting from as low as $30 per year whereas others charge in excess of $100 per year for essentially the same service.

Just because you go with a big company that charges more, that doesn't necessarily mean the service will be better. In fact, I have often found that smaller web hosts offer the best service. The big ones can become cumbersome and impersonal.

Don't be fooled by grand claims and ultra-professional presentation. Just like cheap can sometimes mean cheap and nasty, expensive can be an overpriced rip-off.

If a company is charging more than others you've seen, be careful to check what it is offering that is truly different and worth the extra money — and don't forget to ask your friends about their experiences.

Location, location, location

The Internet is a truly global market. In theory, you can tell where a company is based by its website address. Most countries have their own country codes; for instance, google.co.uk has the country code .uk at the end of its address so you can guess it's in the United Kingdom. On the other hand, google.com.au has .au at the end of it, so you know it's in Australia.

The code gives away a little about the company's location, but it isn't foolproof. Any website with any address can be located on a server anywhere in the world. So just because a website has a German web address, that doesn't actually mean the site is on a server in Germany.

Although data travels around the Internet at incredible speeds, you can expect a definite time delay when talking to a server that is geographically a long way from you.

Ideally you should locate your site on a server that is in the same country as your target audience simply for the benefit to your visitors in speed of access.

Then, of course, there is location within the same country. If most of your web-site visitors are going to be from the East Coast of the U.S., what would be the point of having your server housed 3,000 miles away on the West Coast?

Check with the web host you are thinking of using to find out where its servers are located, just to make sure they're not hidden away in Outer Mongolia or somewhere on the other side of the world.

Back that thing up

One major difference between web hosts is the backup options. I cannot stress enough how important it is to have a good, recent backup of your site. Check with your host what its options are.

Some hosts automatically back up every site they host every night. This is good.

Some hosts do not back up the websites they host at all. This is bad.

Some hosts will back up your sites for you for a small additional fee. As long as that fee doesn't make your overall hosting cost too high, that can often be worth it.

If the server your site is on goes down and neither you nor your host has a backup of your site, then there is absolutely nothing that can be done to get your site back. Nothing at all.

Make sure your host is making regular backups of your site and then also regularly back it up yourself. See Chapter 4 to find out how to create your own backup.

Sometimes the hare beats the tortoise

We all know Aesop's fable of the hare and the tortoise. The two animals race and the hare takes off really fast, while the tortoise plods along. The hare uses too much energy too quickly, though, and decides to take a nap before he reaches the finish line. When he awakes, he finds that he slept too long and the slow-moving tortoise has passed him and won the race.

Sometimes the tortoise doesn't win, though — like in web servers, for instance.

It is extremely rare in web hosting server technology that you're able to sacrifice reliability for speed. In general terms, server reliability doesn't change no matter how much you speed it up.

This means you should look for a host that claims to have or is proven to have faster servers. Factors to look for are as follows:

- ✔ **Does the host limit how many sites are put on one server?**

- ✔ **What specifications do the servers have?** Faster processors and more RAM mean faster machines.

- ✔ **Is the server's uplink port 10Mbit, 100Mbit, or 1,000Mbit?** The uplink port is the physical connection between the server and the Internet. The higher the number, the faster the connection.

- ✔ **What operating system and server software does the server use?** CentOS running Apache server is the most common combination, but the NGINX web server software is becoming more popular as a slightly faster alternative to Apache.

All these things make a difference, but when it comes down to it, don't just take the hosting company's word for how fast the servers are. Ask around because sometimes people's actual experience can differ somewhat from what a company claims.

Not All Control Panels Are Created Equal

With hundreds of thousands of web hosts to choose from, the variety of hosting control panels is significant — and the difference between them in terms of ease of use is even more significant.

Web hosting software, and thus its associated control panels, comes in essentially two different flavors:

- ✔ **Hosting software creators:** These are independent companies that don't provide hosting themselves. Instead, they put all their energy into creating a hosting system that is both powerful and easy to use. These are companies like cPanel and Parallels, which make the cPanel and Plesk hosting systems, respectively. Their systems can be licensed for use by any hosting company.

- ✔ **Proprietary systems:** These systems are developed in-house by the larger web hosts and are unique to that particular host.

Which system you use is totally based on your personal preference. Sometimes the difference between whether you feel a host is good or bad comes down to how easy it is for you to navigate around its control panel.

Control panel designs are changed frequently so what you see today might not be what you see in a couple of months.

The following sections cover some of the most popular control panels.

cPanel

cPanel is the most widely used hosting system and the most customizable.

The cPanel screen in Figure 2-1 is laid out in a series of sections, each containing related functions.

Figure 2-1: The cPanel front screen.

The cPanel control panel is highly customizable and comes with various preinstalled layout options. Many hosts even allow you to select which of the basic layouts you want to use. To change the format of the cPanel control panel, use the Change Style screen. (See Figure 2-2.)

Some hosts even completely redesign the control panel to integrate it with some of their other systems. The implementation by justhost.com is a great example of that. (See Figure 2-3.) Not only has justhost made the control panel blend in with the rest of the site, but it also has added sections to the control panel itself to provide a whole host of additional features and functions.

Plesk

Plesk, which is made by Parallels, is probably the biggest rival to cPanel, offering as much functionality with a very different layout. (See Figure 2-4.)

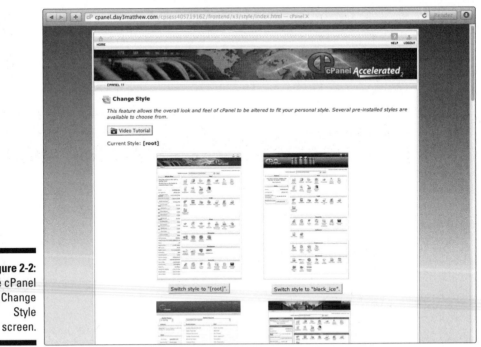

Figure 2-2:
The cPanel Change Style screen.

justhost adds its own sections to cPanel.

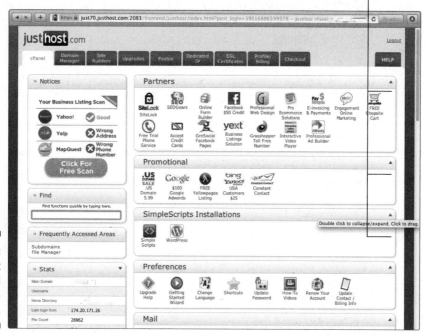

Figure 2-3:
The justhost
cPanel
configura-
tion.

Figure 2-4:
The
Parallels
Plesk con-
trol panel
home page.

GoDaddy

GoDaddy is the world's largest domain name registrar and web hosting provider. GoDaddy has created its own proprietary system to manage all aspects of having an account with it.

This system is quite different from cPanel and Plesk, but it tries to be intuitive and self-explanatory. (See Figure 2-5.)

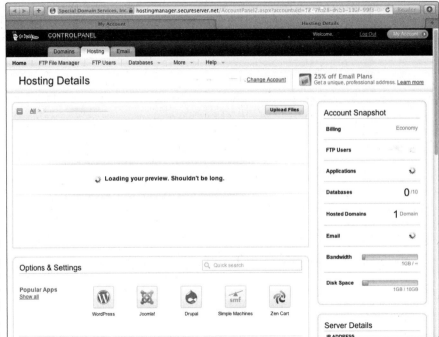

Figure 2-5:
The GoDaddy control panel.

DreamHost

DreamHost has created its own control panel, which is quite unlike anything else on the market.

From the front page, you can go directly to some of the most used functions through the Toolbox at the top left. (See Figure 2-6.) Everything else is easily accessible through a couple of clicks in the menu system.

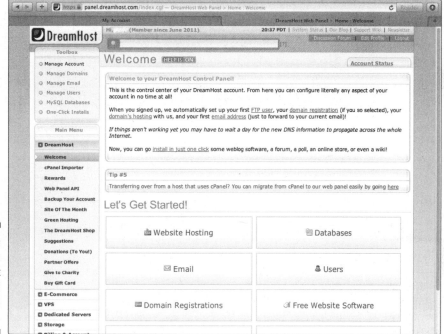

Figure 2-6:
The DreamHost hosting control panel.

1&1

1&1 has been in the online services business since 1988 and has a large presence in the U.K. and the U.S.

The control panel's front page has developed over time to be simple, clean, and easy to use. (See Figure 2-7.)

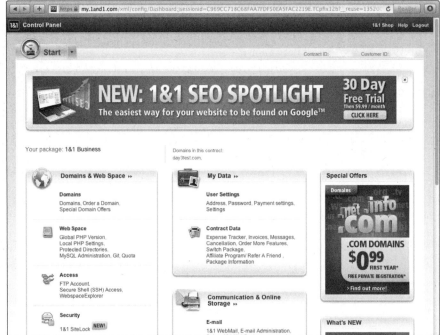

Figure 2-7: The 1&1 hosting control panel.

Part II
Getting to Know the Essential Services

In this part . . .

- ✔ Discover hosted e-mail and how to use it.
- ✔ Manage your website files and back them up.
- ✔ Discover what databases are and how they can help you.
- ✔ Find and read log files to help you see what's going on with your website.
- ✔ Install scripts such as WordPress to make your site better and easier to maintain.

Chapter 3

Using Hosted E-mail

E-mail has become one of the most used (and sometimes overused) forms of communication in the 21st century. I have difficulty corresponding these days with people who don't use e-mail. I barely remember how to stick a stamp on an envelope, let alone know what to do with the envelope when it's ready to send.

Many people have e-mail addresses that end in something like @gmail.com or @aol.com. These addresses are generally free, and e-mail messages are easy to retrieve and send. When you're first starting out on the Internet, taking the free e-mail account that is offered to you is a sensible idea. After all, you have to start somewhere.

When you purchase your own domain name, though, you open a whole new world of possibilities that make your address more memorable, more unique, and more personal. You can have an e-mail address that ends in *@yourdomain name.com*.

For example, I own the domain name PeterPollock.com. (It seemed sensible because it's my name.) So now, instead of being PeterIsAwesome@gmail.com, my e-mail address can be Peter@peterpollock.com. It's far easier for people to remember and is much more personal.

Your web hosting gives you the capability to create e-mail addresses at your domain just like I have with Peter@peterpollock.com. In this chapter, I show you how to create your own e-mail address and explain why you may want to do so.

Enhancing Your Brand with a Personalized E-mail Address

The concept of creating a brand is all the rage these days. Whether that brand is for your business, club, or organization or whether it's your personal brand, people everywhere are telling you that your brand image is important.

When I first started writing this book and was telling my friends about it, one of the first things people said to me was, "Oh, one of those yellow books?" The For Dummies brand is known worldwide for its distinct cover design and its easy-to-understand content — and that's no accident.

Branding helps people identify you in the crowd. Hundreds of people and businesses are competing for consumers' time and attention, and a strong brand image helps some stand out above the rest.

Personalized e-mail addresses are part of enhancing your brand image and brand recognition. For example, if you're in business and your website is `tinycarspares.com` but your e-mail address is `peterthedude2487@aol.com`, then there is a disconnect between you and your business. If you don't trust your own business enough to have an e-mail address related to it, why should your customers trust you to still be in business next month?

Changing your e-mail address to one that connects you directly to the business encourages people to think that you believe in your business, and it gives them cause to do the same.

Even if you don't run a business as such but are trying to promote yourself, your blog, your website, or whatever it may be, aligning your e-mail address with your domain name provides a sense of legitimacy, longevity, and purpose.

Creating E-mail Addresses

Your web hosting control panel is where you create e-mail addresses. You can have multiple addresses, depending on the limits set by your web host, so you can have one for yourself and give one to each of your employees, associates, family members, or whomever you want to give them to.

You need three things to create an address:

✔ The name of the e-mail address you wish to create

✔ A password

✔ The mailbox size

To create an e-mail address in cPanel, use the following steps:

1. **Log in to your control panel and find the section labeled Mail or Email.**

   In Figure 3-1, the section is labeled Mail.

Figure 3-1:
The cPanel
Mail options
section.

2. **Click the Email Accounts icon.**

   The Email Accounts screen opens, as shown in Figure 3-2.

3. **Enter the e-mail address in the top box.**

4. **Enter your desired password in the next two boxes.**

   You can also click the Password Generator button to create a secure password, but the generated password will be quite difficult to remember.

Enter details in these boxes

5. **Enter your desired mailbox quota or click Unlimited.**

   Read the "Selecting the right mailbox size" section later in this chapter for information about how to determine the size of the mailbox.

6. **Click Create Account.**

Your e-mail address is now created and ready for use.

Picking a name

Picking the name to use for your e-mail address can be tricky. Do you want it personalized to you or do you want it more general? Do you want to repeat a word from your domain name or do you think that would look a little odd?

Take my e-mail address, for instance. My domain name is PeterPollock.com, so what should I put before the @ sign in my e-mail address? I was hesitant to use Peter because I already had Peter in the domain name, but eventually I decided to just go for that because I couldn't come up with anything else that was professional and easy to remember. That said, my e-mail address is Peter@peterpollock.com.

I could easily have picked info@peterpollock.com or contact@peter pollock.com but for this particular domain name, those choices seemed too impersonal. When it's your business e-mail address, something more general might actually be better, though. It comes down to personal choice, and there are no real rules that define what you should or shouldn't use. As a general guideline, your e-mail address should be

- ✔ **Memorable.** Your name is memorable. `CEO@` is memorable; `peterthe dude2487@` is not memorable.

- ✔ **Short.** You don't want to make your e-mail address so long it doesn't easily fit on a business card or is a mouthful to say.

- ✔ **Simple.** Avoid tricky spellings, or people may get it wrong when trying to e-mail you and the mail will not arrive.

Picking more than one name

Sometimes the solution to choosing the right name is to have more than one name. Even if there is just one of you behind the website, additional mailboxes can add legitimacy, professionalism, and a way of keeping different types of mail separate.

For instance you may want a personal e-mail address of `Bob@tinycar parts.com` to give to suppliers and your best customers but not want the whole world writing to you there. In that instance, it might be worth creating a second e-mail address of `Service@tinycarparts.com` or `contact@ tinycarparts.com`.

You can then choose whether to have them as completely separate e-mail accounts or whether to forward one to the other. See the "Forwarding Mail" section later in this chapter for details on how to set up a forwarder.

Selecting the right mailbox size

Selecting the correct mailbox size depends very much on your hosting plan. Many web hosts count the size of your mailboxes as part of your web space allowance, which can severely limit what size the mailboxes can be.

Every e-mail that comes in or that you send out has a physical size. That size is made up of how much data is in the e-mail — including how long it is and whether or not it has any attachments.

An average size for an e-mail that is just text is less than 10K. That means a mailbox that is 100MB in size could hold around 10,000 e-mails.

However, if people are sending you images, each image can easily be 2MB so a 100MB mailbox could only hold 50 e-mails with 2MB images in them.

I normally recommend a mailbox size of around 250MB, which gives you plenty of room for mail, including mail with attachments. If you regularly delete unnecessary mail and attachments, a mailbox of that size can keep you going for years. I currently have two full years of e-mails in my 250MB mailbox, and I still have plenty of space left.

If having plenty of space for mail is important, select Unlimited or put in a really high number. You can only use up to whatever your plan limit is, but at least you won't hit an arbitrary limit on the way. (See Figure 3-3.)

Select quota here

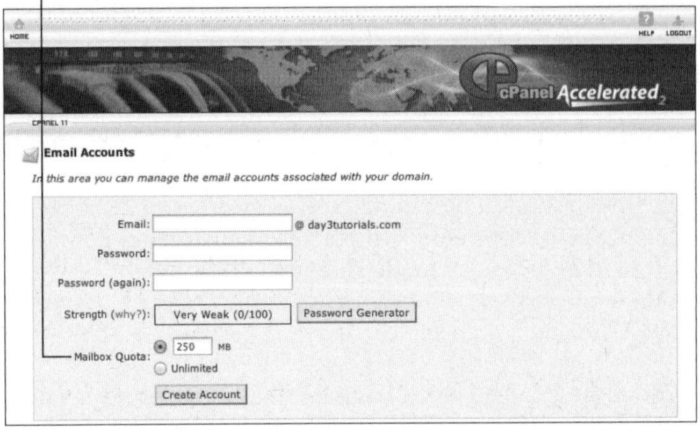

Figure 3-3:
Mailbox
Quota
selection
options.

Reading and Writing E-mail

After you have created your e-mail addresses, you need to be able to read the e-mail that comes in and send e-mail out from those addresses. There are two ways to do this:

- ✔ Webmail
- ✔ A mail client

Each has its own advantages, and you may find there are times where both come in handy. Just because you regularly use one does not mean you can never use the other(s). They work in tandem.

The webmail advantage

Webmail is where you log into your e-mail account through your browser. You normally go to webmail.*yourdomain*.com or mail.*yourdomain*.com, depending on how your particular host configures its servers.

Here are some of the benefits of using webmail with your hosted e-mail addresses:

- ✔ Webmail can be used on any Internet-connected computer with a browser.
- ✔ It's easy to use and you don't need your laptop to be able to read your e-mail.
- ✔ Most hosts have a couple of different webmail interfaces for you to choose between, so you can pick the one that works best for you.

Going offline with mail clients

Webmail is very popular, but it has one big drawback: You can't read or write e-mail if you're offline.

This is an increasingly connected world but there are times when you're out of range of an Internet connection, or your connection goes down for some reason. What do you do then? Many businesses are suddenly disabled because they can't access their e-mail to read customer requests and orders.

The great advantage of using a mail client is that it downloads your mail to your computer so that you can read and write offline. The disadvantage is that you have to configure a mail client on every computer you use, which, if you don't always use the same computer, can be very frustrating.

Reading Your E-mail in a Browser (Webmail)

Webmail is simply a browser interface into your mailbox.

Your mail is stored on the server, and a webmail client (a browser-based application) enables you to see what mail is currently stored and which items have not yet been read.

Many different webmail clients are available, each with its own strengths and weaknesses.

cPanel installations come with four different webmail clients:

- ✔ Horde
- ✔ RoundCube

  ✔ Squirrel Mail

  ✔ AtMail

Your host can select which of those are available to you and can add others.

You can access your webmail in two ways:

  ✔ **Through a direct URL.** Your web host will be able to tell you what the URL is, but it's most likely to be either `webmail.`*`yourdomain`*`.com` or `mail.`*`yourdomain`*`.com`. (See Figure 3-4.)

  ✔ **Through your control panel.** Most control panels have an easy link to click to take you directly to your webmail login screen.

Your login details should be your e-mail address as the username and the password you set up when you created the e-mail address.

After entering your login details, your host should give you a choice of webmail clients if there's more than one option. (See Figure 3-5.) You can use a different client every time you log in, if you want, until you find the one you prefer.

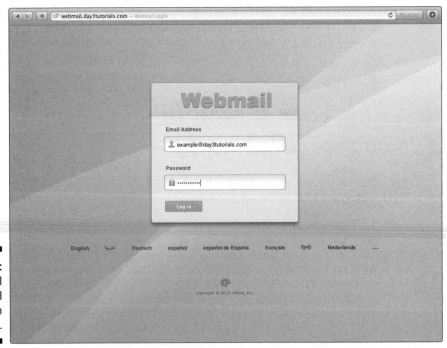

Figure 3-4:
The cPanel webmail login screen.

Figure 3-5:
The cPanel webmail client selection screen showing four available clients.

Select your preferred client and you will be taken to your e-mail.

Some hosts enable you to set your favorite webmail client to automatically load when you log in. For example, in cPanel, just click [Enable AutoLoad] beneath the client of your choice after you log in.

Reading Your E-mail in a Mail Client

Many e-mail clients are available, depending on which operating system you use. Some are free and some are commercial.

On Windows-based computers, the top free clients include Mozilla Thunderbird, Opera Mail, and Windows Live Mail. The top paid clients include Microsoft Outlook, Postbox, and The Bat!

For the Macs, popular free clients include Apple Mail, Mozilla Thunderbird, and Opera Mail. Popular paid clients include Postbox, MailMate, and Microsoft Outlook.

On Linux, all the most popular clients are free and include Mozilla Thunderbird, Evolution, and Zimbra.

Whichever client you choose, you have to configure it to connect to your server for sending and receiving e-mails. There are two ways to connect to your server: POP3 and IMAP. Both are configured through the same configuration wizard in your e-mail client, but they work in an importantly different way.

POP3

When you download your mail using POP3, the mail is downloaded to your computer and the computer remembers the last e-mail it downloaded. That way, the next time your computer checks for new mail, it knows which e-mails it has already downloaded and ignores them.

You then choose in your e-mail client's option settings how often to delete mail from the server. You can do it anytime from immediately to never. (See Figure 3-6.)

Apart from that, what you do with the local copy of the mail after you've downloaded it is up to you — and it won't affect anything on the server.

POP3 can be useful when you find that you've inadvertently deleted one of the e-mails you downloaded and need to get it back. You can log in to the server through webmail or through a different e-mail client and re-download the e-mail.

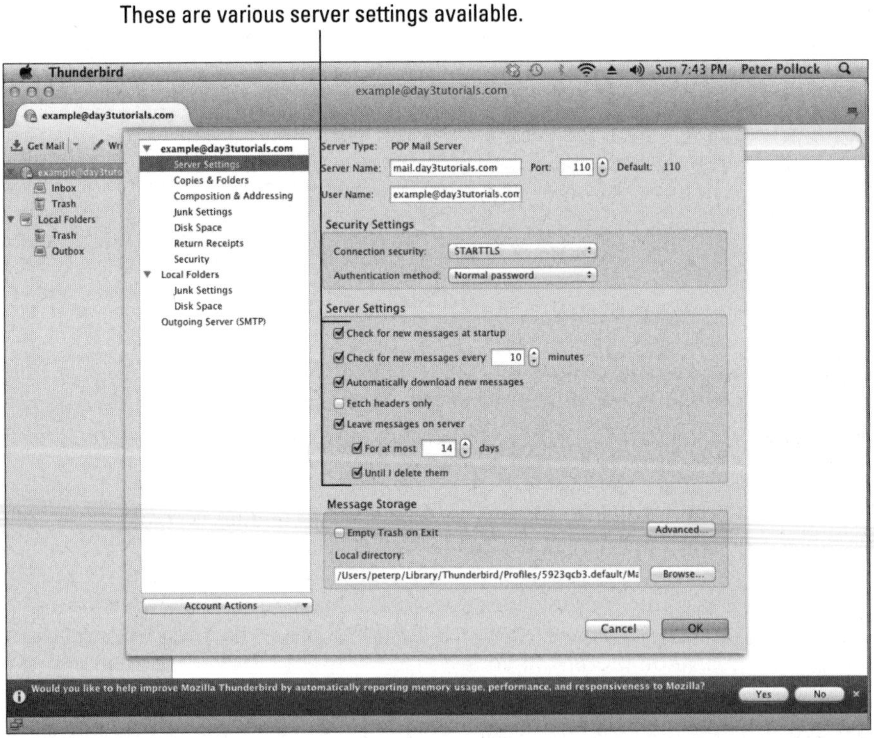

These are various server settings available.

Figure 3-6:
Setting mail deletion options using POP3 in Thunderbird.

The disadvantage of POP3 comes if you read e-mails on more than one device — say a laptop at work and a desktop at home or your desktop and your smartphone. Each client keeps its own record of what it has downloaded and what it hasn't, regardless of what you've downloaded elsewhere. This means that you can download your e-mail at work and go through and delete all the junk to leave only the e-mails you need. When you get home, though, your computer has no way of knowing what you deleted at work and downloads the whole day's worth of e-mails again and tells you they're all unread.

IMAP

IMAP works in a similar way to POP3 except instead of just downloading new e-mails, it synchronizes the e-mail in your e-mail client with what's on the server. When you delete an e-mail locally, IMAP then deletes that e-mail from the server the next time the client and the server synchronize.

This is a great advantage if you read your e-mail on more than one device. Wherever you check your mail, you always see what you've already read and what you've replied to even if you read the messages on a different computer or device.

The disadvantage, though, is that there's no fail-safe system. After you've deleted an e-mail, it's gone, no matter which device you try to look for it on.

Whether you use POP3 or IMAP is up to you. If you are using one and decide that the other would be more suited to you, you can switch without any problems. However, you should not try to use both concurrently or it may cause problems.

Reading Your E-mail on Your Mobile Device

Mobile devices, whether they are smartphones or tablets, can give you full e-mail functionality providing they have an Internet connection.

You can, if you wish, use webmail through your mobile browser, but most webmail clients do not display very well on the smaller screens typically found on mobile devices.

Most mobile devices come with clients preinstalled that handle mail either through POP3 or IMAP. There are some alternative clients that you can download onto your device, but all have their weaknesses.

Becoming Friends with Your Auto-Responder

Auto-responders, or auto-replies, can be really useful tools or the bane of your existence, depending on how you use them. Many people dislike receiving automated replies when they've spent time crafting an e-mail, but used the right way, auto-replies can be helpful.

The idea of an auto-responder is that it automatically replies to every e-mail you receive. This can be useful when

✔ You go on vacation and want to let people know you won't respond until after a certain date.

✔ You're particularly busy and need a way to tell people they may get a delayed response to their e-mails.

✔ The e-mail box is for a customer service e-mail address or something similar. An auto-responder can let the customer know that his query has been received and can give him an estimated response time.

✔ You have an e-mail address that is only used for sending mail and replies are not read by anyone, and you want to notify the sender that she has contacted that e-mail address.

To configure an auto-responder, you have to create an e-mail message that is automatically sent when necessary. The following steps demonstrate how to set up an auto-responder in cPanel. Other control panels differ slightly in the steps necessary to set one up, but the general process is the same:

1. **Log in to your control panel and navigate to the mail section.**

2. **Click Auto Responders.**

   The Modify/Add Auto Responder screen opens. (See Figure 3-7.)

3. **In the Email box, enter the e-mail account you want the auto-responder to be associated with.**

4. **In the From box, type the name you want the e-mail to say it's from.**

   This could be your name or Customer Service Team or whatever is most relevant.

5. **In the Subject box, type the subject line you want the reader to see.**

   This could be something like **Out of Office** or **Thank you for your inquiry.**

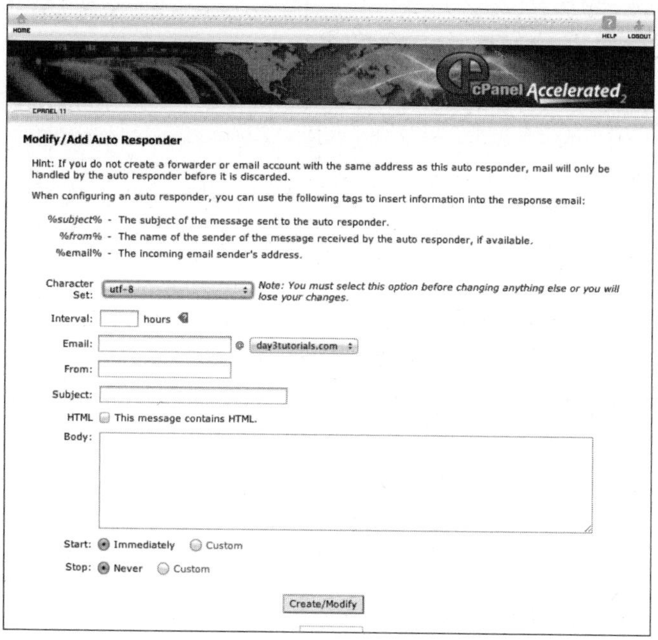

Modify/Add Auto Responder

Hint: If you do not create a forwarder or email account with the same address as this auto responder, mail will only be handled by the auto responder before it is discarded.

When configuring an auto responder, you can use the following tags to insert information into the response email:

%subject% - The subject of the message sent to the auto responder.

%from% - The name of the sender of the message received by the auto responder, if available.

%email% - The incoming email sender's address.

Character Set: [utf-8] *Note: You must select this option before changing anything else or you will lose your changes.*

Interval: [   ] hours

Email: [   ] @ [day3tutorials.com]

From: [   ]

Subject: [   ]

HTML ☐ This message contains HTML.

Body: [   ]

Start: ◉ Immediately ◯ Custom

Stop: ◉ Never ◯ Custom

[Create/Modify]

Figure 3-7:
The cPanel
Auto
Responder
screen.

6. Type the main topic of your e-mail message in the Body box.

What you enter here will vary depending on the purpose of the auto-responder, but in general your message should explain why the auto-response has been sent and give some time frame for a non-automated reply.

7. Set the start and stop dates for the auto-response.

This is important. You don't want your auto-responder still telling people you are on vacation when you've been back a week.

One of the biggest frustrations for e-mail users is getting unnecessary auto-responder messages. Here are a few rules you should follow when using auto-responders:

- ✔ Make sure your vacation notification is off when you get back.

- ✔ Don't set up an auto-responder that says you'll reply within two hours if you rarely reply the same day.

- ✔ Don't give too little information. "I'm on vacation" doesn't tell the recipient anything. He doesn't know when to expect a reply.

- ✔ Don't give too much information. People don't need your schedule for the next two weeks. A simple explanation that you're busy and an idea of when they can expect a reply are sufficient.

Forwarding Mail

Mail forwarding can be useful and can simplify your life dramatically. The following are some examples of when you might want to use a forwarder:

- ✔ **You want to create an e-mail address at your domain for people to use but prefer to use your personal account for sending and receiving messages:** In this instance, you can forward your mail to your personal e-mail address and respond to it from there.

- ✔ **You change your e-mail address and don't want to lose e-mails that come in to your former address.**

- ✔ **People might spell your name wrong and you want to catch e-mails with a misspelled address:** For example, if your name is Michele but you find that people often spell it Michelle (double "l"), then you could forward any mail to michelle@*yourdomain*.com to michele@*yourdomain*.com.

- ✔ **You have more than one domain extension:** For example, you may own the domain name *yourdomain.com* and also buy the names *yourdomain.net* and *yourdomain.org* as well. You can then redirect all the e-mail from the additional domains to your primary domain. That way when someone sends an e-mail to Joe@*yourdomain*.org, it will be forwarded to you at Joe@*yourdomain*.com.

- ✔ **You want e-mails to a particular address to be forwarded to a group of people:** For instance, you may have an e-mail address of complaints@ *yourdomain*.com that is monitored by the customer service manager. The board of directors might decide that they all want to see every complaint that comes in, so you can set up a forwarder to forward the e-mail to a mailing list. See the "Using Mailing Lists without Being a Spammer" section later in this chapter for more details.

Forwarders do not have to have a physical mailbox associated with them, but they can if you want them to.

Here's an example of a way to use a forwarder. Your new orders come into an address called sales@*yourdomain*.com. Someone looks at the orders and enters them into the system. Your warehouse manager gets frustrated, though, because the responsible party never remembers to add the sales into the system until the very last minute, and it's always a rush for the warehouse to find everything needed for the orders. To solve the problem, you could set a forwarder to forward all new orders to the warehouse so they know what's going to be coming their way. The e-mails still go to sales@ *yourdomain*.com, but they're forwarded to a second e-mail address as well.

Here's another example: Kate leaves the company, which means she doesn't need an e-mail address anymore and you delete it completely. You then realize that some customers might only have her now-deleted e-mail address and will no longer be able to contact the company. You do not need to set up the mailbox again; you can simply set up a forwarder to forward any e-mail originally addressed to `kate@yourdomain.com` to another person's mailbox.

The following steps demonstrate how to create a forwarder in cPanel. Other control panels differ slightly in the steps necessary to set one up, but the general process is the same:

1. **Log into your control panel and find the mail section.**
2. **Click the Forwarders icon.**
3. **Click the Add Forwarder button to add a new forwarder.**

   A Forwarders screen opens from which you can set the specifics of the forwarder. (See Figure 3-8.)
4. **Enter the address you want to forward in the Address to Forward field.**
5. **In the Forward To field, enter the address you want the mail to be forwarded to.**

   This has to be a real address, either that of an individual or a mailing list.

Figure 3-8:
The cPanel
add mail
forwarder
screen.

Depending on your host, you may also be able to select some different forwarding options (see Figure 3-9):

- ✔ **Discard with Error to Sender:** Send e-mails straight to the trash after notifying the sender of the message that the e-mail address no longer exists.

- ✔ **Forward to a System Account:** Some system administrators like to use a system e-mail account that is a background account without a real address. Messages can't be sent from this type of account, but it is used to receive important notifications about the server.

- ✔ **Pipe to a Program:** Some software can receive e-mails such as orders and read the details automatically. If you have software that can do this, you need to set up a pipe to receive the e-mail. Your software designer should be able to tell you the correct path for the pipe.

Click advanced options to see more forwarding options

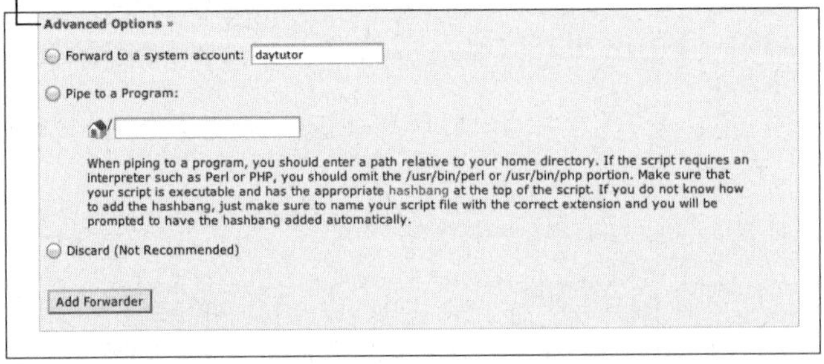

Figure 3-9:
The cPanel
forwarder
advanced
options
screen.

Advanced Options »

○ Forward to a system account: daytutor

○ Pipe to a Program:

When piping to a program, you should enter a path relative to your home directory. If the script requires an interpreter such as Perl or PHP, you should omit the /usr/bin/perl or /usr/bin/php portion. Make sure that your script is executable and has the appropriate hashbang at the top of the script. If you do not know how to add the hashbang, just make sure to name your script file with the correct extension and you will be prompted to have the hashbang added automatically.

○ Discard (Not Recommended)

Add Forwarder

Using Mailing Lists without Being a Spammer

Mailing lists are often associated with spammers — for good reason. People pay good money to buy lists of e-mail addresses so that they can send unsolicited mass marketing e-mails.

Mailing lists are not all about spam, though. They can form a useful and important role in your daily operations.

Some web hosts do not provide a server-based solution to creating mailing lists, but most do in some form or another.

Mailing lists, sometimes called groups, are simply collections of e-mail addresses that can be e-mailed simultaneously by sending just one message.

You can create mailing lists for any group of people, such as

- ✔ Family members
- ✔ Customers
- ✔ Members of your organization
- ✔ Committee members
- ✔ Your staff

Mailing lists can be incredibly useful and time saving. When you use them well, they can enhance your sales, marketing efforts, and community building. Here are a few rules to remember when using lists:

- ✔ Give people an easy way to unsubscribe from the list.
- ✔ Do not send e-mail to a list more often than you say you are going to.
- ✔ Do not send too many e-mails to a list.
- ✔ Do not sell or market your list unless you have the consent of every list member.

In the U.S., you must also abide by the CAN-SPAM Act rules, which cover any e-mail sent with the purpose of advertising a commercial service or product. You can find details of the CAN-SPAM Act by visiting the FTC website at `http://business.ftc.gov` and searching for CAN-SPAM.

Some control panels include mailing list management programs such as Mailman. You can find them by logging into your control panel and looking for the mail section. Mailing list management will be labeled Mailing Lists or Mail Groups.

Using Server-Based Anti-Spam

The single biggest hurdle when hosting your own e-mail addresses is filtering spam.

If you have an account with Gmail, Yahoo! Mail, or one of the other many free e-mail providers, it is almost certainly filtered for junk and viruses by some pretty sophisticated software.

When you first create your own hosted addresses in your control panel, they most likely have no filters on them at all, which can make for a messy — and dangerously vulnerable — e-mail account.

Most web hosts provide optional spam filters that you have to turn on and configure yourself.

These different spam filters work in different ways and require some monitoring and configuration, but they will help you greatly reduce the amount of spam you receive.

Many filters are available. BoxTrapper and SpamAssassin are two of the most common filters.

Find your options by logging in to your control panel and looking for the Mail section. In that section, if your host provides them, you will see some spam protection options.

On cPanel, for example, BoxTrapper and SpamAssassin are almost always installed. Here's how they work.

BoxTrapper

BoxTrapper prevents any e-mail address from sending mail to you unless it is on a *whitelist*.

A whitelist is a list of allowed e-mail addresses. Users can also create a blacklist that contains banned e-mail addresses. The same terms are used to apply to IP addresses when dealing with website security.

E-mail addresses can get onto a BoxTrapper whitelist in two ways:

- ✔ You manually add them to the list
- ✔ The senders verify they are real.

BoxTrapper sends an e-mail to any unverified senders asking them to respond to prove that they are legitimate senders. Spammers who send out e-mails automatically en masse using fake e-mail addresses can't reply to the verification message, and BoxTrapper will block messages that come from those addresses. See Figure 3-10 for the BoxTrapper Configuration screen.

BoxTrapper holds blocked e-mails in a queue for moderation, so you have to remember to log in periodically and check for legitimate e-mails that inadvertently have been blocked. This can be a pain to do, especially if you get large quantities of junk and have to pick through the junk in the queue to find real, non-spam messages.

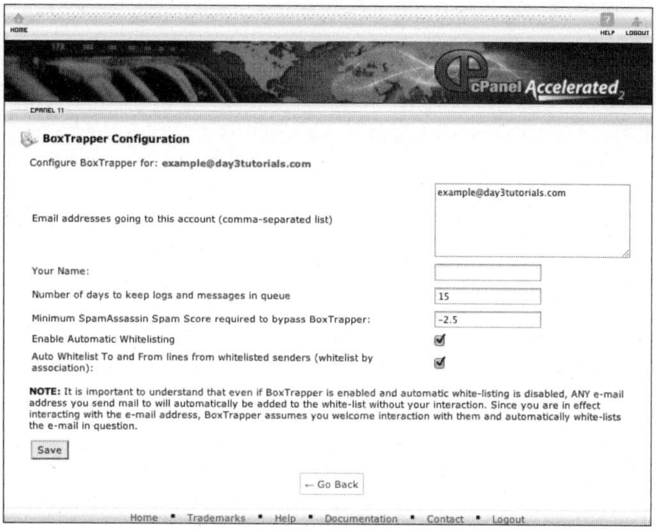

Figure 3-10:
The cPanel
BoxTrapper
Configur-
ation
screen.

I generally recommend using BoxTrapper only if you use your e-mail address for correspondence from a limited number of people. If you're giving your e-mail address to lots of people and particularly to companies that send automated e-mails, BoxTrapper can be more of a headache than a helper.

SpamAssassin

According to its creators, SpamAssassin is "an automated e-mail filtering system that attempts to identify spam messages based on the content of the e-mail's headers and body."

The basic concept is that, when enabled, SpamAssassin reads any e-mails you receive and gives them a score on a scale of one to ten on how likely it is that the e-mail is spam.

The system it uses is complicated but fairly effective. SpamAssassin has a series of hundreds of rules that it tests the e-mail against; the e-mail receives a score for each rule. For instance, SpamAssassin looks at the title and if the title has the word *cheap* in capitals, it gets a score of one. If the subject has something like *replica watch* in it, then it might get a score of somewhere around three. All the scores are added to give the message its total spam score. See Figure 3-11 for the SpamAssassin configuration screen.

When SpamAssassin determines that an e-mail is spam, it alters the subject line of the e-mail to have ***SPAM*** at the beginning so you can set your mail clients to filter out any e-mails with that in the title.

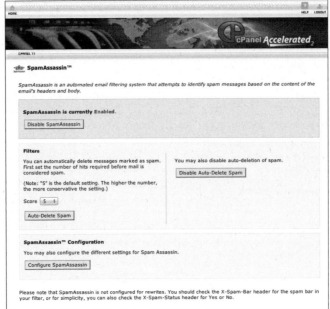

Figure 3-11:
The cPanel
Spam-
Assassin
configura-
tion screen.

SpamAssassin also has the option for you to set a score above which e-mails are automatically deleted. The default value is five, but you can change it to anything between one and ten. Ten is the most conservative setting, so if you set it at ten only the e-mails that are most definitely spam will be automatically deleted. One is the least conservative, so setting the auto-delete value to one means there is a far higher chance that a legitimate e-mail will be deleted.

Using a Remote Mail Service with Your Domain Name

The Domain Name System (DNS) has been designed so that you have almost unlimited ability to control different aspects of your domain's behavior.

This means that although you have taken out a hosting plan for your website, your e-mail for that domain name does not have to be handled by the same server.

Which server processes your e-mail is controlled by what are called MX records. (See Chapter 9 for in-depth details about MX records.) If you want, you can have a different server handle your e-mail addresses. This is actually a good idea, as it means that if your web server goes down, your e-mail still works, and vice versa.

If you want to host your e-mail on a different server than your website, you can either take out another hosting plan just for the e-mail, or you can use one of many third-party companies that specialize in hosting e-mail.

One of the most popular third parties is Google, which will enable you to use the Gmail system with your own e-mail address. This means that if you like the Gmail interface but want to use your own domain name for your e-mail address, you can have the best of both worlds through Google Apps.

Google Apps are free for individuals and small groups. To register for Google Apps, go to `http://google.com/apps`. Google has recently changed the layout of the site to reflect its emphasis on selling the service to businesses, but if you click Pricing in the top navigation on the Apps page, you can find a link to sign up for free as an individual. (See Figure 3-12.)

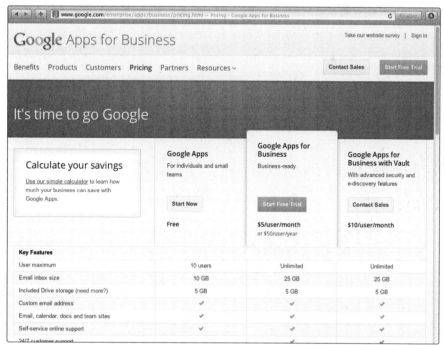

Figure 3-12:
The Google Apps pricing page.

When you sign up, Google walks you through what you need to do to use the service, which normally includes the following:

- ✔ Creating a Google Apps account

- ✔ Uploading a file to your website (see Chapter 4 for help)

- ✔ Changing your MX records to point your mail to Google's server (see Chapter 9 for more information).

Chapter 4

Managing Files

. . . .

In This Chapter

▶ Transferring files to and from your server

▶ Connecting to your server

▶ Securing your files

. . . .

*K*nowing how to manage your files is one of the most important parts of web hosting. Being able to upload new files and download backups is essential to a healthy, up-to-date website.

In this chapter, you find out how to use the File Transfer Protocol (FTP), what software you need to do it, and how to use FTP to protect your website.

As I explain in Chapter 1, FTP is like the loading bay at a store or business. It is how you get files into your site and how you get them out again.

There are a number of protocols used on the World Wide Web, and all are there to help your computer and the web server it connects to understand what you want to do. The FTP tells your computer and the server that you want to copy entire files from one place to another.

When using FTP, your computer will not try to display the contents of a file and the server will not try to process the file's contents at all; the server simply copies the file to the location you tell it to. FTP, and its more secretive cousin, Secure File Transfer Protocol (SFTP), are useful for adding content to and backing up content from your website.

Both FTP and SFTP normally require usernames and passwords, but you can configure FTP to not require a login, which is known as an *anonymous login.*

It is quite dangerous to use anonymous logins because they essentially give free access to your files to anyone. There are situations where anonymous logins are useful, though — just be careful not to give everyone access to essential files.

Unleashing the Power of FTP

To use FTP, you need four things:

- ✔ An FTP client
- ✔ The FTP address for your server
- ✔ The correct port for connecting via FTP
- ✔ Your FTP login details

With these four things, you can log in and see your server in a way you've never seen it before.

Finding your FTP details

When you signed up for hosting with your web host, you should have received an e-mail giving you all the details you need for your hosting account. That e-mail would have provided your FTP details. See Figure 4-1 for an example.

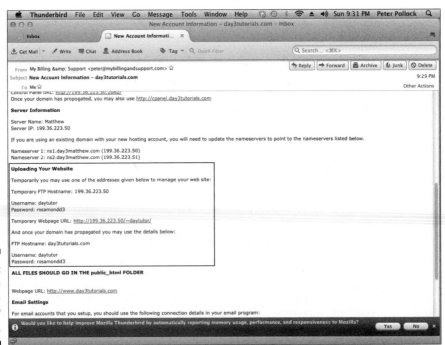

Figure 4-1:
Sample
e-mail giv-
ing FTP
details.

If you didn't receive such an e-mail or no longer have it, your host may have a dashboard where you log in to manage your account, and you might be able to access to that original e-mail through the dashboard.

If you still can't locate the original e-mail, log in to your hosting control panel and go to the Files or Websites section. There you should be able to find an FTP accounts management facility, which will have the details you need.

The details you are looking for are your username and password, the FTP address of the server, and the port it uses.

FTP addresses come in a few different forms and might be one of the following:

✔ Your domain name

✔ Your domain name preceded by ftp — for example, `ftp.your domain.com`

✔ The server's IP address — for example, 192.168.1.1

✔ Your host's FTP domain name — for example, `ftp.yourhost.com`

Generally, even if your host tells you that you should use a real name, such as `ftp.yourdomain.com`, using the server's IP address also works (if you know what that is).

You also need to know the correct port to use. This is normally 21 for FTP or 22 for SFTP — but your host might have changed it for security.

Every server has ports that it can open or close. These are simply connections via which different programs can connect to it. Your host will have configured a port to listen for an FTP connection. You will not be able to connect via FTP to any port that is either not configured for FTP or is closed. For server security, you should only open the ports you need. Imagine it like the doors and windows of your house. If you leave them all open, you are simply inviting thieves in and you can't possibly watch all the windows and doors all the time to spot intruders. Instead, you only open the doors and windows you need — and then lock them when you're away!

Installing an FTP client

An FTP client is a program that enables you to connect using FTP.

Both Windows and Mac OS X have built-in FTP clients, which are useable if you have something quick and simple to do, but are not very feature-rich. You ideally want to install a program specifically designed as a dedicated FTP client.

For Windows, free clients such as FileZilla or Free FTP from CoffeeCup do the job very well. Alternatively, you can go for commercial products such as CuteFTP or CoffeeCup's Direct FTP.

For the Mac, free clients Cyberduck and FileZilla are both quite popular. Commercial clients include Transmit by Coda and YummyFTP from YummySoftware.com.

Although FileZilla is one of the most popular free FTP clients, it has one major problem: It stores your passwords in a plain text file. This means that hackers can navigate to that file on your computer and can easily read your FTP usernames and passwords if they are stored there. The simple way around this issue is to not use FileZilla's built-in facility for remembering your password.

Installing an FTP client is simple. The following example uses FileZilla because it's my favorite FTP client, but you'll find the installation process is essentially the same for any client. Here are the steps:

1. **In your browser, go to** `filezilla-project.org`.

2. **Click Download FileZilla Client.**

   Be sure to download the client and not the server; the two are quite different.

3. **Select the appropriate download for your computer.**

   You can download a FileZilla version for Windows, Linux, and Mac, with variants depending on the hardware you use. If you use Windows, there is also the choice between a zip file and a self-installer. Unless you know you need the zip file, select the installer.

4. **Click on the downloaded file to install the client on your computer.**

   For full details on how to install FileZilla on your operating system, go to `http://wiki.filezilla-project.org/Client_Installation`.

Using FTP

Open your FTP client and you are prompted to enter your server login details. The example in Figure 4-2 shows the initial screen in the FileZilla client.

In the boxes on the screen, enter the following information:

 ✔ Your server name (sometimes called the host or hostname).

 ✔ Your username.

✔ The password.

✔ The port number your server uses. Unless your host has told you to use a different port, the port should be 21.

Click Connect and the client starts to negotiate a connection with the server. After the connection is made, you see a list of files and folders that are available on the server.

I recommend using a client that shows you the files on both your local machine and the remote server side by side (as FileZilla does — see Figure 4-3).

You can use the client to copy, move, delete, and create files and folders just like you can with the file manager on your computer.

Uploading files to the server is as simple as selecting the files you want to upload from the local column (the one on the left) and dragging them with your mouse over to the remote server column.

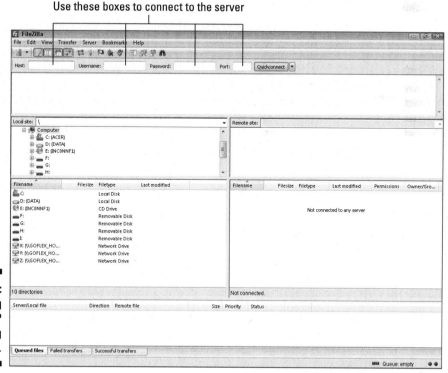

Figure 4-2: Connecting to an FTP server using FileZilla.

Dragging files from the remote column to the local column copies those files to your local machine.

Determining file location

The way web servers work, one folder is designated as the folder that is open to the Internet. This folder is called the Document Root. All files and folders in the document root are accessible to the Internet. Everything outside of that folder is protected from view by anyone online.

Each domain and subdomain in your hosting plan has its own document root. This is the highest level of folder that the Internet can see for that domain or subdomain.

The document roots for each domain or subdomain are found inside the document root for the primary domain.

Your host can tell you which folder is the document root. It is usually a folder called `html` or `public_html`. Any files that need to be visible to one of your visitors' web browsers must be placed within the document root.

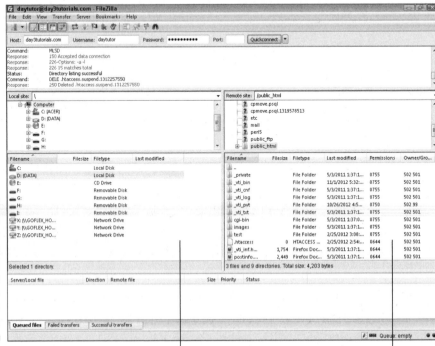

Figure 4-3:
FileZilla shows the local and remote files in side-by-side windows.

Local files

Remote (server) files

Click the folder in your FTP client to open it so that you can upload your files into the correct place.

 FTP accounts can be configured to have the document root as the highest level folder that the FTP user can see. This has the advantage of protecting system files from being accidentally deleted by you or anyone else who gets your FTP details. See the "Creating New FTP Accounts" section later in this chapter, for details on how to set the root folder for new FTP accounts.

Some hosts configure the default FTP account to have the document root as its root. If that is the case with your host, you are automatically taken into the document root when you log in via FTP. You then do not have to click to go into another folder before uploading your files.

Securing FTP

You can make your FTP uploads and downloads more secure in one of two ways: through Secure File Transfer Protocol (SFTP) or Transport Layer Security (TLS).

SFTP

SFTP is a more secure way of uploading and downloading files than FTP. When you use FTP, data is sent unencrypted, so someone who intercepts the data can easily read it. SFTP encrypts the commands and the data to provide a much more secure form of transport.

To use SFTP (also known as secure FTP or SSH file transfer protocol), your host has to have configured the server to be able to accept a secure connection from you. Most shared hosts do not allow this because giving clients SSH access opens doors for clients to get into areas of the server that the host does not want them messing with.

The FTP and SFTP protocols work quite differently, and your host needs to have opened a specific port and allowed you SSH login permission to be able to connect with SFTP. If you do have SFTP access, the following steps show how to make a connection using FileZilla. Other clients may differ slightly in layout but require that you enter the same information:

1. **In your FTP client, select File➪Site Manager and create a new site.**
2. **Select the Protocol drop-down box and click SFTP.**

   The Site Manager dialog box opens, as shown in Figure 4-4.
3. **Enter the Host name, Username, and Password, which are normally the same as you would use with FTP.**

Select SFTP from the drop-down box

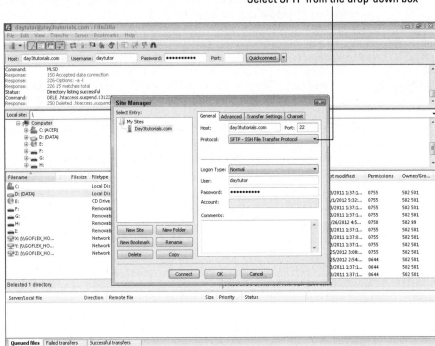

Figure 4-4:
Sample
SFTP
configura-
tion using
FileZilla.

4. **Enter the correct setting in the Port field.**

5. **Click Connect and your client attempts to negotiate a secure connection.**

If the client cannot connect, check with your host to confirm whether it allows SFTP connections.

TLS

TLS offers a similar level of security to SFTP but is favored more highly by hosts because it does not require that the client have SSH access to the server.

The following steps describe how to connect using TLS and FileZilla:

1. **Choose File⇨Site Manager and create a new site or select an existing one.**

2. **Enter your FTP details as normal.**

3. **Click in the Encryption drop-down box (see Figure 4-5) and select either Explicit TLS or Implicit TLS.**

   See the "Explicit TLS versus Implicit TLS" sidebar for more information.

4. **Connect as normal.**

Select your preferred encryption type

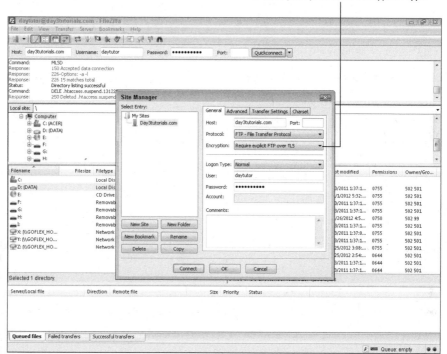

Figure 4-5: Sample TLS configuration using FileZilla.

Explicit TLS versus Implicit TLS

Explicit TLS creates a normal connection to the server and then negotiates with the server for the connection to be made secure when data is transferred.

Implicit TLS creates an immediate secure session. It is implied that every command and data

packet will be secured. Implicit TLS requires that you use port 990 instead of the usual port 21.

Which type of TLS you use is up to you, but for various reasons, explicit TLS is often considered more secure.

Setting and managing file permissions

File permissions are a powerful security tool created to give the server administrator the capability to define exactly who can read, write, and execute any given file.

Each file has its own permissions, which are either expressed in a textual form (drwxrwxrwx) or in numerical form, such as 755. See Figure 4-6 for file permissions shown in three-digit format in FileZilla.

The permissions are set for

- ✔ **The owner:** Usually the owner is the creator of the file, but that can be changed, if necessary.

- ✔ **The group:** Groups are set up in UNIX/Linux to manage permissions. Each user can be added to multiple groups, and each file can be in one group. This enables you to restrict who has access to the file.

- ✔ **The public:** Anybody who has access to the system is classed as a member of the public group. That means all users are in the public group.

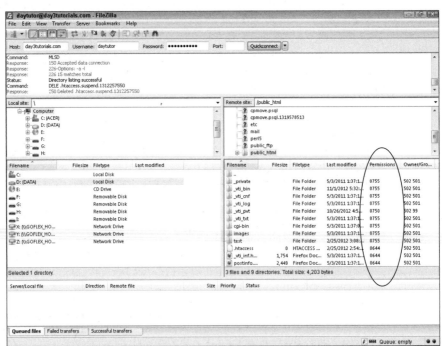

Figure 4-6: File attributes shown in FileZilla.

You can set file permissions any way you want, but generally the owner has the most access, the group has the same or slightly less access, and the public's access is the same as or less than the group's access.

The three permissions for each of these users are

- ✔ **Read:** Permission to read the contents of the file
- ✔ **Write:** Permission to write to the file (or overwrite or delete it)
- ✔ **Execute:** Permission to execute a file if it is a program or script

You might be wondering why someone would ever be given permission to execute a file but not to read it. The answer is simple: Executing a file means that you ask the server to do whatever the file is written to do. That could be displaying something on a screen or running a procedure. The file might contain passwords, usernames, database names, or other sensitive information it needs to perform its function, and although you might want to give somebody permission to execute that file, you might not want that individual to be able to see the usernames and passwords that are held in the file.

Breaking down the textual form

When the permissions are displayed in the format drwxrwxrwx, it's far easier to understand what you're looking at if you break it into four parts:

d | rwx | rwx | rwx

The first character can be (d) to signal that the file is actually a directory or folder, (-) to indicate that it's a file, or (l) to indicate that it's a link.

The next set of three characters indicates the permissions for the owner. All three characters must be represented either by their letter or by a (-). A letter indicates that the owner has that permission. If a dash is used in place of a letter, then the owner does not have that particular permission. For example, rwx means that the owner has Read, Write, and Execute permissions.

In another example, -wx means that the owner does not have Read permission (because there is a - in place of the r), but she does have Write and Execute permissions.

The second instance of rwx sets the permissions for the group, and the last instance sets the permissions for the public.

So if you have a file and you want to give the owner read, write, and execute permissions, the group read and execute permissions, and the public only execute permissions, it would look like this:

-rwxr-x--x

Decoding the numeric form

The other way permissions can be represented is as three numbers. The three-number system ignores whether you're providing permission to a directory, file, or link, and assigns values to each set of permissions. Each file has a three-digit number representing the permissions; the first digit shows the permissions for the owner, the second digit shows the permissions for the group, and the third digit shows the permissions for the public.

The values are

- ✔ r = 4
- ✔ w = 2
- ✔ x = 1

You get the number for each type of user by adding up the values of each of the permissions.

For example, if the owner has full read, write, and execute permissions, the score for the owner would be 4+2+1=7.

If the group had r and x permissions but not w then the score would be 4+1=5.

In the previous example where the permissions are –rwxr-x–x, the numeric representation would be 751.

Your FTP client should include a visually obvious way of setting file permissions, such as check boxes. For example, in FileZilla, you change file permissions by right-clicking the file whose permissions you want to change and selecting File Permissions at the bottom of the pop-up menu to open the Change File Attributes dialog box. See Figure 4-7.

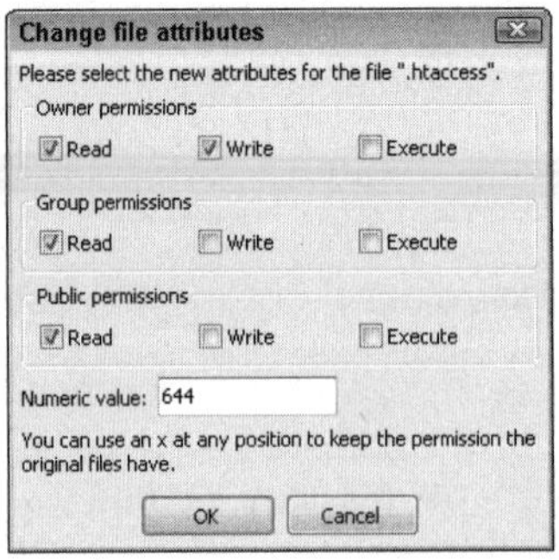

Figure 4-7:
In FileZilla, you edit the permissions of a file using check boxes.

Change file attributes

Please select the new attributes for the file ".htaccess".

Owner permissions
☑ Read   ☑ Write   ☐ Execute

Group permissions
☑ Read   ☐ Write   ☐ Execute

Public permissions
☑ Read   ☐ Write   ☐ Execute

Numeric value: 644

You can use an x at any position to keep the permission the original files have.

[OK]   [Cancel]

If you have SSH access to the server, you can set file permissions, file owners, and file groups from the command line using commands chmod, chown, and chgrp. See Chapter 16 for more information.

Creating New FTP Accounts

You may want to create additional FTP accounts for a variety of reasons, such as the following:

- ✔ You want to give someone else FTP access to your site.
- ✔ You want to give someone FTP access to just a certain part of your site.
- ✔ You add a domain or subdomain and want to create an account with direct access to it.

Your control panel gives you the facility to create additional FTP accounts. The following example uses cPanel to create new FTP accounts:

1. **Log in to your control panel.**
2. **Find the Files section of the panel and click FTP Accounts.**

    An FTP Accounts page appears, as shown in Figure 4-8.

Figure 4-8:
Creating a
new FTP
account in
cPanel.

(Figure 4-8: screenshot of the cPanel FTP Accounts page)

HOME — HELP — LOGOUT

cPanel *Accelerated₂*

CPANEL 11

FTP Accounts

FTP accounts allow you to access your website's files through a protocol called FTP. You will need a third-party FTP program to access your files. You can log into via FTP by entering day3tutorials.com as your FTP host and the username and password of the account you wish to log into.

Add FTP Account

Login: [   ] @day3tutorials.com
Password: [   ]
Password (Again): [   ]
Strength (?): [Very Weak (0/100)] [Password Generator]
Directory: /home/daytutor/ [   ]
Quota: ◯ [2000] MB
◉ Unlimited
[Create FTP Account]

FTP Accounts

[Search Accounts] [Search Accounts]   Results per page: [10 ⬍]

LOGIN	PATH	USAGE / QUOTA	ACTIONS
No accounts found.			

Special FTP Accounts (?)

3. **Enter the username and password you want the new account to have.**

4. **Enter the directory you want to be the top-level directory this account can see.**

   Users of the account will not be able to navigate above this directory. For example, you may have an images folder to which you want to give other people access so they can upload new images. Type the path from the document root to that directory, and that account will only be able to see the images directory and anything in or below it.

5. **Click Create FTP Account.**

You can add as many accounts as your host will allow. To remove accounts you no longer need, go back to the same place and select the delete icon next to the account you no longer need.

For security purposes, it is a good idea to delete any unnecessary accounts and change the passwords at least monthly.

Managing Files through Your Control Panel

Your control panel also gives you a handy way to manage your files without the need of an FTP client. This is something common to almost all control panels but is sometimes labeled slightly differently. For example, most hosts call it the File Manager, but DreamHost calls it WebFTP.

Using the File Manager is pretty much the same with all hosts, although the exact screen sequence to connect varies slightly from host to host. Here is how it is done with cPanel:

1. **Log in to your control panel.**

2. **Click the File Manager icon in the Files section.**

3. **In the pop-up box that asks you which directory you want to start at, select Web Root to go to the document root of your primary domain. (See Figure 4-9.)**

4. **If you want to show hidden files, which are also called dot files, click the option to do so.**

   The hidden files are files whose names begin with a period, such as .htaccess.

   Hidden files are hidden for a reason: so you don't accidentally delete them as they are generally important.

Figure 4-9: cPanel's File Manager opening window.

5. **If instead you want to see the hidden files so that you can move, edit, or delete them, select the Show Hidden Files check box to force those files to appear on the next screen.**

   Be careful with dot files. When you can see them, you can delete or change them just as you can any other file, and you will not be prompted that it is a normally hidden file. If you are deleting a number of files and don't want to delete your dot files, it's best to keep them hidden.

6. **Click Go to open a new window with the files laid out similarly to how they are laid out in your file manager on your computer. (See Figure 4-10.)**

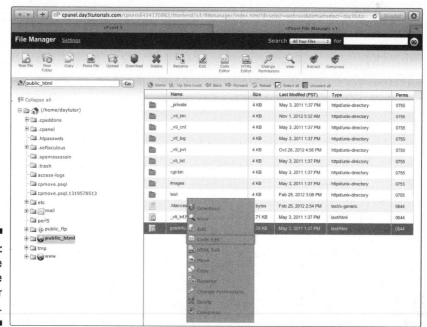

Figure 4-10: Sample cPanel File Manager screen.

You can perform functions on files such as moving, editing, or deleting them by selecting the file you want to change and clicking the appropriate icon at the top of the window. Alternatively, you can right-click the file to bring up a contextual menu.

The File Manager in cPanel is fairly full-featured and can be used in place of an FTP client for simple tasks, but using an FTP client is much easier when you're handling multiple files.

Performing Backups through FTP

If there's one thing you should take away from reading this book, it's the importance of backups. It's easy to be blasé and cavalier about backups — at least until you have a serious problem.

That feeling in the pit of your stomach when you see that your website has suddenly vanished and you start scrambling to remember when your last backup was is unforgettable after it happens.

An online daily (or at the very least, weekly) backup solution is essential. If you don't regularly download a full backup, you're playing Russian roulette with your website.

My advice is to do a full website backup at least once a month and store it on your computer, a backup drive, or a USB memory stick for quick retrieval if you need it.

To do a full backup, log in to your server through FTP and drag everything from the document root to a folder on your computer.

It may take a while, but eventually all the files will be copied to your computer and you can then do what you like with them to store them.

If you have databases connected to your account, you should also back them up. In fact, you should back up your databases more frequently than your files. See Chapter 5 for details on how to back up your databases.

Chapter 5

Working with Databases — It's Essential

In This Chapter

▶ Understanding databases

▶ Figuring out how to use databases

▶ Maintaining databases

▶ Creating database backups

S ay the word *database* and many people run for the hills. The realm of databases can seem like an area that is way too technical and too advanced for most web users. Don't worry, though; by reading this chapter, you find out that databases aren't so scary.

In fact, working with databases is easy when you have the right knowledge, and they are powerful, essential tools for building fast, dynamic, modern websites.

In this chapter, I explain what databases are; how they work; and how you can use, modify, and protect them.

Understanding That Databases Are Information Storage Systems

In essence, a database is simply a structured way to store information (data). We all have and use databases on a regular basis, although we don't necessarily think of them like that.

Your address book is a good example of a database you use regularly. It holds names, addresses, phone numbers, and other information. Your address book has the following qualities:

✔ It stores information.

✔ It is indexed (by alphabet) for the quick retrieval of information.

✔ It has a data retrieval system. In this case, the database retrieval system is comprised of your hands and eyes as you search through the address book.

✔ It sometimes requires a cleanup.

A database is an electronic version of your address book. A database has the following qualities:

✔ It stores information. This information can be anything you want.

✔ It is indexed for the quick retrieval of information. Indexing links pieces of data and keeps data stored in a quickly searchable order,

✔ It has a data retrieval system. The retrieval system is called a query. You make the query and the computer does the hard work of searching for what you want.

✔ It sometimes requires a cleanup. Like your address book, the database can get messy with deleted and changed entries, so some easy cleanup is required every now and then.

Databases can store pretty much any information you want and — as long as you have set up the databases correctly — they can index that information well for extremely fast look-ups.

Every database is made up of three elements:

✔ Tables

✔ Fields

✔ Records

A *table* is a new store of information, and you can have as many tables in a database as you want.

For instance, if you computerize the paper "databases" you use at home, you might have a table for names and addresses, another table for your Christmas card list, and another for recording important events (such as baby's first words, when baby started walking, and so on).

Each table is broken up into *fields*. For example, your names and addresses table might have fields for first name, last name, address, town, ZIP code, birthday, and phone number.

When you first create a database, the table is empty, but it's ready to have information entered into it, just like after you purchased a new address book.

To fill the database, you create *records,* one per person or event inside the table. Each record consists of a set of data in each of the fields.

You can set various properties for each field. For example, the birthdays might have to be in a specific date format, and the ZIP code might have to be five digits long to be accepted. That way, information remains consistent through all the records, which helps in indexing and retrieving data.

You can also set which fields are required and which are optional. A new record cannot be stored unless all the required fields are completed, but it can be stored without any data in the optional fields. For example, in the names and addresses table, you could set the first name and last name of the person as required fields. After all, what is the use of storing someone's address if you don't also store the name of the person who lives there?

You can set many other rules for fields, too, such as that the data in them has to be unique. You don't want the same person's name multiple times on your Christmas card list, so in this instance, you might make the name field a unique field to prevent you from sending more than one Christmas card to each person.

You can also do all sorts of other exciting things, such as linking fields between tables. This task is outside the scope of this book, but you can explore a book that's specifically about databases if you want to learn more. Suffice it to say that databases can be flexible and large, and with them, you can do things you have never previously dreamed possible.

Making Your Site Dynamic with Databases

Databases are great for storing customer details and sales records, and you can certainly use them for that purpose, but databases have another forte, too: generating dynamic websites.

Think back a few years to the early days of building websites. In those halcyon days, sites were built by creating each page individually and crafting each part of every page to look exactly the way you wanted it. If you wanted to make a change to your design across your site, you had to change every single page to update it with the new design. It was monotonous and difficult — especially if you had a big website.

New technologies were created to help make websites more manageable. You could include one page inside another, so, for instance, you could have a file called `header.html`, and make it so that every page you created from then on showed `header.html` at the top of the page. That way you could get a uniform design or menu system across your whole site and only had to change one file (`header.html`) to update the entire site.

Cascading Style Sheets (CSS) introduced more flexibility by enabling you to create a style sheet in which you defined default styles for your whole site. For example, you could define in the style sheet that every time you placed text on a page and called it a header, it would display in a particular font at a particular size.

Style sheets are actually a form of database, though you may not think of them that way. Each section of the style sheet has a unique name and definitions of the style associated with that name. Your browser then references that style sheet and searches through it for the information it needs using the name as the index. A style sheet is a fairly rudimentary database, but it's a database nevertheless.

Websites continued to grow, though, and users wanted websites to have up-to-date information and content. Businesses were creating websites, and their customers wanted to be able to go to the website to find out what was new and exciting.

The result is that companies had to start writing regular update messages and keep an archive of old messages. Each message or announcement was on a different page; as a result, the number of files in a website could rapidly become huge. If you add something new even once a day, by the end of a year you have 365 more pages on the site than you had at the beginning of the year.

Consequently, sites became slow and unwieldy, so some bright spark came up with the idea of using a database to hold the pages. At first glance, that may sound incredibly difficult but it actually is not. What you need to do is separate design and content.

Websites, like everything else, follow certain design rules, and those rules have to stay the same across the whole site to maintain visual consistency.

Therefore there is a basic framework for each page that might look something like this:

- ✔ A *header* area at the top which contains the site logo and name
- ✔ A *navigation* area underneath the header with links to all the different areas of the site
- ✔ A *content* section, where the information specific to that page goes
- ✔ A *sidebar* at either the left or the right to share more links, ads, and additional content
- ✔ A *footer* at the bottom that contains copyright information, credits, and extra site links

The dawn of Content Management Systems (CMSs) made it possible for the text for any particular page to be held in a database while the design of the page is handled separately. The two are automatically melded together for displaying the site on a visitor's computer.

All of a sudden, design and content were separated. People realized that you only had to create the design once and after that, it was just a case of putting the content in the right places.

When you look at most websites, you see a space on the screen for the bulk of the text. This is called the content area. Having an area on the page designated to content is an opportunity for a database to come into play.

You can update your site regularly simply by using a database to change the content in the content area. The design stays the same; only the content changes.

Create a database with a table for content in which each record is a new article and has fields in it for the date and the text or figures you want to change on the site. The content from the database is fed into a file that specifies how the page will look. The database simply looks for the appropriate record and delivers the content from that record.

It can seem a bit magical.

Suddenly, you have a website that only has a few files that define how the site should be displayed and a single database that can hold the thousands of records of content.

By using a database, you also have the possibility of including a search facility on your site so that your visitors can use keywords to search for older content. It's difficult to search a site made up of thousands of different files, but it's quick and easy to search a database.

The database is what makes a site dynamic. The pages don't exist as individual files; instead, they are created when the user wants to view them by pulling data from a database and feeding it into a display template.

Having a database also makes changing the site design easier. Because you don't have to update thousands of files with the new design, you update the one or two files that hold your website design, and the content is automatically pulled from the database into the newly designed pages. Slick!

Choosing a Database Technology

As with all things, there are many database technologies to choose from. In this section, I tell you about four and give examples of when and why you might use them. For more information about databases, I recommend the excellent *PHP, MySQL, JavaScript & HTML5 All-in-One Desk Reference For Dummies* by Steve Suehring and Janet Valade (John Wiley & Sons, Inc.).

SQL (Structured Query Language)

SQL (pronounced as either S-Q-L or "sequel") is a language designed specifically to handle data stored in a Relational Database Management System (RDBMS) database. This sounds complicated, but really it isn't. SQL is simply a way of getting data into and out of a database.

SQL is used in products such as Oracle and Microsoft SQL, which provide tools for using, manipulating, and developing with SQL.

SQL has a set of standards that define how it operates. However, these standards are either ignored or interpreted so differently by the companies that develop SQL products that despite the fact that their databases are written in the same language, there is often little or no portability between them.

Portability refers to the ease of moving something from one system to another. It is also shortened to just the word port, as in, "It's difficult to port the database between systems." In this particular case, an SQL database created with one company's tools might simply not be recognized at all by a similar tool from another company. Hence "there is little or no portability."

In theory, you should be able to develop a database product in Microsoft SQL and then query it using an Oracle system if you want to. In practice, it doesn't work quite that smoothly; the two don't play nicely with each other.

Products that use SQL are commercial and cost money to buy. There are some very powerful tools created by the companies to help you use SQL, though, and so the commercial products are still very popular.

MySQL

If you are really unsure about databases, your best option is to use MySQL. It's free, easy to use, and almost universally accepted by web hosting companies.

MySQL (pronounced My S-Q-L or My Sequel) is a free version of SQL developed by Michael Widenius and David Axmark and named after Michael's daughter, My.

MySQL is based on the SQL standards, but it does not comply with them fully. It was written with its source code freely available under a GNU GPL (General Public License).

You can administer MySQL from a command line or by using one of many Graphical User Interfaces (GUIs). Its popularity has grown incredibly over the last few years because it comes preinstalled by most web hosts, who also install the phpMyAdmin GUI for it.

MySQL is free, easy to use, powerful, and robust enough for most purposes. It is the database used by popular applications such as WordPress, Joomla, Drupal, and phpBB, and it is the database language behind sites such as Google, Wikipedia, Twitter, and Facebook.

Microsoft Access

Microsoft Access is a database technology developed by Microsoft (who else?) for use in its Office suite of products.

Access has been well integrated into Office so that all of the office suite products can easily use databases created with it. Access has been continually updated by Microsoft for many years, so it offers an easy-to-use, integrated system that can be valuable for small businesses.

Access is not well suited to the web, though. It does not offer great portability between systems, so although it is great for in-house applications, it is not the best choice for building a website.

PostgreSQL

PostgreSQL (sometimes called Postgres) is a free Object-Relational Database Management System (ORDBMS).

The differences between MySQL and PostgreSQL are fairly significant in terms of how they work behind the scenes, but fairly small in terms of performance for the average website.

PostgreSQL, like MySQL, has been around for a while now and has proven itself to be stable, full-featured and, more recently, as fast as MySQL.

Creating a New Database

You need to create your database within your control panel and create a special database user who has permission to access it.

When you are installing a web application or script that requires a database from your control panel, the installer will most likely be able to create its own database and user. When you are installing a script from elsewhere or are building your site manually, you need to create a database and user yourself.

The exact steps required to create a database vary from control panel to control panel, but most are essentially the same as the following steps, which are for cPanel. To create a new database automatically, do the following:

1. **Log in to your control panel.**
2. **Click the MySQL Database Wizard in the Databases section.**
3. **Type a name for the database.**

   On most control panels, the name of the database can be a maximum of eight letters.

4. **Click Create Database.**
5. **Type a username.**

   On most control panels, the username can be a maximum of seven letters and should be a word unique to the user.

6. **Type a password for the user and then retype it in the next box.**

   You can use the password generator to generate a very secure password, but don't forget to make a note of what it is!

7. **Click Create User.**

8. **Select the privileges the new user will have on the database.**

   Unless you know of specific privileges you want to exclude the user from having, it's best to click All Privileges.

9. **Click Next Step.**

Alternatively, you can create a database manually by using the following steps:

1. **Log in to your control panel.**

2. **Click MySQL Database in the Databases section.**

3. **Type a name for the database.**

   On most control panels, the name of the database can be a maximum of eight letters.

4. **Click Create Database.**

5. **Scroll down to the section titled MySQL Users and type a username.**

   On most control panels, the username can be a maximum of seven letters and should be a word unique to the user.

6. **Type a password for the user and then retype it in the next box.**

   You can use the password generator to generate a very secure password, but don't forget to make a note of what it is!

7. **Click Create User.**

8. **Scroll down to the Add User to Database section and select your database and username from the drop-down menus.**

9. **Click Add.**

10. **Select the privileges the new user will have on the database.**

    Unless you know of specific privileges you want to exclude the user from having, it's best to click All Privileges.

11. **Click Make Changes.**

Managing Your Database

As the vast majority of database-using websites use MySQL, this section focuses on how to manage a MySQL database. Some of the principles are the same for managing other types of databases, but consult a guide to your particular database product to ensure you keep your database healthy.

Databases, as I say earlier, are simply information storage systems. Imagine a database being like a wall full of mailboxes. Each mailbox can hold one piece of information and there are an infinite number of mailboxes.

As an example, say you are creating a database of all your customers. Each customer takes up one mailbox, and you keep an alphabetical index of which customer's records are in which box.

At first, you only have a couple of dozen customers, so little space is required, making it easy to pull out the record for any given customer fairly quickly. Over time, though, new customers come, some of the old ones go, and, before you know it, you have hundreds or even thousands of customers. Your index is full of records that have been crossed out, and new entries have been squeezed in here, there, and everywhere.

To get to the most recent customer's records, you have to walk miles down the wall of mailboxes to find the right one. Even if you know its location, it takes a long time to get to it.

More frustrating than that, even, is the fact that some of the mailboxes you walk past are empty because the customers' records have been removed for one reason or another.

In short, over time, left unchecked, your mailbox wall becomes a mess that makes finding things slow and laborious.

What you need is a little cleanup and maintenance. Go through the whole wall; move everything together so there are no empty mailboxes in the middle; create a new, clean index; and pick up off the floor any records that might have somehow fallen out of their boxes. With a little work, the system is repaired so that storing and retrieving customer files becomes much easier again.

Exactly the same is true for an electronic database. Over time, things are deleted; some items get re-created at a later date and some do not; records get corrupted; indexes get jumbled; and everything slows way down.

You can use tools, such as phpMyAdmin and MySQL Workbench, to automatically fix, clean up, and optimize your databases and to manually view, edit, and delete records. These tools are powerful and give you a way to look behind the scenes at the content of your database as well as poke around and do whatever you need to do.

Database management is essential, but can also be dangerous. Data can be lost or corrupted easily if you select the wrong command or accidentally click in the wrong place. Always back up your database before performing any maintenance, even automatic maintenance, and proceed with caution.

Four essential commands

You can use four built-in commands in MySQL to keep your database in top condition:

- ✔ **Analyze:** This command improves performance by analyzing a table for key indexing information to help MySQL make decisions on how to join tables and search for data.

- ✔ **Check:** This command checks for corruption in a table. This is mostly used if you have had a server crash or are experiencing weird data inconsistencies or issues.

- ✔ **Repair:** The repair command only needs to be run if the check command finds errors. It goes through and re-indexes and repairs the data in the affected tables. Obviously, the repair command cannot fix data that is completely missing or corrupt, but it is a useful tool for fixing many problems.

- ✔ **Optimize:** Running the optimize command regularly keeps your database running quickly and smoothly by defragmenting it, sorting the indexes, and updating the index statistics.

If you are proficient with using a command line, these options can be run from there. If you are a beginner, the easiest and safest way to run these commands and to do other maintenance work on your database is through a GUI. I recommend two: phpMyAdmin, which is used through a browser, and MySQL Workbench, which is a program you install on your computer.

phpMyAdmin

phpMyAdmin is *the* go-to tool for quick, easy MySQL administration. Installed automatically on most web servers, it offers an intuitive and easy way to manage your databases through your browser.

phpMyAdmin is available on almost all control panels. Use the following steps to log in to phpMyAdmin:

1. **Log in to your control panel.**

2. **Click on the phpMyAdmin icon, which may be in the databases section or may be somewhere else, depending on your control panel.**

3. **If asked, enter the user details for your database.**

   You set up the user details when you create the database (refer to the earlier section, "Creating a New Database"). If the database was set up automatically by a script you are using, there is usually a configuration file that holds the username and password. For example, if you are using WordPress, the wp-config.php file in the root of your WordPress folder has the details you need. Some hosting software does not ask for a username or password to give you access to the management areas.

The phpMyAdmin front panel opens and you see a page similar to Figure 5-1.

Left column shows databases.   Right column shows software and server details.

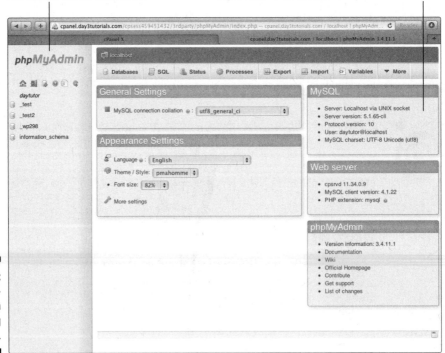

Figure 5-1: The php-MyAdmin opening screen.

A column on the left side lists your databases. Depending on your hosting plan limits, you could have a number of databases listed here, one for each web script you have installed.

There may also be a database listed called information_schema. This is a kind of master database that holds information about the makeup of your other databases. It should be impossible to edit or delete it, but steer clear of it, just in case.

The right-hand column displays information about the server and options for what you can do.

To start managing your database, in the left column click the name of the database you want to manage.

Be sure to select the correct database. Over time, you may have created more than one database, and it's important to select the right one. Check your web script's configuration file for the name of your database if you are not certain.

Click your database to bring up a list of the database tables in the left column and also in the right (see Figure 5-2). How you use all the options on this page is out of the scope of this book. *PHP, MySQL, JavaScript & HTML5 All-in-One For Dummies,* by Steve Suehring and Janet Valade (John Wiley & Sons, Inc.), is a good source of information about the functions in phpMyAdmin, but there are a few specifics I will point out:

- Select the Browse option next to any table to see and edit the data held in that table.

- *Do not* click Empty or Drop. These commands completely empty or delete the table. Unless you are sure you want to do this, you should avoid these options completely to minimize the risk of doing damage.

- The column labeled Rows shows the number of records in that table. This can be useful to help you find the table you're looking for. For instance, if you have a blog, the table with the most rows is probably your blog posts.

- The Overhead column is important for maintenance. The Size column shows you how much space the table is taking up. The overhead is then calculated by taking the actual amount of data in the table from the table size. If there is a number in the Overhead column, it shows you that there is wasted space and the table needs to be optimized. (These columns are not shown in Figure 5-2.)

Left column shows database tables.   Top row gives options to perform on database.

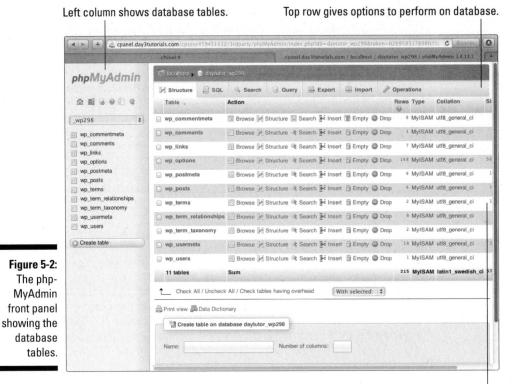

Main column gives options for table and table info.

You can run the table maintenance commands using one of two ways. Use the following steps to use the first method:

1. **Click on the name of the table.**

2. **Click Operations on the menu along the top of the window and scroll to the bottom of the page until you see the Table Maintenance section.**

3. **Click the command you want to run.**

    A Flush option is also available. This command flushes the internal caches, which can sometimes help speed up the database. (See Figure 5-3.)

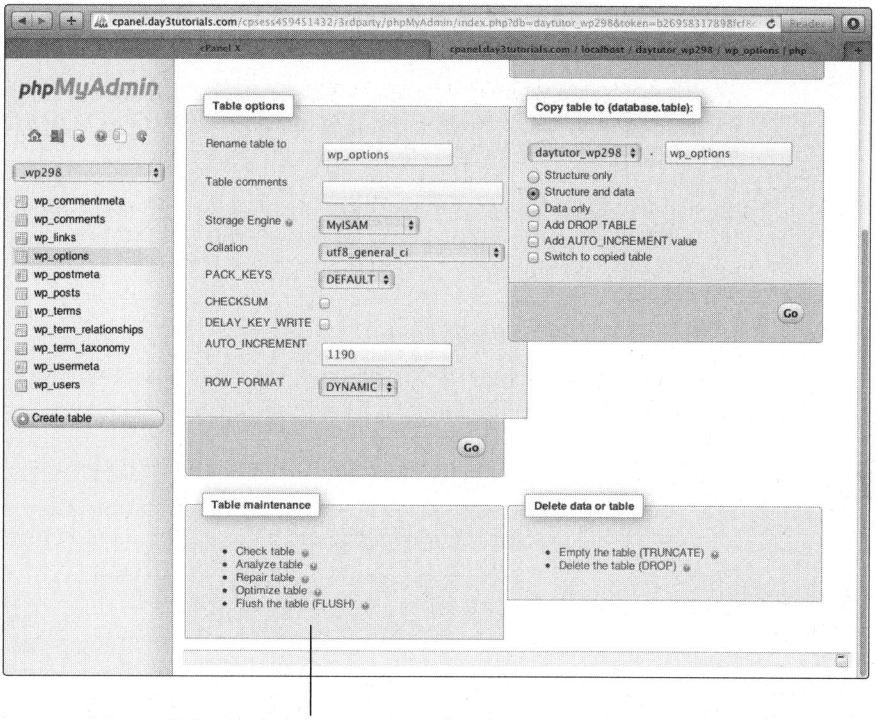

Figure 5-3:
The database table maintenance options in phpMy Admin.

Select maintenance command

Alternatively, you can use the following steps when viewing the database structure:

1. **Select the table(s) you wish to work on.**

2. **Scroll to the bottom of the table list and click the drop-down list (see Figure 5-4).**

3. **Select the command you want to run from the list.**

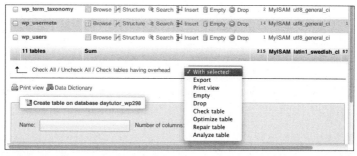

Figure 5-4:
Selecting maintenance commands from the Structure tab.

MySQL Workbench

Although phpMyAdmin and other browser-based tools for managing databases are good, there may be times when you want something a little more powerful. That's where MySQL Workbench comes in.

MySQL Workbench is a free database design and administration tool made by Oracle that joins together two previous products: MySQL Query Browser and MySQL Administrator.

Installing MySQL Workbench

To download and install the Workbench for most operating systems, use the following steps:

1. **Go to** http://dev.mysql.com/downloads/workbench/.

2. **Scroll down the screen to the download section, and then select your operating system (OS) from the drop-down box. (See Figure 5-5.)**

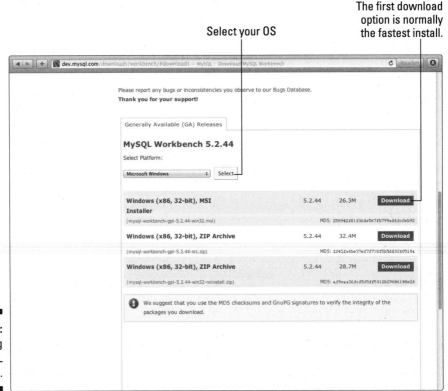

The first download option is normally the fastest install.

Select your OS

Figure 5-5:
Downloading MySQL Workbench.

3. **Click the Download button for the appropriate installer.**

4. **Install the software as appropriate for your OS.**

Open MySQL Workbench and you are presented with the three columns shown in Figure 5-6:

- ✔ **SQL Development:** This section gives you an SQL window where you can run any SQL commands you need on your database. This is useful for manually running maintenance commands, querying data, and editing data.

- ✔ **Data Modeling:** Useful for more advanced database users, this section helps you design and analyze databases. This is a design tool rather than a maintenance tool, but it can be very handy when you're creating and dealing with complex database structures.

- ✔ **Server Administration:** Some of the facilities in this section require remote administration to be switched on at the server, and many hosts won't allow that. Even without that, though, the Server Administration section shows you some useful information about the health of the server and provides an essential database backup facility (see the later section, "Backing Up Your Database," for more details.)

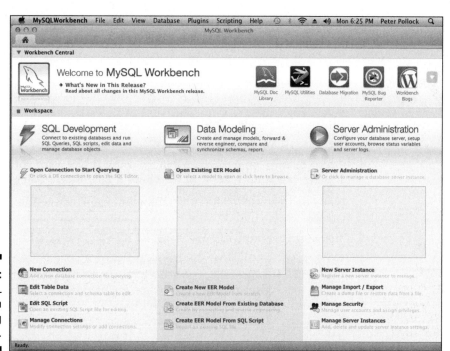

Figure 5-6: MySQL Workbench opening screen.

Configuring MySQL Workbench

After you open MySQL Workbench on your computer, the next thing you need to do is set up a connection to your server. Follow these steps:

1. **Click New Connection in the left column.**

2. **Give your connection a name and select your connection method. (See Figure 5-7.)**

   You can find out the correct connection method for your server from your host.

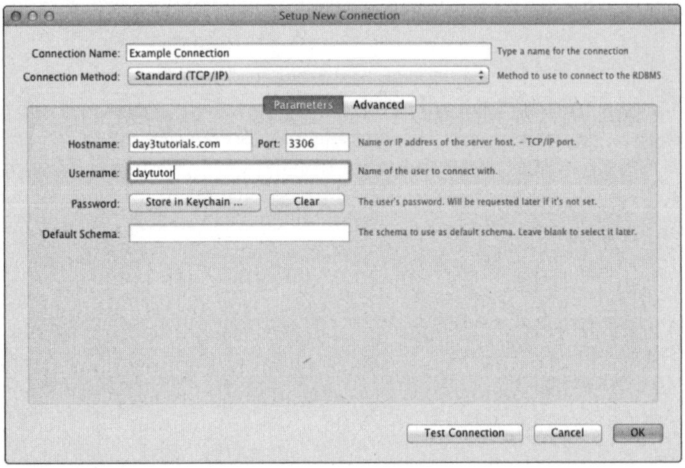

Figure 5-7: The MySQL Workbench Setup New Connection dialog box.

3. **Enter your hostname, port, and username.**

   The port is usually 3306, unless your host advises you otherwise.

4. **Choose to store your password in the vault if you want your computer to remember it for you (or in Keychain if you're on a Mac).**

   If you don't choose to store the password, you are asked for it every time you connect to the server.

5. **Click Test Connection.**

   The software attempts to connect to the server using the details you entered. If it is successful, you see a message telling you that the connection was successful and the connection parameters are correct. You can then click OK to complete the setup.

   If the connection is not successful and the error message says that "Host xxxxxxx is not allowed to connect to this MySQL server," (see Figure 5-8) move on to Step 6.

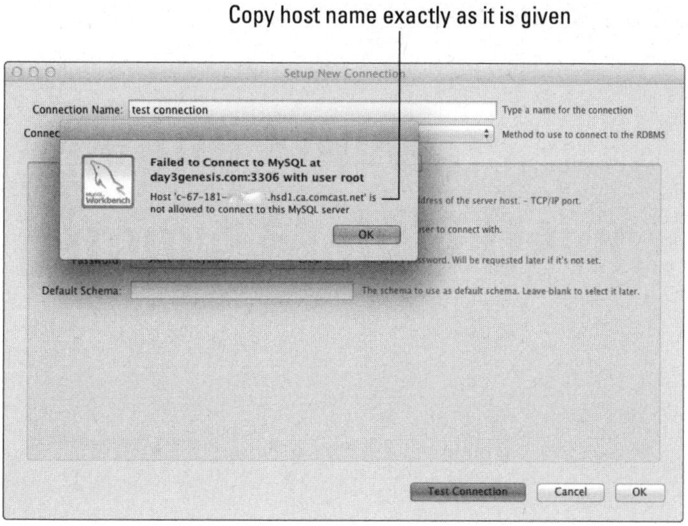

Copy host name exactly as it is given

Figure 5-8:
The MySQL
Workbench
Setup New
Connection
error
message.

6. Make a note of the name of the host it says is not allowed to connect.

7. Log in to your hosting control panel.

8. Look for an option labeled Remote MySQL and select it.

9. On the Remote Database Access Hosts page, enter the hostname exactly as you copied it down from the error message.

10. Click Add Host.

11. Return to MySQL Workbench and test the connection again.

12. If it still fails, check with your host to confirm that you are allowed remote connections.

Next, use the following steps to set up a connection to the server in the Server Administration section:

1. Click New Server Instance in the right-hand column of the Workbook home page.

2. Select Take Parameters from Existing Database Connection, and select the connection you just created from the drop-down box. (See Figure 5-9.)

3. Click Continue.

4. When the connection check is complete, click Continue again.

5. Select whether to use remote management and click Continue.

6. Enter a name for the Server Instance and click Finish.

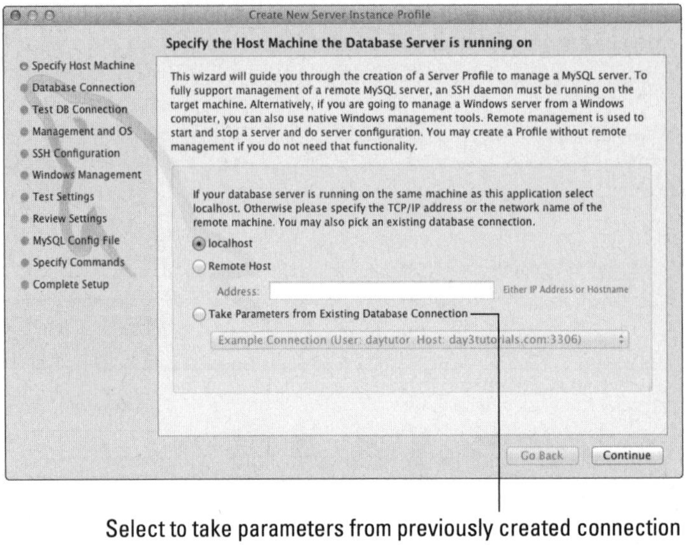

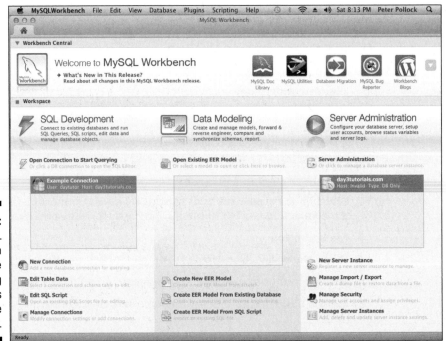

Figure 5-9:
The MySQL
Workbench
Setup
Server
Instance
dialog box.

Select to take parameters from previously created connection

Return to the home page, and your connections will appear in the boxes on the screen (see Figure 5-10). To use the SQL Development or Server Administration tools, click the connection you just created.

Figure 5-10:
The MySQL
Workbench
homepage
showing
connections
ready to be
used.

If you have more than one server, you can create multiple connections. Just make sure to give them obvious names so you can tell which is which.

Backing Up Your Database

Sites that use databases must make database backups a priority. The site design can be easily re-created in the event of corruption or loss, but the data in databases is much harder to rebuild — unless you have a good backup.

Your host may already back up your database as part of its normal backup routines, but it is still wise to ensure that you have a recent copy held locally just in case.

Your web script may have the facility to back up your database automatically or you may be able to use a plug-in to create a backup. Back up your database either to another server (Dropbox or a similar service is a good place to back up to), or you can have a backup e-mailed to you if it isn't too large.

Do not make the backup of the database on the same server as the master copy. If the server goes down, you will not be able to access either the master *or* the backup. Not good!

If you cannot back your site up automatically — or even if you can and you're a little paranoid about your precious data (like I am about mine) — you can also back up the data manually using one of the tools I mention earlier in this chapter.

Backing up using phpMyAdmin

Use the following steps to make a backup using phpMyAdmin:

1. **Log in to phpMyAdmin.**
2. **Click the database you want to back up.**
3. **Click on the Export tab (see Figure 5-11).**
4. **Click Go to download a complete database backup.**

   Alternatively, you can select only the options you require and then click Go.

The database downloads to your default download folder. Store it in a safe location — in a different folder on your hard drive, on a USB memory stick, or on a DVD.

Select Custom to modify backup options

Select Quick to use default options

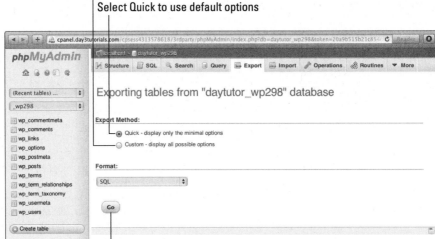

Figure 5-11:
Running a
database
backup
using php-
MyAdmin.

Click to start export

Backing up using MySQL Workbench

You can also make backups using MySQL Workbench by following these steps:

1. **Open MySQL Workbench and open a connection to your server in the Server Administration section.**

2. **In the column on the left of the Admin area, click Data Export.**

3. **In the right column, select the database(s) you want to back up.**

4. **Select whether to Export to a Dump Project Folder or a Self-Contained File (see Figure 5-12).**

5. **Select the folder you want to save the backup in.**

6. **Click Start Export.**

The Export Progress screen appears and notifies you when the export is complete.

The difference between exporting to a project dump folder and exporting to a self-contained file is that the first option creates a folder with separate files for each table in your database. This enables you to modify and restore any individual table without touching the others. The second option, however, creates a single file that holds all the tables. Which you choose is a matter of personal preference.

Select Data Export

Choose export options

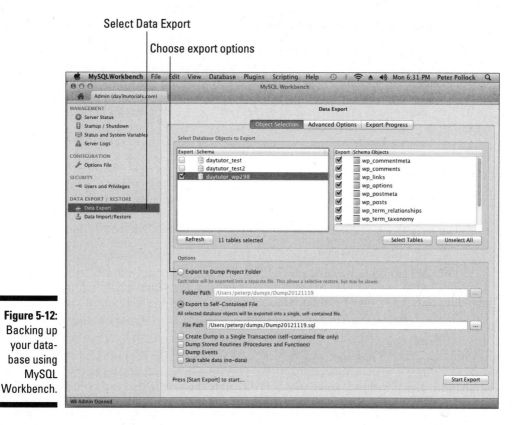

Figure 5-12:
Backing up your data-base using MySQL Workbench.

Restoring from a Backup

Restoring a database from a backup can be one of the most nerve-racking and risky tasks you can undertake as a website owner. Use the following two simple rules, though, and it will be a lot less stressful and intimidating:

✔ Remember to make a backup of your database before doing anything to it.

The database may have corruption or may be causing issues of some kind, but, if possible, always make a backup of what is there, just in case you need it later.

✔ After you have made a backup, remove any tables that you are going to restore. You can do this using the Drop command.

MySQL will not just overwrite data in a table; it will attempt to append the new data to the end of the table, meaning you can end up with dupli-cated data and a bigger mess than when you started.

Do not just empty the table because the issue may be in the structure of the table itself. Drop the table completely so it is completely re-created when you do the restore.

After you've done these two things, you will have the peace of mind that you have a backup of the original data, or what's left of it, and a have created a clean, empty space to upload into.

Restoring from a backup is simply the reverse of creating a backup.

Restoring a backup using phpMyAdmin

Use the following steps to restore a backup using phpMyAdmin:

1. **Open phpMyAdmin.**
2. **Select the database you want to restore to.**
3. **Click on the Insert tab.**
4. **Select the file you want to restore from by clicking Choose File.**
5. **Click Go.**

All tables in the file you selected are restored to the database. If you have not dropped all the tables you are restoring, the restore may fail with an error due to duplicate records being created.

Restoring a backup using MySQL Workbench

Use the following steps to restore a backup using MySQL Workbench:

1. **Open MySQL Workbench.**
2. **Under Server Administration, click the server you wish to restore to.**
3. **On the right column, click Data Import/Restore.**
4. **Select whether to import from a dump folder or self-contained file, depending on how you backed it up.**
5. **Browse to the file you want to restore from and select it.**
6. **Click Start Import.**

It is important to make regular backups of your database so that if you do ever have to restore from the latest backup, the amount of data lost is minimized.

Chapter 6

Protecting and Speeding Up Your Site by Understanding Logs

*J*ust the mere mention of log files is enough to send better men than I running for the hills. Log files are big, scary-looking, and seem like they're written in a foreign language. Even I still feel like I have to take a deep breath before diving into one.

They're really not that scary, though. Log files are full of useful nuggets of information and can quickly help you make your site faster and more secure — when you know where to look!

Log files are created by the server and the software that runs on it to literally keep a log of everything that happens. Each piece of software, if it's well written, will keep logs of events, particularly errors, so that you can go back to see what the server was doing when it got the error and exactly what error occurred.

Reading Logs

There are, essentially, two types of logs:

✔ **Logs that can be displayed graphically.** These are logs that record details of activity, which can then be read and analyzed by a program to display the results in a more easily readable form.

✔ **Logs that must be read manually.** These are generally logs that record events such as errors or access attempts.

Most control panels come with graphical log-reading software installed called stats. The following are some of the most popular programs:

- Awstats
- Logaholic
- Webalizer

There are many other programs, and some hosts design their own stats packages, but they all essentially do the same thing. They read the visitor logs and use statistical tools to create an analysis of what's been happening on your site.

You may be surprised at the breadth of information that can be gathered by the server from visitors without their knowledge. Statistical tools collect the following information:

- The page where the visitor arrived (the landing page)
- The pages the visitor went to and how long he spent on each
- The site he had been on before arriving at your site
- What search terms he used if he found you because of a web search
- Which links on your site he clicked
- Where in the world he is located (down to the city)
- What browser he used to view your site
- The screen resolution of the device he visited the site with
- How many colors the screen was set to display
- What operating system was used
- How often the visitor has come to your site

The trick is not in gathering the data; your server will do that for you automatically. The trick is in reading and analyzing the data to help you improve your site.

Using Logs to Identify Speed Bumps on Your Site

Everybody hates speed bumps in the road. You have to slow your car to cross a speed bump, and still everyone inside gets shaken up like gelatin in an earthquake. Nobody likes having to slow down, and speed bumps make the traveling experience less enjoyable so you try to avoid them whenever possible.

The same goes for websites. People don't like slow websites. We're all getting spoiled these days by fast Internet connections, and research shows that web users will click away to another site if yours takes more than two seconds to open. A faster site retains more visitors; with a slower site, visitors may click away to a competitor's site.

In the same way that drivers avoid streets with speed bumps, web users avoid sites with speed bumps, too.

A number of factors affect the speed of your site, including the following:

✔ **The server you are on.** Generally, being on a dedicated server means your site will be delivered faster than on shared servers.

✔ **The platform you use to build your site.** Some platforms are faster than others, but speed also depends on your site design and the type of server it is on.

✔ **The size and number of images you use on your site.** Bigger pictures take longer to load — it's that simple.

✔ **The number of bells and whistles you beautify your site with.** Cool effects and widgets can make a site look good, but they can also slow the site down to a crawl if you use too many.

✔ **The geographical location of your server.** The farther away your server is from your visitors, the longer it takes the information to get to their screens.

The information your server gives you can revolutionize how you manage and develop your site, and it's fairly easy to read. In the next couple of sections, you find out how analyze your stats for speed bumps.

Opening web stats

To demonstrate how to read stats, I'm going to focus on the Webalizer stats program, which is installed on most cPanel and Plesk systems. All stats programs display the information differently because their focus differs depending on what their developers think is most important.

I generally view at least two stats programs whenever I'm doing site analysis because little bits of information often are displayed on one program and not another.

Use the following steps to open Webalizer:

1. **Log in to your control panel.**

2. **Search for the stats or logs section.**

   In cPanel, the section is usually called Logs and is about halfway down the screen. (See Figure 6-1.)

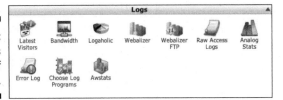

Figure 6-1: The logs section of cPanel.

3. **Click Webalizer.**

4. **Click the magnifying glass next to the domain for which you want to view statistics.**

   If you have multiple domains hosted in the same account, Webalizer enables you to pick the one you want to view statistics for.

5. **Select the month you are interested in from the 12-month summary page.**

   The summary page gives a broad overview of various statistics by daily average and monthly total. This can be useful to spot trends, but the real gems are hidden on the next page.

You've opened Webalizer, so the trick now is to glean useful information from it. I now walk you through it section by section.

Mastering the terminology

First you need to learn what each term in the statistics means. In the statistics, you see the following headings:

- ✔ **Hits:** The total number of requests received by the server in that period.

- ✔ **Files:** The total number of files delivered by the server. This is lower than the number of hits because the server doesn't deliver a file if the user's computer already has a cached copy of it or if the request is for something that doesn't exist.

- ✔ **Pages:** This is the total number of actual page views, not a count of all the component parts that make up a page.

- ✔ **Visits:** The number of times your site has been visited. The way it calculates this is by counting all page requests from one person within a certain time period as one visit. So if you go to a site and read four pages, four page views are recorded, but only one visit is recorded. If you do not request to see another page within 30 minutes of your last request, your next page view is classed as the first in a new visit.

- ✔ **Sites:** The number of unique IP addresses that have requested pages from your site. This figure can be misleading because multiple people in the same office can have the same address; in this case, multiple people may view your site but they are recorded as just one individual. On the other hand, one person could look at your site from her phone and her computer, both of which might have different addresses; in this case, you see two site records for only one real person. The Sites statistic gives you a rough idea of the number of unique visitors to your site, though.

- ✔ **Hostname:** Every device has its own unique hostname. It can have multiple IP addresses but can only ever have one hostname.

- ✔ **Kbytes:** Every file that makes up your site and every page has a physical size, measured in bytes. The number of bytes of data that need to be sent to deliver a file or page is added up by the server every time it receives a request. This figure is a measure of the total amount of data that was sent in response to requests from visitors for pages and files. This figure is also referred to as the amount of *bandwidth* used. If your host gives you a certain amount of bandwidth per month, that is calculated by the total number of bytes of data requested from your site during that month.

- ✔ **Response code:** When a request is made for data from the server, it logs a response code relating to how successful it was in completing the request, called a HTTP response code. For example, a code of 200 means OK — in other words, it did exactly what it was asked to do. On the other hand, code 404 means Not Found, meaning the request was for a file or page that doesn't exist.

HTTP response codes were defined in the HTTP/1.1 standard (RFC 2616) and are thus standardized across the Internet. There are dozens of possible codes, split into five categories, each starting with one of the numbers 1 to 5. The number 1 provides informational codes, the number 2 shows success codes, 3 refers to redirection codes, 4 indicates client error codes, and 5 identifies server error codes. See Chapter 10 for details on how to create custom error pages that will display to the user when a specific error code is generated.

Reading your web stats

Now you know what all the terms mean. Next, I explain each section on the Webalizer page and how you might use it.

- ✔ **The first section of data gives you overall monthly statistics.** The following sections all break down the details in this first section.

- ✔ **The next two sections show you the daily usage of your site.** The details are shown in graph form: The days are numbered along the bottom axis, and three lines plot statistics for three types of data. Those results are then given in numerical form, by day, and show how many hits, files, pages, visits, sites, and KBytes were recorded. It also gives a percentage of the total monthly usage for each day. This is very useful for determining if a day or days had particularly high usage. If so, you should investigate why that was and see if there are ways you can spread the visits out more evenly. In simple terms, the more visitors you have at once, the slower the site goes. It's like a shopping mall: When nobody is around, you can get in and out quickly, but on Black Friday, it's a whole different story!

- ✔ **The next two sections look at data transfers across the month and break them down by hours of the day.** You can also analyze this to see if the site is particularly busy during certain hours.

- ✔ **The next section shows you the top 30 Uniform Resource Locators (URLs) requested in the month.** This basically identifies the most frequently requested pages and files.

- ✔ **The next section shows the top ten URLs by KBytes.** This is one of the most important sections for speeding up your site because it shows which files and pages contain the most data and take the longest to load. Figure 6-2 shows the top ten URLs by KBytes from one of my customers' sites. If you look at the first line, one file has used more than 39 percent of the data but has had only 0.22 percent of the hits. Looking along the line, you can see it's a PDF file so that's not unreasonable. It's a download and visitors understand that downloads can take time. The next line, though, shows that one image has had 3 percent of the total hits but has used 13 percent of the KBytes. Looking further down, this is a disproportionately high amount of data, so it suggests that this image is a lot larger (in file size) than any of the others on the site and thus loads slower than the others. Seeing that suggests that you look at what that image is and why it's using up so many resources, and maybe find ways to optimize it so it doesn't slow the site down so much.

Figure 6-2:
Top ten
URLs in
KBytes as
shown in
Webalizer.

#	Hits		KBytes		URL
			Top 10 of 1342 Total URLs By KBytes		
1	96	0.22%	322467	39.03%	/dinosaurs/wp-content/uploads/2012/11/What-I-Remember-About-Dinosaurs-Kickstarter-Backer-Exclusive.pdf
2	1335	3.11%	107365	13.00%	/wp-content/uploads/2012/03/tumblr_lyqbuqRvsX1qhwyiio1_500.jpg
3	1604	3.74%	36626	4.43%	/
4	7335	17.09%	31442	3.81%	/wp-login.php
5	577	1.34%	14180	1.72%	/feed/
6	33	0.08%	12784	1.55%	/wp-content/uploads/2012/08/website-graphic-design-book-just-breathe.png
7	27	0.06%	12158	1.47%	/wp-content/uploads/2012/08/intel-software-marketing-graphic-design.png
8	35	0.08%	12003	1.45%	/wp-content/uploads/2012/08/dinosaurs-illustration-childrens-book.png
9	2	0.00%	8988	1.09%	/arkwood/wp-content/uploads/2012/10/2012-05-30-Master-Chief-Goes-On-A-Date.gif
10	2954	6.88%	8300	1.00%	/wp-content/uploads/2012/03/email.png

✔ **The next section shows the top ten entry pages.** An entry page is the first page viewed on any given visit. For blogs, this will show which post was most popular in the month. For other sites, though, this can really help you with your site Search Engine Optimization (SEO). Ask yourself why visitors are arriving at those pages first and whether those pages then make people want to stay to browse around. Discovering why certain pages are more popular can help you optimize other pages on your site to increase their popularity. Additionally, if you'd rather that people first land on a different page, it can help you modify the site accordingly.

✔ **The next section shows you the top ten exit pages.** The exit page is the last page a person sees before leaving your site. If the entry and exit page lists are fairly identical, then it means visitors are only viewing one page on your site before leaving. The site is not drawing them in to go to other pages. If the exit pages are not all the same as the entry pages, you might ask yourself why people leave the site after going to those top ten pages. Is there something offensive on them or do they maybe need some work to make them more "sticky"?

✔ **The next two sections show the top visiting sites by hits and by KBytes.** For most of us, this is fairly meaningless, but it can show you if one person is visiting a disproportionate number of times and you can investigate why.

✔ **The next section shows the top *referrers*.** Referrers are pages that request a page or file from the server. Most referrers will be pages from your own site because pages on your site have multiple objects on them and so when a page is displayed, it has to request every object it needs to be complete. For example, if you have ten images on a page, every time that page is viewed, it has to make ten requests from the server and thus has referred ten files. It can be useful to look through and find the top referrers that are not *internal* (on your site) so you can see which sites — and which pages from those sites — are sending the most visitors your way.

✔ **The top 20 search strings show up next.** This refers to the searches people did on search engines that resulted in those individuals clicking on a link to your site. This information can be very eye-opening because it reveals how people find your site.

✔ **The next section is the top 15 *user-agents*.** That's simply a big name for *browsers* — the programs you use to view web pages. Every browser will potentially display your website slightly differently. When you design your site, you should test it in multiple browsers to ensure that it looks right in all of them. Knowing which browsers your visitors use most can help you optimize your site for each browser and show you which browser you should concentrate on when redesigning your pages.

✔ **The final two sections show what countries your visitors are in.** Knowing where your visitors are can help you both in the marketing and ongoing design of the site and also in knowing where your server should be located. For instance, if the majority of your visitors are in Europe, then hosting your site on a server in Europe may be a good idea. That way, you will help speed up server response times to those visitors.

Other stats programs show slightly different statistics. Look around at the programs available to see what useful information you can glean from them.

The data you see displayed in any stats program will be fairly accurate, but you might find that the results differ between stats programs even on the same server. The reason for this is that these programs use statistical analysis tools and formulas to come up with the data they display. None is perfect.

Finding Your Logs

Log files are everywhere — and I do mean *everywhere*. Finding the right ones can be a chore, but here are some of the main files and locations:

✔ Linux has a main log folder located at /var/log/. A quick look in the /var/log/ folder on one of my servers showed more than 50 different log files with a further 10 subfolders that contain more log files. Those log files include everything from which software updates have been run to what mail has passed through the server.

✔ Depending on the control panel software installed, there may be File Transfer Protocol (FTP) logs somewhere. In cPanel, they are in the root of your hosting space in the /access-logs/ folder. In Plesk, they reside in /usr/local/psa/var/log/xferlog.

> ✔ Each different control panel generates its own log files. cPanel has logs in `/usr/local/apache/logs/`, `/usr/local/apache/domlog/`, and in `/usr/local/cpanel/logs`.
>
> ✔ Your web platform and scripts may generate their own `error_log` files too, which will be scattered around your hosting space.

To view most of the log files, you need root access to the server. You won't be able to get to those log files you're on a shared server, but you should have access to them on a Virtual Private Server (VPS) or dedicated server.

Error logs in your hosting space should be freely available to you without root access. They can help you find and fix problems that are occurring in your website.

It is important that you familiarize yourself with the log files so you can track down the source of any problems that might occur.

Spotting Security Breaches Using Your Log Files

The big question is always about security. How can you keep your site secure and guarantee that it won't get hacked?

The short answer is this: You can't.

Everything is hackable given enough time, devious brains, and resources. There are things you can do, though, to protect yourself somewhat. I discuss those things in Chapter 8. Here, though, I open the door a crack and show you some things you can do to track down the source of your problems if you do get hacked.

The first thing to do is to check your FTP log files. In cPanel, those are found in `/home/youraccount/access-logs/`.

If you have been hacked, then it is most likely that some of your files have been altered. Use FTP to look at the date stamps on your files to see when the affected ones were last changed and thus find out when the attack happened.

Then download the logs to your computer via FTP and open them. I recommend the free Notepad++ (`http://notepad-plus-plus.org`) software for editing and viewing logs.

The FTP log should have lines of data looking a little like this:

```
Fri Nov 16 11:11:33 2012 0 97.182.220.213 248 /home/daytutor/public_html/.
          htaccess a _ o r daytutor ftp 1 * c
```

The information in that line of data breaks down like this:

- ✔ `Fri Nov 16 11:11:33 2012` is the date and time, obviously.
- ✔ 0 is the number of whole seconds the transfer took. This transfer took less than a second.
- ✔ `97.182.220.213` is the IP address of the computer that did the transfer.
- ✔ `248` is the size of the file transferred (in bytes).
- ✔ `/home/daytutor/public_html/.htaccess` is the file transferred and the full path to it.
- ✔ a is the type of transfer. It can be either a for ASCII or b for binary.
- ✔ _ [underscore] represents the action taken. The _ means no action, C means compressed, U means uncompressed, and T means Tar'ed.

Tar originally meant Tape ARchive and was a system developed for converting data into a single stream for recording onto backup tapes. The technology is still used today but it's mostly used to collect files into a single archive file and store them on any media. A tar file usually has the file extension `.tar` and is uncompressed. You can use additional compression software to compress `.tar` files, in which case the file extension is changed to indicate what compression software was used. For example, a `.tar` file compressed using the gzip program will have the extension `.tar.gz`.

- ✔ o is the direction of the transfer. The o is for outgoing, i is for incoming, and d is for deleted.
- ✔ r represents the type of user. r is for a real user, and a is for an anonymous user. *Note:* "Real" does not mean human; it means the login used a username/password combination.
- ✔ `daytutor` is the username used to log in.
- ✔ `ftp` is the service used (this normally will be FTP).
- ✔ 1 is the authentication method. The 1 is a valid authentication method as defined by RFC931. A 0 means no authentication was used.
- ✔ * indicates the user ID of the user who made the transfer (if said user were logged into the server at the time). The * means the user was not logged in.
- ✔ c is the completion status. A c means the transfer was complete. An i means it was incomplete.

In the example, you can see that it was a file called `.htaccess` that was transferred out using FTP by user `daytutor` on November 16, 2012, at 11:11.

However, the big question is *who* did the transfer. All you know is that the person used the username `daytutor` and had the IP address 97.182.220.213.

The first thing you should do is go to `http://www.whatsmyip.org`, which will tell you what your IP address is so you can compare the two. If the IP address in the file is not the same as yours, it may signal a security breach.

If the IP address is not yours, does anyone else have FTP access to your server? Do you use a backup system on another server that uses FTP to connect to this one?

Go to your preferred search engine and enter the IP address. This will give you a list of sites that can show you the geographical location of the device that uses that IP address. If the IP address is for a server, it should also show the hostname of the server.

You can also go to a site such as `http://network-tools.com` and enter the IP address there. If the IP address is connected with a server, you may get more information about the server from Network Tools.

There's little else you can do to track down who uses that IP address, unfortunately, but you might be able to draw some conclusions from what you learn about the IP address. For example, I once helped a client whose site had been hacked, and the IP address told us which city the hacker was in. As it turned out, it was a small city and just happened to be the city where someone who had a vendetta against him lived. Coincidence? I don't think so!

Next, go to your server's firewall settings and deny that IP address access to your server. This won't stop some hackers because they can simply switch IP addresses, but at least it stops attacks coming directly from that IP address again.

The battle against hackers is a never-ending one. I wish I could say that wasn't the truth, but it is the reality in which we live. Although the battle may be ongoing, the prognosis is not that grim. Applying good security to your site and regularly checking your logs for suspicious activity can help you keep your site running healthily. Read more about securing your site in Chapter 8.

Chapter 7

Building Your Site Using Scripts

*Y*our web host's only concern is providing you with the space and facilities to house your website. The design and functions of the site itself are not your host's responsibility.

In earlier chapters, I compare your host to a landlord. The landlord provides the building, but adding furniture and decor is your job. Most hosts help by providing you with easy access to some free *scripts* that help you build your site. Scripts are prewritten pieces of website code that you can use to add functionality to your site. They range from small add-ons such as a contact form or guest book to full-blown site creation tools that enable you to create a whole site in minutes.

Most web hosting control panels include a set of installable scripts designed to help you build awesome, highly functional websites with little or no programing knowledge. You can also find countless other scripts available to download online.

Although your host may provide some easy-to-install scripts, it will not generally give you free support in using the scripts.

In this chapter, I tell you what kinds of scripts you can find, where to find them, how to install them, and how they can help you.

Making Life Easier with Scripts

Why reinvent the wheel? In the case of websites, why try to create something from scratch when you can skip the hard part and get straight on with customizing your site to look, work, and feel the way you want? Literally hundreds of scripts exist, and you can install them to do everything from control your entire site to add small pieces of functionality.

All scripts provide you with a customizable framework that you can adapt to give your website functions you otherwise wouldn't have — unless you learned to code the functions yourself.

In this ever-changing world of computer and mobile technologies, terms are being coined and used interchangeably fairly indiscriminately. You may hear scripts referred to as *apps, applications, programs,* or *solutions.* In general, they all mean the same thing; it just depends on what terms the speaker is familiar with. You may also hear the word *platform,* which normally refers to a whole-site script, such as WordPress or Joomla. Scripts help you incorporate specific functions into your website. For example, you can find scripts that fall into the following categories:

- **Blogs:** Scripts such as WordPress, which give you complete blogging solutions, really come under the platform title but are lumped together with other scripts because they are free and easy to install.

- **Portals/Content Management Systems:** Joomla, Drupal, and Mambo are probably the most well-known content management system (CMS) scripts, and they provide you with an easy way to create a site and keep it regularly updated.

- **Forums:** Scripts such as phpBB and Vanilla provide a complete solution to anyone who wants to have a bulletin board or forum system on his or her site.

- **Image Galleries:** Image gallery scripts enable you to easily add rotating image galleries and slide shows to your site.

- **Calendars:** Calendar scripts enable you to do everything from displaying and managing a calendar of upcoming events to creating an online reservations system.

- **Polls:** Polls and surveys are popular tools for reader engagement, and many scripts are available that enable you to add a poll to your site wherever you want it.

- **E-commerce:** E-commerce scripts add sales, client management, and invoicing capabilities to your site. The e-commerce title covers scripts from generic systems like osCommerce to custom-made scripts for specific industries.

This list of script categories isn't comprehensive: You name the functionality you want, and there's a script to help you get it. And if you don't find what you need in your web host's control panel, you can search online for hundreds more that you can download.

Most scripts are free, but some may be free only for a trial period, after which you have to pay a subscription fee to use them fully. Check first whether you will have to pay to use a script before committing the time and effort to testing it.

Choosing the Right Script

With such a variety of scripts available, making the right choice can seem overwhelming. When you use the following steps, you can quickly find the right script for your needs:

1. **Break down exactly what you want to achieve with your website.**

   Be specific. Separate the functionality you need into parts, if necessary. You may want a site where you can share information about your organization or group, but also want a forum where your visitors can chat about certain things. You probably need two different scripts to do both.

2. **Do some research online.**

   Open your search engine of choice (Google, for example) and search for phrases such as "best site creation script" or "top website poll script." Phrases like these can help you find the type of script you need to achieve your goals.

   You can also search your web host's control panel for likely scripts. All control panels are laid out slightly differently, and so it can sometimes take a little bit of hunting to find the installable scripts. Even with standard control panels like cPanel, the hosting company can customize the headings and the look and feel of the menus.

   What you're looking for is an area that has a list of different categories or names similar to the list in the section "Making Life Easier with Scripts," earlier in this chapter. See Figure 7-1 for an example list in a standard cPanel installation.

3. **When you find scripts that seem like they might do what you want, search again for people's opinions on those scripts.**

   A good way to look for opinions on the scripts is by searching again for the name of the script plus the word "review" or "issues." You'll quickly find which scripts work well and which ones just frustrate people. Pick two or three scripts so that you can evaluate the differences between them.

Figure 7-1:
Softaculous
menu in
cPanel.

4. **Install and test the scripts. (See the later section, "Installing Your Chosen Script," for information on how to install scripts.)**

   Take a little time to try to master each script; don't get discouraged just because you don't understand how it works at first click. You'll quickly see which script has the best functionality for your needs and which is easiest to work with.

After you choose your script(s), take a step back and ask yourself whether incorporating the script's functionality will really help you achieve your goals for your site. It's easy to get awestruck by the functions scripts can give you and start building something that isn't exactly what you need to achieve based on cool features you've discovered.

Installing Your Chosen Script

You can install scripts either through your control panel or by downloading them from the web and installing them manually.

Each method has both advantages and disadvantages, but where possible, I recommend installing scripts through your control panel.

Installing from your control panel

Installing scripts safely is easy, when you know how. Just follow these simple steps and you'll breeze through it in seconds. Most control panels use either the Softaculous or Fantastico script installer systems, but they are not necessarily labeled that way.

If you install a script into the root of your hosting space, it could overwrite any files you already have in there. So be careful where you install your scripts.

1. **Look through the script installation area of your control panel to find the script you want to install.**

2. **Click the script icon or name to view a page that gives you a little more information about the script and what it can do for you.**

3. **Click on the Install tab.**

   If your control panel is using the Softaculous installer, you see an Install tab at the top of the screen. Clicking on the tab takes you to the Install screen. Other installers also have an Install tab or button prominently displayed.

4. **Install your script in a test folder.**

   As part of the install process, you should be asked which folder you want to install your script into. Softaculous labels it `In Directory`. Type a new folder name into this box. At this stage, I suggest using a naming system for the folders that will enable you to test multiple scripts independently without disturbing anything else on your site. You might want to call it *xxx*-`test` (where *xxx* is the name of the script). You can then easily find where your test installations for each script are.

5. **Complete any other information the installer asks you for.**

   This might include a username and password (don't forget to note what they are) and your site name.

6. **Click the Install button at the bottom of the page.**

After you've picked the script or scripts you need for your site, run the install again and install a fresh copy in the folder you are actually going to use it in and start customizing it to fit your needs.

Watch the tutorial on the For Dummies website at www.dummies.com/go/ webhostingfd to see how it's done.

Installing from a downloadable script

Installing scripts that you find online is a little trickier than using the installers in the control panel, but don't get discouraged. It's easy enough when you know how.

You need the following things to install a downloaded script:

- ✔ The script downloaded from its online location.
- ✔ A File Transfer Protocol (FTP) client and your FTP details.
- ✔ For some cases, a manually created database.

When you find the script you want to test or use, the website you find it on should have installation instructions. Here are some things you need to check:

- ✔ **Server requirements:** Most script authors tell you the minimum server specifications required to run their scripts. Compare those to what you know about your server before attempting an install. If you aren't sure what your server's specifications are, contact your web host to find out.

- ✔ **Find the installation instructions:** If there are no installation instructions on the website, double-click the file after you have downloaded it to your computer to open the file in your file manager. You should see a text file labeled something like InstallInstructions or Readme.txt.

  If you can find no installation instructions at all, it's probably best to steer clear of using the script. The authors of well-written scripts generally take the time to document their work. Scripts where the author hasn't taken the time to write instructions are often more sloppily written — and potentially harmful.

- ✔ **Is the script safe?** If you install a script on your site that causes the server problems, your host may delete the script without warning you, or the host may even suspend or cancel your account. Try to first find some reviews of scripts you are going to test to make sure other users haven't had problems with them.

- ✔ **Download it in the right format:** Most scripts can be downloaded in multiple formats. If you are unfamiliar with the terms .tar and .gz, then the best format to download is a .zip file. You can open these files directly on both PCs and Macs.

Although the installation instructions differ between scripts, the following directions are basically what they are going to tell you to do:

1. **Download the script .zip file from the website.**

   The zip file is like a suitcase. Everything you need is packed into it. Downloading a script is normally as simple as clicking a Download button on the website where you found it.

2. **Extract the files from within the .zip file.**

   In Windows, double-click the file to open it and then click Extract All from the menu at the top of the screen.

3. **Upload the files to your hosting space.**

   You need to create a folder and use FTP to do this. See Chapter 4 for information on how to use FTP.

4. **Navigate to a certain file to activate or install the script.**

   The instructions may tell you to Open install.php, which means you need to open your web browser and go to http://yoursite.com/your_script_folder/install.php.

There may also be other instructions about tasks you need to do, like create a database and edit a file to put the details of your database in. For these, you need to either use the database wizard in your control panel or manually create a database. See Chapter 5 for details on how to create databases.

Typically, .tar and .gz files are smaller than .zip files, which means faster downloads. You can also open them on Linux machines. If you don't have the choice of downloading a .zip file and you don't have a way to open the file, you can download free .zip extractors, such as 7-Zip (www.7-zip.org), which will open it for you.

Part III
Managing Security and Access

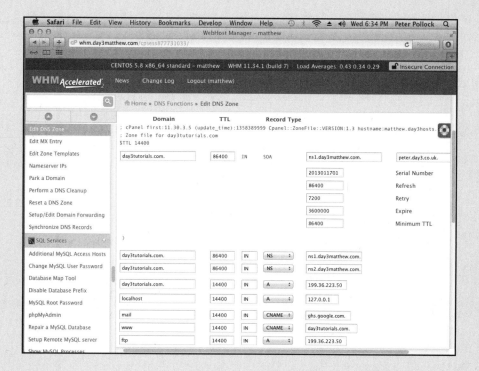

Learn how to create a secure password you can actually remember at
www.dummies.com/extras/webhosting.

In this part . . .

- ✔ Understand website security and what you need to do to protect your site.

- ✔ Master the DNS (Domain Name System) and unleash its power.

- ✔ Install and configure some of the advanced functions in your hosting.

- ✔ Manage your hosting on the go with your Internet-enabled mobile device.

Chapter 8

Taking Command of Website Security

● ●

In This Chapter

▶ Understanding your role and responsibilities in site security

▶ Knowing when and how to use SSL certificates

▶ Assessing the need for SSH access

▶ Using password-protected folders

▶ Protecting your site from viruses

● ●

*N*obody likes viruses and malware, but they're a fact of online life. Sticking your head in the sand and pretending that the malicious elements of the online world don't exist isn't going to help.

In this chapter, I help you see where some of the potential security holes are and provide steps you can take to shore up your defenses before you become a victim.

Accepting That Security Is Your Responsibility

"Security! Security! Come help me, someone's attacking my site!"

You can shout and scream all day, but no one will run to help. This is your site, your hosting plan — and you're the head of security. If you haven't put the security guards in place then you've left yourself exposed and it's too late now.

If you are using a managed hosting service (where you have specifically paid extra for increased server management from your host) some of the security will be covered by the host, and it should be your first port of call in an emergency. Check in advance to find out what the host does and doesn't do, though, to ensure that you don't leave your site exposed.

Attacks come in all different shapes and sizes. Viruses, malware, Distributed Denial of Service (DDOS), phishing, creating zombies for botnets, spam sending, and data theft are just some of the types of attacks your server will face.

Attackers can be anyone from a school kid who's trying to prove that she's smart enough to hack a server to an organized syndicate that will use your server in any way it can to make money and cause Internet havoc. Attacks can also come from *bots,* which are servers that run automated programs to scour the Net and find servers so that a set of basic hacks can be tried on each one.

In the same way that there is no way to stop the most resourceful and determined burglar from getting into your house, ultimately there is no way to completely prevent hackers from gaining access to your server. However, just as you can beef up the security in your house to thwart the vast majority of would-be thieves, you can also do a great deal to secure your server and website against all but the most dedicated hackers.

You need to protect two groups of people when creating a website in your hosting space:

✔ **Your visitors.** People using your site need to know that any personal information they give you is secure and that browsing your site is not going to cause their computers to become infected with viruses or malware.

✔ **You and anyone else on the same server as you.** If you are on a shared server, it isn't just your site that is affected if you get hacked. Hacks often result in huge resource usage on the server, which slows everyone's sites down. If your site is hijacked and used to send spam e-mail, the result can be that the whole server and all the sites on it are blacklisted, meaning they can no longer send e-mail.

If you don't take steps to protect these two groups, you *will* eventually get hacked, and your visitors and neighbors on the server will feel the pain of it as much as you do.

Act now to build the barricades before the barbarians get in!

Protecting Your Visitors with SSL Certificates

Secure Socket Layer (SSL) certificates are easy to buy, and they give your customers the peace of mind that any personal information they send to you is encrypted and secure.

The purpose of an SSL certificate is to show that the site the visitor is looking at is trustworthy (that is, made by a legitimate person or company) and also to encrypt information as it is exchanged between the visitor and the server to prevent anyone from intercepting and stealing that data.

Recognizing when you need SSL

SSL certificates are not needed for any sites that are purely informational. You only need to install an SSL certificate if you are asking customers to supply you with personal information.

Here are a few example scenarios that illustrate when you do *not* need an SSL certificate:

- ✔ **Your site simply shares news about your organization or is there to promote your business visually without taking customer feedback.**

- ✔ **You have a blog on which people leave comments including their names and e-mail addresses.** For the majority of web users, a name and e-mail address are fairly impersonal. If someone steals that information, there's not much the thief can do with the information to hurt the owner. An SSL certificate is an option for protecting comments, though, if you're really security-conscious.

- ✔ **You have a contact or feedback form on your site that asks for the person's e-mail address and name.** Again, these details are not sufficient to require encryption.

And here are some scenarios in which you *do* need an SSL certificate:

- ✔ **You have a form on your site that *requires* extra information, such as a username, phone number, or ID number.** Many sites request information like a phone number but do not make it mandatory. SSL certificates will help protect their visitors, but because giving the information is optional, the site is not exposing itself or its visitors to too much risk if there is no SSL certificate. If the information is required, though, you should definitely protect the transfer of that information using an SSL certificate.

✔ **Your customers/clients can create an account on your site into which they enter personal details such as their addresses, birth dates, or phone numbers.** If you don't have a certificate, your visitors may as well take out an ad in the newspaper to tell everyone their personal information. The risks are simply that high.

✔ **You accept payments by credit card.** Although most sites that accept credit card payments already have SSL certificates because they are receiving and storing personal data, there are some sites on which you can use a credit card without creating an account. These sites need SSL encryption so that the credit card details cannot be intercepted and stolen.

Store as little customer information as possible. The more personal data you have on your server, the higher the risks and consequences to your customers if your server is hacked. Even if you accept credit cards, it's safer for everyone when you don't store the details.

A good rule of thumb is to consider whether the data you are taking from your customers is something you'd want to say out loud in a public place if it was your information. Your name and e-mail address are fairly inconsequential, but anything more than that you probably wouldn't want the world to know.

If you wouldn't say it out loud in public then you need to get an SSL certificate to protect it.

How SSL certificates work

Without getting overly technical and in-depth, your browser goes through four basic steps to ensure that the connection is secure:

1. It checks the address of the site and its IP address against the details on the certificate.

2. The server and the browser interact to determine what encryption types they can both support and agree on one to use.

3. The server and the browser supply each other with unique codes to use when encrypting and decrypting data sent between them.

4. The browser displays a confirmation in the address bar that the connection is secure, and all data is then sent encrypted.

When a connection is secured, it uses a slightly different connection protocol known as HyperText Transfer Protocol Secure (https). This replaces the standard http protocol and you will notice that the web address now starts `https://`. If the `https://` is colored red, it means the site is attempting to use the secure protocol but the certificate is not valid or not recognized so the connection may not be secure.

Depending on the level of security you purchase, the visitor's browser displays different confirmations in the address bar:

✔ A low-level security certificate displays a padlock before the site name in the address bar (see Figure 8-1).

Figure 8-1:
A padlock in a browser address bar indicates basic https security.

Padlock shows basic security.

✔ A certificate fully confirmed to legitimately belong to a legal entity with the right to use that domain name either turns the whole address bar green or displays the company's name in a green block before the web address (see Figure 8-2).

Figure 8-2:
A green browser address bar indicates Extended Validation (EV) https security.

Green bar indicates EV security.

SSL certificates must be purchased from a recognized Certificate Authority (CA); otherwise, your visitors' browsers will not authenticate them. There is an extensive list of trusted CAs, each of which can have multiple brands attached to it.

The three main international players in the certificate market have a number of different brands associated with them, including the following:

✔ **Symantec:** Equifax, Thawte, VeriSign, and Geotrust

✔ **GoDaddy:** GoDaddy.com and Starfield Technologies

✔ **Comodo:** Comodo CA and UTN-USERFirst-Hardware

Your browser can give you a list of its trusted certificate authorities. For example, in Firefox, go to Options⇨Options⇨Advanced⇨Encryption⇨View Certificates.

Choosing the right level of security

SSL certificates come with different levels of security, ranging from very basic security all the way to air-tight-no-leaks security, with prices ranging from free to hundreds of dollars per year.

Although there are some standards in place for Extended Validation (EV) security, which is the highest level of security, each company defines its own security levels for its certificates and its own prices.

One of the biggest differences between the security levels is the way that they validate who the purchaser of the domain is. The simplest form of validation is done immediately online and is essentially self-validation. The certificate issuer takes it on faith that you are who you say you are. The highest level is EV security, a level for which standards have been agreed upon between the companies that issue the certificates. Validation can take weeks because they check, among other things, whether your company physically exists and is operational, if it currently has control of its own domain name, and if you are an authorized agent of that company.

The following list includes three security levels and what they might entail so that you have an idea of how to compare the different certificates. Each level is more trustworthy than the one preceding it and thus is more expensive.

- **Basic:** Purchased with online automatic validation, no paperwork, no faxes needed. 2048-bit digital signatures and 99.9% browser recognition with a $250,000 warranty.

- **Wildcard:** Full business validation, 2048-bit keys with 128/256-bit encryption, 99.9% browser recognition, and covers all subdomains for your domain with a $1 million warranty.

- **Extended Validation (EV):** The highest level of business validation plus a green address bar and $1.5 million warranty.

As you look at the different certificates that are offered, bear in mind how big your customer base will be and how critical the data you will transfer and store is.

You may feel you need a certificate to cover a feedback form that collects a user's name and address, but a top-of-the-line extended validation certificate is probably overkill for just those details.

Sourcing an SSL certificate

You can buy certificates from a whole host of different places, and you are free to shop around and buy your certificate from your preferred seller. Buying a certificate from your web host, though, is sometimes best because installing a certificate isn't always easy, and your host will be able to help you with certificates purchased through it.

You can purchase SSL certificates directly from the CAs, although this is sometimes the most expensive way to do it because they often are available at discounted prices through resellers such as your host or your domain name registration provider.

There is no real advantage to buying certificates directly from a CA. Where you get your certificate is a matter of whom you prefer to do business with.

Installing an SSL certificate

Installing an SSL certificate may be one of the trickiest functions you will ever have to perform in your hosting. Depending on the level of access your host gives you, you may not even be able to install one on your server, in which case you have to request that your host do it for you.

The installation procedure is different for every CA, every brand, and every certificate level. There is justification for this because, to provide the user with the best level of security, the CA has to make it as difficult as possible for fake websites to trick browsers into believing there is a valid certificate for their fake site.

Correctly installing an SSL certificate correctly involves three required elements — and sometimes a fourth element:

- ✔ A Certificate Signing Request (CSR)
- ✔ The certificate itself
- ✔ A private key
- ✔ An intermediate CA certificate (sometimes required)

The purchase and installation procedure may or may not require you to generate the CSR and private key.

I'm sure I'm making this sound incredibly complicated, and that's because it is. There is no way to give you a generic step-by-step guide that will work regardless of the combination of CA, server software, and certificate type you choose. You should follow the certificate provider's instructions — and follow them to the letter; otherwise, the certificate will not work.

Firewalls

The term *firewall* is often used in computing without much of an explanation. In simple terms, a firewall is a digital wall protecting a computer that allows legitimate users in and repels any unwanted invaders.

I always picture it like a scene from the old *Batman* TV show. The Batcave had a secret door which opened in a rock wall to allow the Batcar through, which then closed again behind it. I imagine a wall of fire instead of a rock wall protecting the Batcave. In this imaginary scene, Batman and Robin are being chased by a bad guy. As they approach the firewall, Batman presses a button on a remote and for a brief moment the fire disappears to give him time to pass through unscathed. The fire then rises again and stops the bad guy from catching him.

This is in effect what happens with the computer firewall. Unfortunately though, your assailants are more resourceful than the bungling villains on *Batman* and, given enough time, will find a way past the defenses.

That said, firewalls are essential because they hold off any but the most determined attackers.

If you are on a shared server, your host should already have a firewall installed. There are both hardware and software firewalls, and shared hosts should automatically install both.

If you are on a Virtual Private Server (VPS) or dedicated server, your host should have provided a hardware firewall that is built in to the router. Your host may or may not have switched on a software firewall for you, so you should check with the host or examine your control panel to see if a software firewall is running.

With cPanel, you cannot install a software firewall unless you have access to the backend administration panel called Web Host Manager (WHM). You should have access to WHM if you are using cPanel on a VPS or dedicated server.

Use the following steps to check in WHM to find out if you have a firewall installed:

1. **Log into WHM using the details your host provided.**
2. **Scroll to the bottom of the page.**

3. **Look for a heading named Plugins in the menu on the left.**

4. **Look for ConfigServer Security & Firewall (CSF) in the Plugins section.**

   CSF is the default firewall for WHM and should be listed under Plugins (see Figure 8-3).

CSF link in the Plugins section

Figure 8-3:
The link to
CSF security
in WHM.

It is possible that your host may have installed a different firewall program. If that is the case then that firewall should be listed under Plugins.

If your server is not running a software firewall, follow the install instructions at www.mysql-apache-php.com/csf-firewall.htm.

After CSF is installed and running, you should go back to the WHM Plugins section and click CSF (see Figure 8-4).

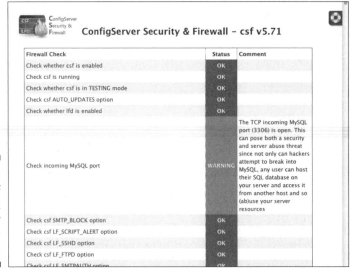

Look at a couple of things in here:

✔ **Click the Check Server Security button.** When you click the button, you see some of the areas where your server may be vulnerable to attack. Go through each one individually and close any holes you can. You may need to leave some holes open because of the website software you're running, depending on what facilities your website needs (see Figure 8-5).

Figure 8-5:
The CSF
Check
security
level page
in WHM.

✔ **Click the Firewall Security Level button and select the level of firewall security you require.** Most websites run with a medium or even high level of security selected. Due to the nature of some sites, some may require a low level of security. The easiest way to find out is to select High and test your website for functionality. If it is functioning correctly, then leave the security on high; otherwise, turn it down to medium and try again, going down to low only if necessary for your site (see Figure 8-6).

Figure 8-6:
The CSF
Firewall
Security
Level
section
in WHM.

ConfigServer Security & Firewall – csf v5.71

Firewall Security Level

Setting (see the Firewall Configuration for more information)	Current	Low	Medium	High
Block outgoing SMTP connections except for root, exim and mailman	1	0	1	1
Allow outgoing SMTP connections from localhost (127.0.0.1)	1	1	1	0
Enable IP range blocking using the DShield Block List	86400	0	86400	86400
Enable IP range blocking using the Spamhaus DROP List	86400	0	86400	86400
Enable Connection Tracking	0	0	400	300
Permanently block Connection Tracking triggered IPs	0	0	0	1
Enable Directory Watching	300	300	120	60
Remove suspicious files	0	0	1	1
Enable Process Tracking	0	60	60	30
Enable User Process Tracking	0	0	15	8
Enable User Process Tracking for all system accounts	1	0	1	1
Skip Apache Process Tracking	0	1	1	0
Ignore IPs in /etc/relayhosts (cPanel only)	1	1	0	0
Port Scan protection	10	20	10	5
Temporary to Permanent IP blocking	0	0	0	1
Permanently block IPs by network class	0	0	0	1
System Integrity Checking (md5sum checks)	3600	0	3600	3600
Select quick firewall protection level		Low	Medium	High

Return

csf: v5.71

✔ **If there is an Upgrade button, click it.** This installs the latest updates to the firewall system, which are essential for keeping the firewall as up-to-date as possible to afford you the highest level of protection it can (see Figure 8-7).

Figure 8-7:
The CSF
Upgrade
section in
WHM.

Upgrade button appears only when an upgrade is available.

Upgrade

Upgrade csf   A new version of csf (v5.71) is available. Upgrading will retain your settings
View ChangeLog

CSF also provides options to allow or deny certain IP addresses and to show the status of the firewall and restart it if necessary.

I have found that it is wise to tell CSF to allow access from your IP address. If you don't allow access from your IP address, then sometimes CSF will think that you are an attacker and will lock you out. Use the following steps to quickly allow CSF access from your IP address:

1. **Go to** www.whatsmyip.org.

   The site tells you at the top of the page what your Internet IP address is.

2. **Copy the IP address.**

3. **Go back to the CSF manager in WHM and scroll down to Quick Allow.**

   Refer to Figure 8-7 to see where the box is on the page.

4. **Paste your IP address into the green box and press Enter.**

You can do this for any IP address that you know requires access to the server. Taking this action will save headaches in the future.

A server firewall is not enough for complete security. Ensure that you have a firewall installed on any computer you use to access the server. If you have an internal network at your office, then each computer should have its own firewall to help prevent the spread of any viruses that do get through.

Protecting Your Site by Locking the SSH

Secure SHell (SSH) is a network protocol to allow secure data communication. In effect, it is like a back door into your system — one that should remain locked unless you really need to use it.

There is no point in locking and bolting the front door of your house if you're going to leave the back door wide open. Any thieves who are thwarted by the front door will find another way in simply by walking around the outside of your house.

In fact, if a burglar sneaks in the back door, you are less likely to notice him than if he walks through the front door.

This is also very much the case online, and so backdoor security is something you really need to take seriously.

SSH enables you to create a secure connection to log in to your server remotely and to execute commands on it. If a third party gets your password, that third party will also have unrestricted access to your server.

In Chapter 16, I show how to connect to your server through SSH and give you some basic commands to use. For now, you just need to decide whether SSH is necessary for you and figure out how to switch it on and off.

Determining whether you need SSH

Most hosts do not allow SSH access on shared servers simply because it is too powerful and opens the door to too many potential abuses and risks. If you are on a shared server and require SSH access, contact your host to discuss granting you access.

If you have a VPS or dedicated server, in most instances your host allows you to decide for yourself whether you want to allow SSH access and, if so, who has access and how access is granted.

Look at the following four things when securing SSH:

- **Does anybody need SSH access to your server?** If not, then simply deny all users SSH access so nobody can use it regardless of who she is.

- **If only certain users are to be given access, you can limit access by username so that only approved users can gain entry.** If, however, hackers can discover an allowed username, this provides a potential entry point for them.

- **You can allow only certain IP addresses SSH access.** This then limits where SSH access can come from and the users would still be required to provide authentication. The disadvantage of this is that most home users do not have a fixed IP address. Although that IP address may stay the same for a long time, their Internet service providers (ISPs) can change the IP address at any time. If that happens, you would have to reconfigure SSH to allow the new IP address.

- **SSH access can be granted by username and password or by a username and key system.** Keys are generated in pairs; the server holds a public key and the user provides a private key that only allows access if it matches the public key. The public key and private key are not the same. They are like a jigsaw puzzle, and when a user tries to access the server using a private key, access is only granted if the private key and public key fit together like two pieces in a puzzle.

Configuring SSH

Naturally, exactly how you configure SSH is different on every variety of web hosting software, but as an example, here is how to configure it using cPanel.

1. **Decide who, if anyone, will be allowed shell access.**

   Each control panel handles access slightly differently, but essentially there are three levels of shell access: Disabled, Jailed, or Normal. Disabling shell access for all users effectively means that SSH is unusable on the server. Jailed shell access allows users access but only to areas of the system. (Only advanced users should attempt to configure this as it can be more trouble than it's worth.) Normal shell access allows full SSH access to the server to that user. As an example, here is how to configure access in cPanel.

   1. **Log in to WHM (if you do not have access to WHM, ask your host to enable shell access for your user).**

   2. **Scroll down on the left-hand side to Account Functions, under which you click Manage Shell Access.**

   3. **Select for each user on the system whether they will have normal shell access (SSH), jailed shell access, or disabled shell access. (See Figure 8-8.)**

Figure 8-8: Managing shell access page in WHM.

Do not assume that because shell access has been disabled for all users that it is completely unusable. Although it is an effective method for denying users access to SSH, a skilled hacker may still be able to sidestep this restriction. As with any security measure, this should only be used as one of a set of security measures on your server.

2. **Decide which IP addresses will be allowed to connect via SSH.**

   Most control panels enable you to allow access only to certain IP addresses. This adds another layer of security, but it is not foolproof. To allow SSH access to only certain IP addresses in cPanel, do the following:

   1. **In WHM, scroll up to the Security Center and click Host Access Control.** Here you can allow or deny specific IP addresses access to any of the services on the server.

2. **Type** SSHD **in the box labeled Daemon.**

3. **Under access list, type the IP addresses which are allowed access.** You can enter multiple IP addresses or just one. Find your IP address at www.whatsmyip.org

4. **In the first action box, type** allow**.**

5. **On the next line, type** SSHD **as the daemon,** all **in the access list and** deny **in the action.** When a user requests access, the server checks their IP address and then starts at the top of the list to see whether that IP address is specified or not. If it is, it performs the action associated with that IP. If it does not find the IP address listed, it will move down the list searching every line for that IP address until it reaches a line that includes the word *all.* At that point it will do whatever the "all" line commands. That way, you can essentially tell the server to allow access to specific IP addresses but then deny it to all others. (See Figure 8-9.)

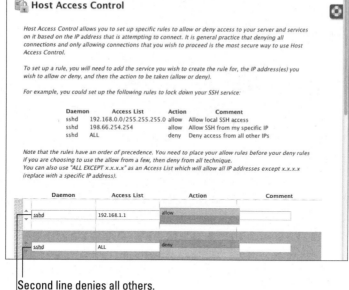

Figure 8-9:
Configuring allow/ deny SSH access by IP address in cPanel.

Second line denies all others.

First line allows certain IP addresses.

3. **Still under the Security Center, click SSH Password Authentication Tweak.**

Now decide whether or not you wish to allow access via username and password or whether all allowed users will be required to use a username and key combination. The screen will tell you whether or not password authentication is currently enabled, and if it is you can click the Disable Password Auth button to disable it and vice versa. (See Figure 8-10).

Figure 8-10: SSH password authentica- tion tweak page in WHM.

🔒 **SSH Password Authorization Tweak**

Password Authentication is currently **enabled**. For security reasons it is recommended to disable password authentication and use the "Manage root's SSH Keys" feature to generate, import, and/or authorize your keys.

Disable Password Auth

Click to enable/disable password authorization

4. **Whether or not you have SSH password authentication enabled, you can still generate keys and use those to connect.** This is a more secure method of connecting. To set the key for the root user in WHM under the Security Center, click Manage root's SSH Keys. In here you can generate a new key. Other users must generate their own keys by logging in to cPanel as the user and under the Security section clicking SSH/Shell Access. (See Figure 8-11)

Click to configure SSH access

Figure 8-11: SSH/Shell access icon in cPanel.

Security

Password Protect Directories | IP Deny Manager | SSL/TLS Manager | SSH/Shell Access | HotLink Protection | Leech Protect | GnuPG Keys

Generating SSH Keys is fairly simple in any control panel and the information required is always the same. Here's how it's done in cPanel and WHM:

1. **In cPanel, click SSH/Shell Access, then Manage SSH Keys; in WHM, click Manage root's SSH Keys, then Generate Key.**

2. **Provide a name for the key.**

   This name is for your benefit in the future so you know which key is which. Name it something which will be self-explanatory to you when you return in the future.

3. **Type a password for your key, and then confirm it in the next box.**

   Using the password generator will give you a very secure password, but it will be hard for you to remember if you ever need it in the future. The password strength indicator shows you how strong your password is. The system can be set to only allow passwords over a certain strength.

4. **Now select the key type.**

   This is either Digital Signature Algorithm (DSA) or RSA (RSA stands for Ron Rivest, Adi Shamir and Leonard Adleman, the original creators of the algorithm). Both are encryption algorithms. DSA generates keys faster, but RSA is faster for verification when you log back in again. Which you choose is up to you.

5. **Select your choice of Key Size from the drop-down box.**

   The key size can be 1024, 2048 or 4096; this is the length (in characters) of the key. The longer the key, the more secure it is. It is recommended that you use at least 2048 for RSA key types; I recommend always using the highest number possible to make the key as secure as possible.

6. **Click Generate Key.**

   This returns you to the list of keys that have been generated. If your new key does not appear in the list, then your user has not been granted SSH access.

7. **Keys must be authorized before they can be used, so under Public Keys, click Manage Authorization in the list of keys.**

8. **The next screen tells you that key is not currently authorized for use to connect to this account.**

   Change that by clicking Authorize. Likewise, you can deauthorize a key using the same method. (See Figure 8-12.)

Click to create a new key

Click to view or download this key

Click to authorize this key

Figure 8-12: Authorize a key in cPanel.

You can generate multiple keys for each username. If a number of people log in using the same username, you can generate a key for each person so that if any damage is done in the future, you can see which key was used to log in. Having multiple keys for each username can also be useful if you log in from multiple locations. You can generate a separate key to use at each location, so if one key is compromised you know which location is the source of the problem, and you can strengthen your security there.

9. **Download your private key by clicking the View/Download key under private keys.**

   This will display your key.

10. **You can either copy and paste the text into a file you create on your own computer or you can click Download Key to download a text file.**

    Depending on how you are connecting using SSH, you may require a key in Putty Private Key (PPK) format, the format used by PuTTY to store keys. If so, type the password you used when creating the key into the box and click Convert. This generates the key in PPK format for you to copy and paste or download as necessary.

If your SSH software has generated a set of keys for you, import these keys through the key manager by clicking the Import Key button.

In some control panels — such as the latest version of WHM — you cannot directly add or delete keys for other users. You can, however, delete the keys by navigating to the .ssh directory within the user's home directory. Deleting any files in there with a .pub extension will stop the user from being able to authenticate that key in the future. See Chapter 15 for details on how to find a user's home directory.

You can also add security to SSH by changing the port required to connect to the server via SSH. The default port number is 22.

It may be tempting to simply disable the SSH service altogether. Although this is possible and shouldn't damage your system, it may make your system harder to administer in the event of a failure. Very occasionally, major errors occur, and the only way to fix them is through SSH. If that is the case, there would be no way to restart the SSH service to allow you to connect: You would be completely stuck.

Securing Uploads with SSH

SSH is good for creating a secure connection through which you can remotely manage your server, and it can also be used to provide secure File Transfer Protocol (FTP) access, too.

FTP, which I explain in detail in Chapter 4, is used to transfer files to and from your server. It is a quite insecure method of transfer and can be exploited with such things as man-in-the-middle attacks to enable external users to read the data that is passing between you and the server.

Secure File Transfer Protocol (SFTP) overcomes this by creating a new FTP protocol that sits on top of the SSH protocol and derives security from the SSH protocol.

Strangely, on most hosting systems, SFTP works even if SSH has been disabled for all users. This is because SFTP allows only certain commands to be sent, which means that even though it is using SSH for security, it is not providing the exploitable access that using SSH to remotely connect normally provides.

For details on how to use SFTP, see Chapter 4.

If you want to disable SFTP then you need to edit the `/etc/ssh/sshd_config` file and comment out the following line:

```
Subsystem sftp /usr/libexec/openssh/sftp-server
```

You then need to restart the Secure Shell Daemon (SSHD). In cPanel, do this by logging into WHM and scrolling down on the left to Restart Services and clicking SSH Server and then Yes. (See Figure 8-13.)

What this does is disable the SFTP subsystem. This basically means that when a user attempts to connect via SFTP the initial handshake will be done but then the connection will be closed and no commands can be sent.

If you do not wish to use SFTP you should disable the SFTP subsystem but not the SSH service. Although disabling the SSH service would have the same effect, it could cause problems in other areas and ultimately could result in your whole system being disabled.

Click to restart service

Figure 8-13:
Restarting
the SSHD
service in
WHM.

Select for SSH server service restart

Protecting Folders with Passwords

One of the most overlooked functions of server security is the capability to password-protect certain folders at the server level.

In the UNIX/Linux operating system, you can protect folders and files using file permissions. You can add an additional level of protection for web users, allowing them access only to the pages in a folder if they have the correct password.

Sometimes people want to protect certain areas of their websites and they do this by using a password-protection system on the site itself: This is a perfectly valid way to achieve that level of protection. However, you do not need to add the extra software to do that through the website; the server already has the facility built in.

All web servers provide this functionality, and it is activated in a similar way across-the-board. In cPanel, you complete the following steps to add password protection to files and folders:

1. **Log into cPanel and scroll down to the Security section.**

2. **Click Password Protect Directories.**

3. **If a box pops up, select the domain that you want to protect.**

4. **Select the folder you want to protect.**

   In cPanel, directories can only be protected if they are directly in the web root. Note that all subfolders of the folder you protect will also be protected by the same password.

   Note that in cPanel the word *Directories* is often used, but in this case the term is *folders*. The two words can be used interchangeably. Techies tend to call them directories, but when you are viewing a directory structure using a Graphical User Interface (GUI), icons are used and the icon for a directory is a picture of a folder. Therefore, for ease of understanding for web users, the word *folder* is used to match the picture.

5. **On the password protection page, click the Password Protect This Directory box, give the directory a name, and then click Save.**

   This name appears when someone tries to access the directory and is prompted for a username and password.

6. **Create at least one user for the password-protected directory. Type the username and the password (twice).**

7. **Click Add/Modify Authorized User.**

   A confirmation screen appears.

8. **Click Go Back and at the bottom of the screen you see the name of the authorized user you just created.**

   You can now add additional users if necessary. All users created for each folder have the same level of access (see Figure 8-14).

That directory is now password-protected; anyone who attempts to access it at any time will need to provide the authorized username and password.

There is no default or override password. If you forget the password you created, you need to go back into cPanel and modify it or create a new user.

The password protection does not apply to users connecting via FTP or using the file manager through cPanel. It is only for web users viewing pages within the folders.

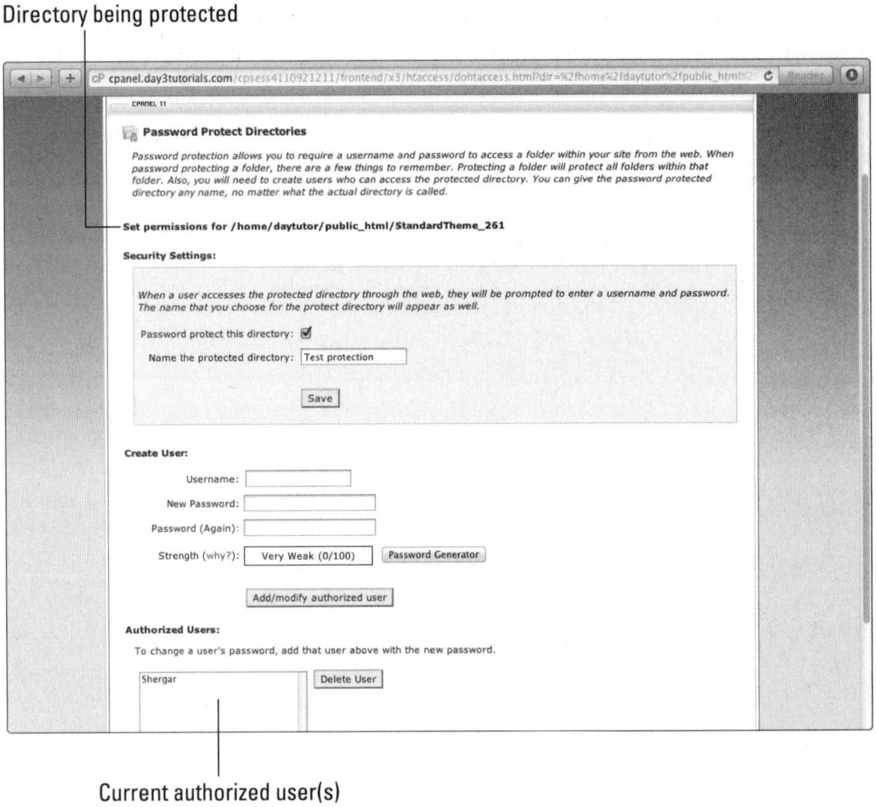

Directory being protected

Figure 8-14:
Screen
showing
authorized
users of
Password
Protected
Directories
in cPanel.

Current authorized user(s)

cPanel's password protection is created using an .htaccess file. This file is placed within the folder to be protected. Although web users cannot access this file, it can be overridden by another .htaccess file in the public_html directory. Do you think it sounds insecure? Don't worry; the public_html directory .htaccess file may be able to override the password protection, but a hacker cannot change *that* file unless he already has root access in the file system. When he has root access, the password protection doesn't apply to him anyway.

Securing Your PHP

PHP security is the nemesis of all website creators. Everyone is convinced that there must be a way to secure a PHP website against all attacks, but no matter what level of security exists, there is always a hacker somewhere who works out a way around it.

That doesn't mean you should just throw your hands up and surrender, though. You can do plenty to protect your site, although nothing is ever foolproof.

Remember, most website hacks are done by automated systems, which are written to cruise around the web and try a series of commands for a specific known exploit. To put that in real-world terms, imagine somebody made a master key that could open any lock produced by a certain lock manufacturer during the period November 1998 to June 1999. If locks from that manufacturer were widely used by households, all the criminal would need to do (if he could get a hold of one of these master keys) is go around and try his key in every lock on every house until he found a lock that was made by the right manufacturer during the right time period.

Protecting your house against this attack would be quite easy. You simply need to update your lock, and you can be certain that the key would no longer work.

Most small websites are never going to be attacked by a hacker directly. The attacks come via automated tools that are just poking around to find a site that is vulnerable. This means that you can protect yourself against the majority of attacks by following a few simple rules:

- ✔ **If you have your own server, keep your PHP version up-to-date.** How to do this varies by system. With a cPanel server, for example, either type `/scripts/easyapache` at the command line or go into WHM and select EasyApache under the Software heading.

- ✔ **If you are writing your own PHP scripts, research how to secure your scripts.** You may not think your scripts have security holes and are vulnerable to exploits, but think again! Plentiful resources online explain how to ensure that your scripts are as secure as possible. Simply search for **securing PHP scripts.**

- ✔ **If you're running web scripts or applications such as WordPress, keep them up-to-date, including any additional plug-ins and theme updates.**

- ✔ **Do not install any scripts or PHP modules that you don't absolutely need.** The less PHP you are using, the less chance there is of an exploit being found.

- ✔ **Use the most restrictive file permissions possible without interrupting the normal running of your site.** See Chapter 4 for details on setting and managing file permissions.

- ✔ **Install mod_security, if you are able to.** You can freely download mod_security to add a level of PHP security. You do have to configure it correctly to allow your software to run. Contact your host for advice on how to configure it.

✔ **Lock down your PHP installation as much as possible.** There are many configuration options for PHP that you can adjust, depending on what your website requires. A lot of available online resources can help you secure your PHP, including the PHP Security Guide from the PHP Security Consortium, which you can find at `http://phpsec.org/projects/guide/`.

✔ **Be proactive.** Sticking your head in the sand is not a good security measure. Keep your eyes and ears open to learn about new attacks and what steps security companies recommend that you take to protect against them.

Appreciating Your Security Guard — the .htaccess File

I mention `.htaccess` files earlier in this chapter, but I haven't yet mentioned how useful and powerful they can be. The `.htaccess` file is one of a number of files called *dot files*. This clever name comes from the fact that the names all start with a dot (`.`). This is unusual because normally the dot indicates the separation between the filename and the file extension (for example, `index.php` or `home.htm`).

Dot files are essentially hidden files. The system can access them, but they are normally hidden from view or access by general users. In Chapter 4, I explain how to view dot files using FTP or your file manager. You cannot navigate to dot files through websites, so the files can securely hold configuration information and other security-related commands and data.

The `.htaccess` file is one that is used to provide an additional level of security to the folder it is in. The directives in an `.htaccess` file also apply to any subfolders below the folder they are placed in.

Directory trees are hierarchical, and commands in `.htaccess` files in higher folders will override commands in `.htaccess` files lower down the tree. The result of this is that sometimes you can create an `.htaccess` file in a lower folder and find that it seems to do nothing. The first thing to do in this instance is to check higher up the tree to see if there is a command that is overriding the `.htaccess` file you just created.

The `.htaccess` file can do many things to help you with website security, such as the following:

✔ **Adding authorization/authentication.** As the word *access* in the filename suggests, you can use the `.htaccess` file to password-protect files and folders often in conjunction with another file called `.htpasswd`, which stores the valid login details.

✔ **Blocking users via IP address or domain name.** The .htaccess file can contain a list of IP addresses, domains, spiders, bots, and referrers who are automatically locked from accessing any files in the folder. This can be a good second line of defense even if you have the same users blocked in your firewall.

✔ **Controlling directory listing.** If a web folder is called by a browser without specifying a filename, by default the user's browser displays a list of files within that folder. This is sometimes useful, but there are other times that you do not want web users to see all the files in a folder; your .htaccess file can deny permission to list those files.

✔ **Rewriting URLs.** Due to the nature of how websites and the pages are created, sometimes filenames or the paths to files can become extremely long. The .htaccess file essentially makes a new index that enables users to use a shortened version of the file path that the server can understand and take those users to the correct place. It also can be useful if you make a change to the file structure and want to redirect incoming links to old filenames to the new filenames.

With .htaccess files you can add a level of security and perform certain functions and commands, but .htaccess files don't always provide the fastest solution in terms of website access speeds.

Some people argue that if you have a VPS or dedicated server and have access to the httpd server config file, it is faster to use that file instead of .htaccess. This may be true. The problem with .htaccess files is that they are read with every http request and, with each request, the server must look in every folder above the current folder in the directory tree for .htaccess files, which may have commands that override the .htaccess file in the current folder. This results in more file reads and disk searches for every web page that is viewed, slowing down the whole system.

On the other hand, given the global nature of the httpd config file, it may be safer for the novice website owner to steer clear of that file so other settings are not accidentally messed up. Also not everyone has access to the httpd config file, so .htaccess provides a more universal way for site owners to add security and make certain changes.

You can modify .htaccess files using a command-line editor, such as vi, or via the file manager or FTP.

The changes you should make depend entirely on your server setup and your website. Research what you need, including the correct commands and syntax to use for your specific application.

Some control panel functions automatically add lines to your .htaccess file. You should not remove these unless you want to disable that function. For example, when creating password-protected directories, the directory protection is set up by creating an .htaccess file in the directory you want to protect. Deleting a file or removing the lines that have been added to it will remove that protection or, even worse, stop legitimate users from being able to authenticate themselves.

Doing Your Part in Avoiding Viruses

The final necessity for becoming the king (or queen) of network security is that you do your part to avoid viruses and malware. This means doing a handful of things, which are really just common sense:

- ✔ **Follow the suggestions I explain in this chapter on securing your site.** Many hackers do not try to extract information from your site, but rather attempt to gain access so that they can place viruses or malware on your site, which will then attack your users and other servers.

- ✔ **Be cautious about what sites you visit and what you download and install, both on your server and your own computer.** Quite often, you can become infected by a virus without any warning and without knowing it happened. Increasingly, though, your browser warns you if the site you are visiting is known to harbor viruses or malware. If you continue to visit those sites and ignore the warnings then do not be surprised if you later find that your computer and your website become infected.

- ✔ **Keep your login names and passwords as secure as possible.** Do not give them out to anyone you don't trust. You should also change passwords and even usernames on a regular basis and delete any usernames that are no longer required. Making these changes minimizes the chances of a virus or malware network getting hold of your usernames and passwords and exploiting them.

- ✔ **Maintain updated antivirus software and firewalls on all the devices you use to connect to your website.** Computer viruses are like human viruses — they are infectious and spread on contact. Running up-to-date antivirus software keeps you inoculated against all but the newest viruses and thus saves you from becoming a carrier who infects other devices.

Please remember that the web server you are hosting is on is just a computer. You may be the only user of that computer or you may be one of many. Either way, it is your responsibility to do all you can to ensure that you keep that computer safe from the viruses, malware, and hackers that will try to attack it.

Chapter 9

Decoding Domains and DNS

In This Chapter

▶ Breaking down DNS so anyone can understand it

▶ Figuring out when to buy extra domain names — and what to do with them

▶ Altering and updating DNS records

*W*hen designing the architecture of the Internet, the single most important requirement was that it had to work. By work, I mean it had to enable anybody who connects to it to easily navigate to any resources on it. The second most important requirement was that it needed to keep working with as much resilience and redundancy as possible, while being fast enough to be useable.

To the human eye, the Internet is simply a place where you type in recognizable names and those names take you to websites; however, a lot goes on behind the scenes to make it work in computer terms and yet keep it as simple and intuitive as possible for human users.

This chapter starts by delving behind the scenes to show you how the Domain Name System (DNS) works and what it does for you. Then it shows you how to manipulate the DNS to make your website faster, more resilient, and generally more awesome.

Understanding DNS

Every device attached to the Internet has a unique Internet Protocol (IP) address, just like every house has a unique address.

Plenty of houses in the world have the number 1600 and there are probably quite a few with addresses of 1600 Pennsylvania Avenue. That said, there is definitely only one with the complete address of 1600 Pennsylvania Ave., Washington D.C.

So, while having only part of an address could lead you to the wrong place, when you have the *complete* address you know that you're looking at an absolutely unique address.

You can give that address to anybody, anywhere in the world, and he or she would be able to use it to travel to and locate the building you want that person to find. IP addresses are designed to be just as unique as complete snail-mail addresses. You can give an IP address of a device anywhere in the world to any machine connected to the Internet and the device that receives that information will be able to navigate its way there due to the way the Internet is designed and the uniqueness of each IP address.

The server your website is on has an IP address, and the unique nature of this address is critical to enabling web users to find your website.

For normal use, you don't have to type IP addresses into your browsers to find websites because the DNS maps website names to the IP addresses of the servers they're on. So instead of saying, "I want to go to 74.125.224.103," you can simply say, "I want to go to Google.com."

We do the same translation in real-world addresses. You would not normally say, "I'm going to 1600 Pennsylvania Ave., Washington D.C., U.S.A." You would simply say, "I'm going to the White House." The only time you need to use the White House's address is if you don't already know where the White House is.

Remember the days when, if you wanted to know where somebody lived, you looked up his name in the local (and often cumbersome) phone book, in which his address and phone number were listed beside his name? If I wanted to go to Joe Schmoe's house and I didn't know where Joe Schmoe lived, I would simply open the phone book, search through the alphabetically arranged names for Joe Schmoe, and the phone book would show Joe's address. (Okay, okay — I know sometimes addresses are unlisted even when a phone number is provided, but work with me here as I provide this generalization to help make my point.) The Internet provides a system very much like this, the DNS, albeit it's a little larger and more complicated than a simple phone book.

Is your address fully qualified?

For the Internet to be able to give you the IP address of the exact server you need to connect to in order to visit the site you want, you need to provide a complete website address. This is called a *Fully Qualified Domain Name (FQDN)*.

An FQDN is comprised of three parts:

- A hostname
- The domain name
- The extension, which is also known as the Top-Level Domain (TLD)

For example, the domain www.dummies.com has the following components:

- The hostname is www.
- The domain name is dummies.
- The TLD is .com.

Here in the Western world, people read from left to right, but when searching for a website your computer actually reads the address from right to left — and here's why:

The foundations on which the Internet is built are a set of servers called the Internet Root Name Servers. There are 13 root nameservers and they have a critically important job: Root nameservers deliver one fairly small file (the Root Zone File) to any computer that requests it.

The Root Zone File contains the IP addresses of another set of servers called the TLD nameservers. There are a number of types of TLD, the most common of which are the following:

- **Country-Code Top-Level Domains (ccTLD):** These are comprised of two letters preceded by a dot and they are internationally recognized as the code for a specific country. These were set up by the International Organization for Standardization (ISO) and are known as the ISO 3166 codes. For example, .au represents Australia and .uk represents the United Kingdom.

- **Internationalized Top-Level Domains (IDN TLD):** These are ccTLDs in non-Latin character sets (for example, Greek or Chinese characters).

- **Generic Top-Level Domains (gTLD):** These domains usually include three letters preceded by the dot (for example, .com, .org, and .net), but may contain more (for example, .info).

Each separate TLD has its own "Authoritative Nameserver" with its own unique IP address. The simplest definition of a nameserver is a server that holds a directory of domain names mapped to the IP addresses of the servers those domain names reside on.

The term Authoritative Nameserver defines a server as the one that is kept the most up-to-date. You can have secondary nameservers, which hold a copy of the records from the Authoritative Nameservers, but if there are any discrepancies, the authoritative server is treated as the correct one. Authority is defined by a Start of Authority (SOA) record.

So, for example, the Authoritative Nameserver for the TLD .com holds a list of all the .com domain names and their IP addresses, the nameserver for the TLD .org holds a list of all the .org domain names, and so on. (See Figure 9-1.)

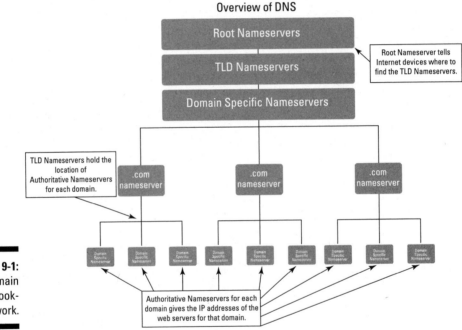

Overview of DNS

Root Nameservers

TLD Nameservers

Domain Specific Nameservers

Root Nameserver tells Internet devices where to find the TLD Nameservers.

TLD Nameservers hold the location of Authoritative Nameservers for each domain.

.com nameserver

.com nameserver

.com nameserver

Authoritative Nameservers for each domain gives the IP addresses of the web servers for that domain.

Figure 9-1: How domain name look-ups work.

When you type an FQDN into your browser — for example, www.google.com — your browser goes to a DNS server (normally one owned by your Internet Service Provider, or ISP) and asks if it knows the IP address of www.google.com. If the DNS server does not know the address then your browser requests a *recursive search,* which means the DNS server must search every resource it can for the answer and either come back with the address or a failure message.

The DNS server then starts an *iterative search,* which goes a little something like this:

First it goes to a Root Name Server and asks, "Do you know where I can find www.google.com? If not, can you suggest where I should look?" The Root Name Server says, "No, but I know where the .com server is; go ask the .com server." It then supplies the DNS server with the IP address of the .com server (in the form of the Root Zone File I mention earlier).

The DNS server then goes to the .com nameserver and says, "Do you know where I can find www.google.com? If not, can you suggest where I should look?" The .com server replies, "No, but I know where the google.com server is." It then sends the DNS server to the Authoritative Nameserver for google.com.

The Authoritative Nameservers for the domain (and there must be at least two) are the ones that hold the exact details of where to find the hostname you are searching for.

When the DNS server queries the google.com nameserver, the DNS server first checks that the nameserver is authoritative for the domain (the SOA record), and, if it is, asks, "Do you know where I can find www.google.com? If not, can you suggest where I should look?" The google.com nameserver checks its zone record for that hostname and either returns an IP address or tells the DNS server the hostname does not exist.

Confused? See Figure 9-2 to get a visual idea of the process.

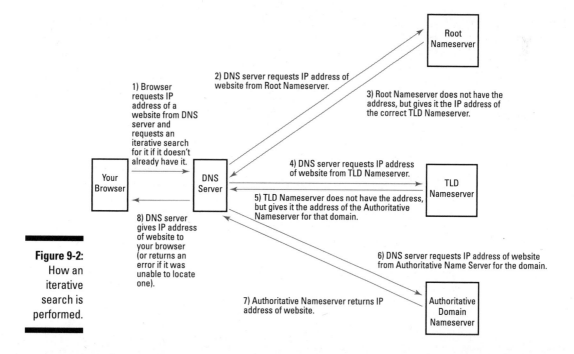

Figure 9-2:
How an iterative search is performed.

Part of the iterative search is for the DNS server to be given the IP address of the next server to ask. If that IP address does not respond to the query, it returns to the previous server and says, "That server is not responding; do you know of another server I can try?" This is why there are multiple servers to try in each part of the process, so if one is down, the DNS server should, in theory, be able to find another way through.

You may think of a website address as being something like `google.com` or `dummies.com`, but, as I mention earlier, to make the name fully qualified it requires another part before the domain name, such as `www.`, which is the *hostname.*

Because of the way the DNS works, this extra element, the hostname, is important. In most cases, by default, if you type a domain name into a browser and do not include a hostname, it will assume a default hostname of `www.`

Most websites now are built so that an empty hostname and the hostname `www.` both point to the same front page of the website, just to make things easier. They don't have to, though; you can configure `www.` to go to a page other than the empty hostname!

The Authoritative Nameserver for the domain holds an index of all the host-names configured for that domain and the IP addresses where those host-names are found, called the DNS Zone File. The way the majority of websites are configured, the server that actually houses the domain name (and most or all of its hostnames) also acts as the nameserver.

This is just for simplicity and cost purposes, but it is not the most advisable way to do things.

As I mention earlier, resilience is the key to the continued functioning of the Internet and so, all the way through this process, multiple servers are actually in play. There are 13 Internet Root Nameservers; if one or two were to go down for some reason, plenty would remain that your browser could find. Actually, 13 is slightly incorrect: Each of those 13 "servers" is a cluster of servers that provide another level of resilience. Root Nameservers are physically located in more than 130 locations around the globe, and there could be multiple servers at each location for added redundancy.

Each TLD actually has multiple Authoritative Nameservers for redundancy and, as I mention earlier, each domain name requires at least two Authoritative Nameservers for the same reason.

At any stage of the iterative search if the DNS server exhausts the possible IP addresses it is provided, and then it returns an error and your browser displays that error message. The sheer size of the infrastructure behind the Internet Root Nameservers and TLD servers makes it unlikely that your browser or the DNS server will ever fail to find one of them. Normally if an error message appears, it is either because the Authoritative Nameserver for the domain could not be found or because the IP address the Authoritative Nameserver said the website is at is incorrect.

The trouble with caches

Just to make things a little more complicated, the system is actually sped up by the use of what is known as DNS caching.

There are a number of caches, the most important of which are the following:

- ✔ **Your computer's cache:** Whenever you search for a new website, your computer stores the IP address in the computer's local cache. This means that the next time you request to visit that website, the browser does not have to spend time redoing the search for the correct address; it simply pulls the address from its cache of stored addresses.

- ✔ **Your browser's cache:** In addition to the cache your computer keeps, each browser you have installed on your computer (for example, Internet Explorer, Safari, Firefox, or Chrome) can keep its own cache of website IP addresses. There have been many times when different browsers on my computer have shown different results for a website because the site has moved and one of the browsers hasn't updated its cache.

- ✔ **Your DNS server's cache:** The configuration of the DNS ensures that, when your computer starts a search for a domain name, the search is routed through your ISP's DNS server and is not done directly by your computer. For this reason, your ISP keeps a cache of the domain names all of its users have searched for. This reduces traffic from the Internet by lowering the number of iterative searches that are performed. If one of your neighbors has already looked up `google.com`, the DNS server doesn't need to search for it again when you want to go there; it just tells you where it found `google.com` the last time it looked.

Other caches may be held by programs on your computer to enable them to provide faster access to places you commonly visit on the Internet. For example, if you have a mail client, such as Outlook or Thunderbird, it holds its own cache that is renewed every time the program is started.

This is why, if you have ever moved a website from one server to another, it can take a while for your browser to see the change. The ISP caches are cleared out regularly but may retain information for 48 hours or more. You can refresh your own cache fairly easily, but you can still be misdirected by your ISP for a while.

Confused? Don't be.

Remember the example of a phone book. You look up a name in the phone book and the phone book gives you the person's address. You then cache that address in your own memory. The next time you need that person's address, you don't have to look it up in the phone book because you already know it. You only look it up again if you forget it.

The phone book is also a kind of cache because, when somebody moves, the printed phone book is not automatically updated. If the address in the phone book is incorrect, you have to wait for the cache to be updated (a new phone book to be printed and delivered) before you have the correct address. You then update your personal cache (your memory) with the new address.

Obviously, it's a little quicker to update caches and addresses on the Internet than in print, but the concept is still the same.

Manipulating Your Domain Name

You now know the basics of how the DNS works with regard to finding websites. The DNS Zone File held by the Authoritative Nameserver for a domain is actually quite extensive, and later in this chapter you find out how to manipulate it. For now, I'm going to switch to the side of the Internet visible to web users and show you how subdomains work (and can improve your website) and how using the DNS for domain parking and redirects can be useful to you.

Getting creative with subdomains

As I explain earlier, an FQDN requires a hostname as well as a domain name. This means that any domain name can actually be split into multiple subdomains.

Picture it like an apartment building — not just any old apartment building either, but a fairly swanky apartment building.

The first floor of the apartment building has an open space that has plenty of comfortable seating and refreshments available. It's a common area that can be used by all residents of and visitors to the apartments.

If somebody told you she lived at 123 Example Street, Exampleton, then you would assume that when you arrived you simply needed to go through the front door to find her. However, in this swanky apartment building that would only get you to the communal area on the first floor. To find the actual apartment, you would need to know the specific apartment number.

So the complete address would be Apartment 45, 123 Example Street, Exampleton. After you have this correct, full address you can navigate straight to the apartment.

This is also true of websites. If you give somebody your website address with no hostname at the beginning, it is like providing your apartment address without your apartment number. That's okay if you live in a house rather than an apartment (or, in website terms, you only require a site to have the default hostname). However, the flexibility of the DNS means that at any time you can create a subdomain by creating a new hostname, you can have a second, third, and fourth (and so on) website all underneath one domain name.

For example, you may convert the upstairs of your house into an apartment for your mother-in-law to live in. Your mother-in-law can then get her own mail and give out her own address as Apartment A, 456 Sample Street, Exampleton.

Likewise, say you're running a website for your local football team, `example footballteam.com`, and the coach decides he wants to have his own blog. You can create a subdomain with its own hostname of *coach*, which will give him his own unique address to make his own site, still under the umbrella of `examplefootballteam.com`.

In this example, the FQDN of the coach's blog would be `coach.example footballteam.com`.

Both `coach.examplefootballteam.com` and `www.examplefootball team.com` are FQDNs, meaning they are both unique and can therefore point to different places online.

In theory, you can have as many subdomains as you need under your domain, but some of the cheaper web hosts may limit the maximum number they allow you to create.

You can get as creative as you like with your subdomains and are limited only by your imagination and your requirements. Some people never require a subdomain, whereas others create a seemingly endless stream of them.

Just to get your creative juices flowing, the following list includes a few ideas of how you might want to use subdomains:

- ✔ You may have purchased the domain `yourfamilyname.com` and created a personal website there. You may then want to give your children the opportunity to have their own websites and so you create a subdomain for each of them — for example, `Sandra.yourfamilyname.com`, `Philip.yourfamilyname.com`, and `Alex.yourfamilyname.com`.

- ✔ Your company's website may be `yourawesomebusiness.com`, and you may want to create another site where you give support for your products, which you could call `support.yourawesomebusiness.com`. You may wish to create another site where you have a forum for your customers to talk about how awesome your products are, called `forum.yourawesomebusiness.com`.

- ✔ Say your name is Gemma and you spend all your spare time doing arts and crafts and have built a website called `gemmasartsandcrafts.com` to show people some of your beautiful items. Only after you started building the site did you realize that the papier-mâché models you create are really of little interest to the people interested in needlework or oil painting. You can create separate sites for each type of craft, each with its own subdomain, such as `oilpainting.gemmasartsand crafts.com` and `needlework.gemmasartsandcrafts.com` as well as having your main site at `gemmasartsandcrafts.com`.

Creating a new subdomain

Most control panels provide you with a simple way to create new subdomains. In the later section "Setting Up DNS Effortlessly," I show you how to manually create a subdomain, but that's generally more effort than it's worth when you can do it through an automated system.

The process for setting up a subdomain is essentially the same for most control panels. As an example, here's how you do it in cPanel:

1. **Log in to cPanel with the details your host provided when you opened the account.**

2. **Scroll to the Domains section and click Subdomains.**

3. **Type the name of the new subdomain you want to create in the box.**

4. **Select the domain for which you want to create a subdomain.**

Any add-on or parked domains you have set up will be available in the drop-down box. See the later sections "Expanding your presence with add-on domains" and "Parking domains in your parking lot" for an explanation of add-on and parked domains.

5. If you want to, type the path to the document root of the domain.

By default, the system selects /public_html/TheSubdomainYouTyped, but you can change it if you need to. See Figure 9-3.

Figure 9-3:
Setting up a
subdomain.

Do *not* change the document root unless you are certain you know what you are doing. Changing the document root can make the setup very confusing.

6. Click Create.

The subdomain shows up in the list at the bottom of the page. You can remove it by clicking Remove or, if you need to, you can redirect it (see the later section "Redirecting domains like a traffic cop" for more information on redirection).

If you need to redirect a subdomain for a domain, it *must* first be set up as a subdomain, either through the automatic process or manually. Otherwise the DNS does not know of its existence and the redirect does not work.

Expanding your presence with add-on domains

Sometimes subdomains just aren't enough. There are times when a new product or project requires its own domain name with its very own website. This may mean that you need to purchase a new hosting plan for the new domain name, but if your web host allows you add-on domains you can save yourself some money by hosting multiple domain names under one hosting account. There are positives and negatives to using add-on domains rather than purchasing separate hosting packages for each domain name.

Some positive aspects of using add-on domains include the following:

- ✔ **Cost savings.** Obviously, it's cheaper to pay for one hosting plan than two. That's a no-brainer.

- ✔ **A single hosting plan means you have just one control panel login to remember and you can administer all your domain names from there.**

- ✔ **Depending on your host's configuration and which control panel it uses, add-on domains are often held in directories that are part of the main domain's file structure.** This means that when you back up the files from the main domain, you can automatically back up the files from the add-on domains with them.

Using add-on domains has some drawbacks, too. Following are some negative aspects of add-on domains:

- ✔ **Even unlimited hosting plans normally have some limits to the amount of resources you can use.** Add-on domains share resources with the main domain and so, if any or all of the domains become popular, they could use up all the resources allocated to you, thus affecting all the domains you have hosted under that one package.

- ✔ **If your add-on domain is part of the directory tree of the main domain, viruses can potentially jump from one site to another.** You also may accidentally delete files or even entire sites.

- ✔ **Things can get messy if you want to shut down or sell one or more of your websites.** You can end up having to do a lot of jiggery-pokery to extract and rehouse the domains you want to keep, particularly if your main domain is the one that you want to sell or dispose of.

It's always a Catch-22 situation trying to decide which way is best for your domain names. I've had situations where I have created add-on domains and then had to move everything around within a couple of months because my business focus changed. On the other hand, I have some sites that have been running for years on separate hosting plans, and I could be saving money if I had put them together on one hosting plan because I rarely, if ever, need to move them around or do anything out of the ordinary.

Sometimes it's just necessary to have another domain name to do something different and, if you don't have any immediate plans to shut down your main site, using add-on domains can be an easy and cost-effective way to increase your online presence.

Each control panel has its own way of adding and handling add-on domains. Some control panels do not even have the facility to include add-on domains, in which case you need to contact your host to discuss your options for adding a second domain name.

In cPanel, you configure add-on domains using the tools on the Addon Domains page (see Figure 9-4), which you access by clicking the Addon Domains icon in the Domains section of your control panel. When you have configured an add-on domain, you'll find that its folder tree is in a subfolder of your main domain. The subfolder's name is the domain name of the add-on domain.

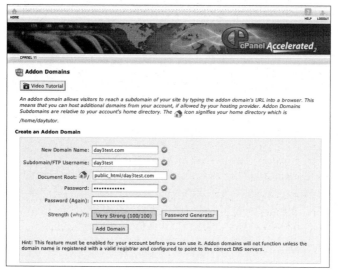

Figure 9-4: Creating an add-on domain.

Figure 9-5 shows an add-on domain to day3tutorials.com, called day3test. com. In the figure, you are looking at the document root for `www.day3 tutorials.com` in the cPanel file manager, and it is showing the website files for day3tutorials.com. In there is a folder called `day3test.com`. That folder is the document root for the `day3test.com` domain so, if you go to that folder, it would then show you the website files for that domain name.

All files for add-on domain day3test.com are inside the day3test.com folder.

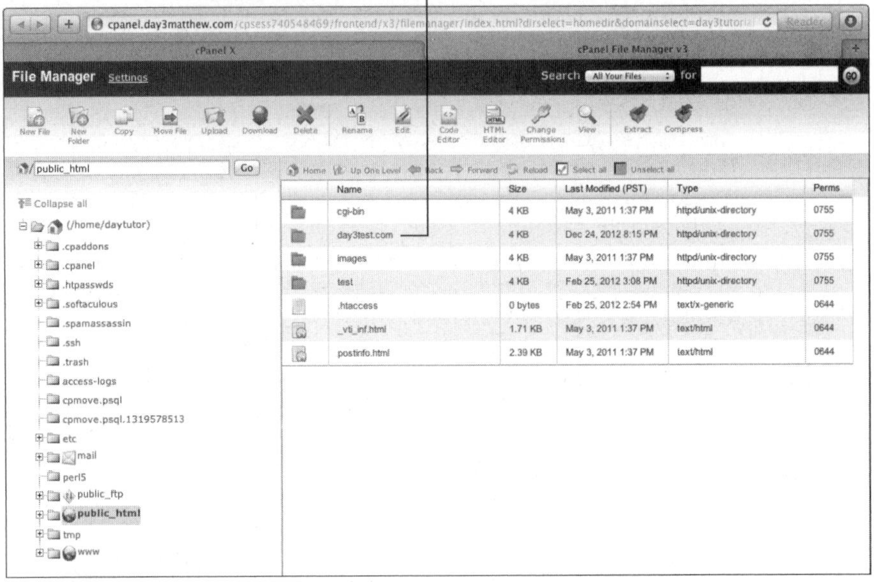

Figure 9-5:
File
Manager
showing the
document
root for
day3
tutorials.com.

Parking domains in your parking lot

Sometimes you need a second, third, or fourth domain name, but that domain name doesn't need its own website. What you need to do in this instance is to park the name somewhere until you need it or redirect it to somewhere else. Most hosting plans allow you to park domains in a proverbial domain name parking lot.

As discussed earlier in this chapter, every domain name requires at least two Authoritative Nameservers. When you register a domain name through your domain name registrar, you have the option of selecting what nameservers you want the domain name to point to.

You have a few options at this point:

✔ **Use your domain registrar's default nameservers.** If you don't intend to do anything with the domain name straightaway, this can be a reasonable option, but generally it means that your registrar's nameservers point the name to a dummy site (pun not to be confused with the *For Dummies* brand, by the way!) that says "this domain name is currently parked here awaiting its site to be built," or something to that effect. That dummy site often also has ads and links on it that have the potential of earning your registrar some money if anybody finds that page and clicks on the ads.

✔ **Make up some fake nameservers.** Some registrars don't allow you to do this because their systems automatically check that the nameservers actually exist before allowing you to select them. If you can get away with it, though, it simply means that your domain name points to nothing, and anybody who types it into her browser gets an error.

✔ **Use the nameservers of one of your current domain names and park the domains there.** This option gives you a little flexibility and the opportunity to choose what exactly happens to any traffic that tries to visit the parked domain.

If you want to set up your own dummy website for a parked domain, then you'll probably find that your host will class that as a complete website in itself; if so, you would need to set it up either as an add-on domain or purchase a hosting package for it.

You can, however, simply park it and leave it going nowhere, or park it and redirect it using the DNS.

Some people make a lot of money through parked domains by placing advertising with affiliate links on the sites they redirect to. There is an art to getting this right. You have to target the ads to appeal to the people who might visit that domain name, but some people buy thousands of domain names and have developed their own systems for placing the right ads under the right domain names to bring in a large, steady monthly income.

Redirecting domains like a traffic cop

Instead of parking a domain and leaving it pointing nowhere, or even worse leaving it making money for someone else, you can park it somewhere where you have the capability to modify its DNS settings. Some domain registrars allow you to do this through your domain registration control panel, or you can do it through your hosting account.

There are a number of reasons for using domain redirection and a number of different ways in which it's used. The following examples help you see why you might want to redirect some domain names:

✔ **To help people find your site it can be useful to buy different variations of your domain name.** These variations include purchasing the name with different TLDs, purchasing the name with different spellings, or in some cases even purchasing different names because users might guess incorrectly what your domain name is. For example, the *For Dummies* brand of books has its own website, and if you were to guess what the address of the website is, it might be logical to think that it would be fordummies.com. In fact, that's the name I normally think of when I try to go to the website. The *For Dummies* website, though, is actually `dummies.com`, so the publisher has purchased the `fordummies.com` name and set it up to redirect to `dummies.com` so that visitors go to the right site, whichever name they type in. Perhaps the most famous example of someone who should have also bought the domain name with other extensions (TLDs) is the White House. The official website for the White House is found at `whitehouse.gov`. When the White House staff registered the domain name, they did not buy the name with different extensions such as `.com` or `.org`. This resulted in other individuals registering those domain names and for a number of years, the `WhiteHouse.com` domain hosted pornography. Many potential visitors who were trying to guess the name of the website of the White House typed in **WhiteHouse.com** because it was often the first thing they thought of. This resulted in quite a lot of embarrassment for the White House when web users, especially children, tried to view the White House website and ended up seeing porn instead. With a little forethought and $10 a year, the White House staff could have prevented quite a few blushes and angry letters from parents.

✔ **Redirecting an old domain name.** You might decide at some point to change your domain name because you come up with something better or your focus changes. You might want a domain name that better reflects your website, but still want to continue to own the previous domain name so you can redirect it to your new domain name. That way, people who know you by the old name can still find their way to your new site.

✔ **Buying a domain name for a specific project.** You may be running a specific project or putting on an event, or you may have a specific product that you don't want to create an entire website for but you want to be able to direct central customers or visitors directly to the right place on your site. For example, Apple has a product called iTunes. The correct website address for iTunes is `Apple.com/itunes`. A web user wanting to find out more about iTunes, though, might assume that iTunes is found at `itunes.com`. That's why Apple purchased the name `itunes.com` and redirected it to `Apple.com/itunes`. Apple then did the same with `itunes.org`. Interestingly, it seems the company purchased the name `itunes.net`, but at time of writing, `itunes.net` is not redirected to go anywhere. Instead, it leads to a blank white page. That may be a missed opportunity for Apple.

✔ **Redirecting a URL to a specific domain name.** This is actually the reverse of the preceding item in the list. For example, there may come a time when Apple wants to move the iTunes website away from the `Apple.com` site. iTunes would then have its own site at `itunes.com` and Apple may want to redirect `apple.com/iTunes` to send people straight to that site.

✔ **Domain squatting.** Although domain squatting is frowned upon by many web users, there are pros and cons to both the arguments *for* domain squatting and *against* domain squatting. Most web users would argue that purchasing a domain name in the hopes that one day somebody might want to use that domain name and then buy it from them for a large amount of money is a little unethical. On the other hand, there are times when you might come up with a brilliant idea for a site, or what you think is a brilliant name, but you don't have time to use it immediately; still, you want to register it before someone else comes up with the same brilliant idea. Whatever your reason for purchasing extra domain names, when you purchase them, redirecting them either to your main website or another site of your choice is generally a better idea than leaving them doing nothing.

You may be wondering now if I'm suggesting that you should spend all your hard-earned cash on every domain name that you can think of. Don't worry; that's not exactly what I'm suggesting. It is good to think about your visitors and try and put yourself in their shoes for a moment and consider whether purchasing additional domain names would be useful to both them and you. You don't need to bankrupt yourself on just-in-case domain names, though.

Exactly how you redirect the domain name differs depending on the facilities your domain name registrar gives you. If the registrar does not give you the right facilities, it then depends which control panel is used for your hosting. As an example, I show you how to redirect domain names using cPanel and, regardless of which system you use, the basic concept is the same.

There are two ways to set up a redirection. The first is to park the domain with a blanket redirect; the second is to get a little more creative with URL redirects.

Setting up a blanket redirect

Use the following steps to park and redirect a domain name using cPanel:

1. **Purchase the domain name you want to use.**

   During the purchase process, set the nameservers to the same as the ones for your current hosted domain.

2. **Log into cPanel using the details your host gave you when you first signed up.**

3. **Scroll to the Domains section and click Parked Domains.**

4. **Type the name of the domain you want to park into the box and click Add Domain.**

It is important to note that cPanel does not allow you to do this until the domain is registered and the nameservers point to the server. If you have only just registered the domain name, it can occasionally take a little while for the registration to go through and the information to propagate around the Internet. You therefore may have to wait a couple of hours after purchasing the domain before you can park it.

5. **Change the redirection, if necessary.**

At this point, the domain is parked and automatically redirects to the primary domain in the hosting account. So web users who type in the domain name are automatically redirected to your primary domain. If you want the domain name to redirect somewhere other than the root of your primary domain, then click Manage Redirection. (See Figure 9-6.)

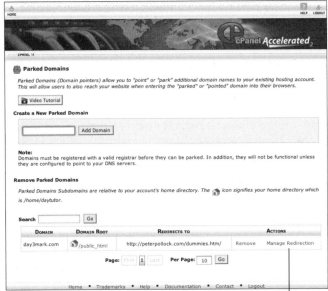

Figure 9-6:
Manage
parked
domains.

Click Manage Redirection to change the redirect.

6. **Type the full URL of the domain or file you wish it to redirect to in the box on the Parked Domain Redirection Page.**

If you are redirecting to a file, then you need to end the URL with a trailing forward slash (/).

 To remove the redirection, click Disable Redirection on the Parked Domain Redirection page. To remove the parked domain completely, click Remove on the main Parked Domains page.

URLs are case sensitive after the TLD. The FQDN is not case sensitive (`www.dummies.com` is the same as `www.DUMMIES.com`), but the file path, which is everything that comes after the slash, is. So `www.dummies.com/store.html` is a valid file, but www.dummies.com/Store.html is not. You can choose to use capital letters in your paths and filenames if you want, but remember to always capitalize them the same when referencing them or you will not be able to navigate to the correct pages.

Creating URL redirects

Sometimes you might want to get a little more creative with your redirects and set up a specific URL to redirect somewhere. I actually used this method just now as I was sitting down to write. I have a link to give people introductions to a membership community for entrepreneurs. The link is extremely hard to remember (`https://founderscard.com/membership?code=FCPETER093`) so, to make it easier for people to remember, I set up a redirect at `peterpollock.com/fc`, which redirects them straight to the right page. It took just a few seconds to do and yet made the URL shorter, more memorable, and easier to spell.

The following steps explain how to get more creative with redirects using cPanel:

1. **Log into cPanel using the details your host gave you when you first signed up.**

2. **Scroll to the Domains section and click Redirects.**

3. **Choose the type of redirect you want.**

   Redirect choices are 301 and 302. These are standard numbers that the server uses to inform your browser of the redirect and give it more information so it knows what to do. A 301 redirect is a permanent redirect. This means that, as far as you know, this redirect will never change. Your browser then knows that it should update any bookmarks you have to the original URL with the details of the redirect. A 302 redirect is only a temporary redirect, which means you're purposefully redirecting for a short time and this may be due to some maintenance or for a short-term project. The browser knows not to update its bookmarks because it needs to check every time you use the URL whether the redirect is still in place.

4. **Choose the domain name you want to redirect from the drop-down box.**

   The drop-down box includes your primary domain and any add-on or parked domains under the account.

5. **Type the rest of the path to the file or folder you want to redirect.**

   For example, if you want to create a redirect so that everyone who types in **yourdomain.com/myfavoritebooks** gets sent to the *For Dummies* website, in this box you'd type **myfavoritebooks**. (See Figure 9-7.)

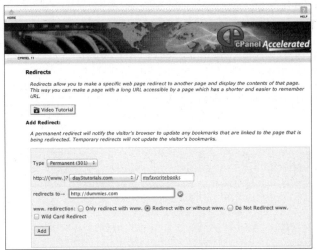

Figure 9-7:
A sample
redirect.

6. **In the Redirects To box, type the full URL of the site, file, or page that you want to redirect to.**

   You also need to include the protocol for the URL, which will normally be `http://`.

7. **Select what type of www. redirection you require.**

   Normally this will be redirect with or without www. As I explain earlier in this chapter, www. is normally simply the default hostname in your URL and your browser treats no hostname and www. as the same thing. It is possible to configure this differently, though, so that www. is a different page on your site. If that is the case on your site, you may need to choose one of the other www. redirection options.

8. **Select the Wildcard Redirect option, if desired.**

   Wildcard redirects can be useful in certain circumstances, but are not always necessary. A wildcard redirect redirects to the same filename in the destination directory. This is useful if you change your domain name, but otherwise have your directory structure the same. For example, you might have a contact form for which your old URL was `yourdomain.com/contact.htm` and the correct new URL might be `yournewdomain.com/contact.htm`. The file structure is the same; only the domain name differs. In this case, if you do not use a wildcard redirect when somebody clicks a link or types into the browser **your domain.com/contact.htm**, instead of being redirected to the contact form on your new domain, that person would be redirected to the main page on your new domain (`yournewdomain.com`). If you do select wildcard redirect, though, the visitor will be redirected straight to the new contact form. This will not work if the filenames have changed.

9. Click Add.

Your redirect appears at the bottom of the screen.

You cannot edit redirects; instead, you have to delete and re-create them.

Redirects are done using commands placed in the .htaccess file in the document root of the main domain. When you create the redirects, they are automatically entered for you by the system at the end of that file. If redirects are not working, check the .htaccess file because other software may have placed commands before them that are overriding the new redirects. For example, when you install WordPress, it creates a redirect that ensures that visitors can find the main page of the site. If this is the case, you should move your new redirects to be at the beginning of the .htaccess file because commands in that file are acted on in the order in which they are read.

You can create redirects for any path or filename within any domain you have added on or parked, and you can add and delete them any time you want. This means that you can easily redirect users for a short time when necessary and can also make shorter URLs to share with potential visitors that redirect to less memorable URLs on your website.

Setting Up DNS Effortlessly

I'm going to take you behind the scenes now and show you how things work in the background to make the DNS function so effectively. When you look at a clock, you see the face and hands; the hands move around and point where they're supposed to point. Most of the time, that's all you need to see; you don't need to see what makes the hands turn or how the cogs and springs work together. If the clock didn't have a face, maybe an expert would be able to tell what time the workings were indicating, but to the average person it wouldn't make any sense.

The Internet has its own face, which is there to make it easy and intuitive for humans to navigate. When you have your own website, however, it's important to see and know how it works behind the scenes so you can modify or correct things that aren't working quite right.

Using DNS to your advantage

Your nameservers hold a series of records, called the DNS Zone Records, which tell visiting browsers where to find the various services and parts of your website. To break it down simply, your domain name covers two main services. Each has its own type of record to help speed Internet navigation.

✔ **Mail exchange records:** The e-mail service for any domain name requires what is known as a *mail exchange,* which is something like a mailroom or a post office. This mailroom can be on any server you choose, although most default setups have it running on the same server as the website. The DNS uses what are called MX records, which stands for *mail exchange,* to denote which records are specifically referring to where the mailroom is. See Chapter 3 for more details about hosted e-mail.

✔ **Address records:** Virtually all other records are designated as A records, which simply stands for Address records. These records have a hostname and an IP address to direct visitors to the right places.

There are other records, such as NS records and CNAME records, which I explain later, but the most important for most general usage are the A and MX records.

Knowing how to create and manipulate DNS records can help you add speed, versatility, and resilience to your website quickly and easily.

Here are a few ways you can use DNS to your advantage:

✔ **Use an external mail server.** I explain later in the chapter exactly how to configure this, but for now what you need to know is that if the server your website is on is also the server that handles your mail and your website goes down, then it is most likely that your mail will go down as well. In that case, if people try to e-mail you to tell you your website is down, those e-mails won't get through to you.

Services like Gmail enable you to use their systems to handle your mail and keep it under your domain name even though it's running through their system.

✔ **Set up an external secondary nameserver.** The default setup from many hosting providers is to have the server your website is on act as both primary and secondary nameserver. This completely defeats the object of having a secondary nameserver. If one goes down, they both go down. If you have access to another server, you can use the DNS to keep a copy of your DNS zone records on the other server and configure your nameservers with the Authoritative Nameserver for your TLD to look first at your server and then at the other server if it cannot contact your server. The best setup, in fact, is to have separate servers for your primary and secondary nameservers (you can even have a third and fourth nameserver if you want) and to have both nameservers be on entirely different servers from where your website is. In Figure 9-8, you can see the domain day3matthew.com configured with four nameservers, to provide redundancy.

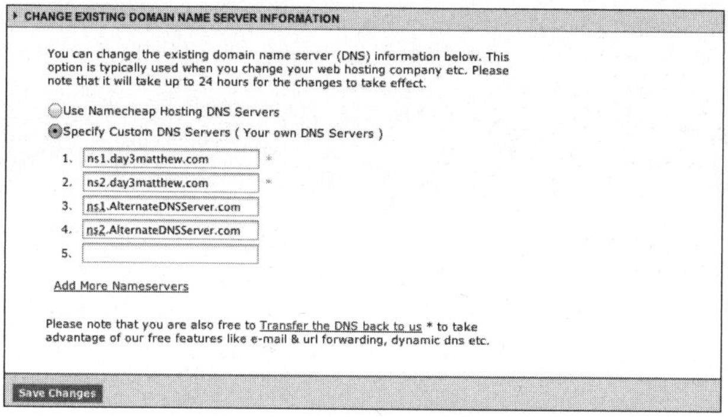

Figure 9-8:
Configuration
of remote
secondary
nameservers.

✔ **Host a subdomain on a separate server.** I talked about some of the
reasons for using subdomains and sometimes a subdomain in itself may
take up so much server resources that it needs to be on its own server.
For example, if you have a support site at `support.yourdomain.com`,
that site might provide downloads and other forms of resource-intensive
assistance. You can use the DNS to point users to your primary server
for your main website and then to a secondary server for your support
site even though they have the same domain name.

An overview of a DNS record

A typical DNS record for a domain might look a little like what's shown in
Figure 9-9.

Each line of the record requires a domain, a time to live (TTL), and a
record type.

As shown in Figure 9-9, most of the lines look essentially the same, except
the first.

The first line is a special line that has the record type Start of Authority
(SOA). This line confirms that this is the authoritative DNS record for this
domain name, also known as the Authoritative Nameserver. The DNS zone
records may be cached elsewhere or even listed elsewhere, but the DNS
system knows that this is the most up-to-date list and therefore takes prece-
dence over all others.

The first part of the record is the domain name or hostname.

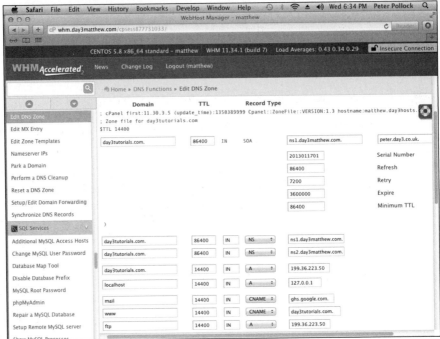

Figure 9-9:
A DNS zone
record.

The TTL is a figure supplied to other computers that do a DNS lookup here to tell them how many seconds to store the current DNS information. In other words, it says this is how many seconds you should wait before checking back to see if the record has changed.

The default value for TTL is 86,400 seconds, which is 24 hours. And it is from this number that your host calculates the figure of 48 hours for domain propagation.

Each record in the DNS file can have its own TTL. Unless you know that you will be updating the records or an individual record frequently, you should leave the value as a fairly high number. The convention seems to be at least 14,400 seconds (4 hours) for A records and up to 86,400 seconds (24 hours) for NS and CNAME records.

Although you do have control over the TTL for each of your records, and it may be tempting to make the TTL shorter to ensure faster updates, in reality zone records are not normally updated frequently. Making the time shorter just puts a higher load on your server and the Internet in general because devices on the Internet will have to come and check for updates more frequently. Some DNS caches ignore your TTLs completely and use their own — often making it three days or more to reduce DNS queries as much as possible.

The next part of the record is the class, which is a two-digit code. In Internet DNS records, the class is almost always IN (which stands for InterNet). There are two other possible classes, CH and HS, but unless you're a UNIX administrator or a company intranet administrator, it's unlikely you will ever come across those.

Do not change the class unless you are absolutely certain that you need to.

The Record Type column is next and, in the first line, this cannot be changed because it must be SOA.

The contents of the next box are dependent on the record type. Sometimes it will be a domain name and sometimes it will be an IP address.

The SOA record also has certain other information. Next comes the administrator's e-mail address. Notice that in the address a period is used instead of the @ (at) symbol. This is a constraint of the system, and you cannot change it.

The SOA then has a "serial number," which is incremented each time the zone file is changed. This number is important because when DNS servers cache the zone record, they take note of the current serial number. When they come back at the end of the TTL, they compare the noted serial number to the current serial number provided by the DNS server. If the two serial numbers match, then the server knows to continue to store the same information for another cycle; if the numbers do not match, the servers request the updated DNS records from the server.

Next comes the "refresh time," which is the amount of time any secondary nameservers wait before checking for changes to the zone file.

The refresh time is followed by the "retry time." If the secondary server attempts to verify that it has the latest zone file but fails to contact the primary server, the retry time is the amount of time it will wait before trying again.

The secondary server is also given an "expire time." This tells it, if it can't contact the primary server, how long to continue to serve the information it already has. Note that the secondary servers do not go by the TTL but rather by the refresh time and, failing the capability to refresh, the expire time. The default expire time is 86,400 seconds, but many servers are configured with the default expire time much higher than this, often in the region of 30 days or more.

After the secondary server reaches the expire time, if it has been unable to contact the primary nameserver, it refuses to give out the DNS zone records anymore. Therefore, you do not want to make the expire time too low because if something goes wrong with the primary nameserver the secondary holds the fort until the primary is fixed. You don't want the secondary shutting off too quickly and thus stopping people from being able to find the site. On the other hand, you don't want to make the expire time too long because generally if the primary DNS server has a problem, the website itself also has a problem (because by default the server that houses the website is also the primary nameserver).

The last part of the SOA record is the "minimum TTL." This should really be called the default TTL because it is the TTL that is used if for some reason a record does not have its own TTL. Calling it the minimum TTL is a bit of a misnomer because the TTL listed in any record in the DNS zone file overrides the minimum TTL, so the minimum can be shorter than what the minimum TTL suggests.

In the last sections of this chapter, I show you how to use and configure some of the different types of DNS zone records. See Figure 9-10 for a screenshot of these records.

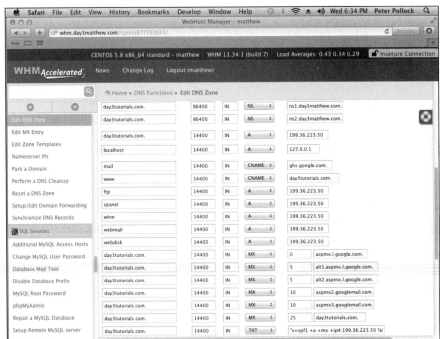

Figure 9-10:
A variety
of different
DNS Zone
records.

Nameservers

When a device on the Internet is trying to find your website, it goes to the TLD nameserver and asks where the nameservers for your domain are located, but your nameservers must be listed in the zone records held on your nameservers. It can seem a little confusing because to be able to read them, most devices on the Internet have already found their way to your nameserver and don't need to know where it is because they're already there. However, the TLD nameservers need to be able to access that information so they can check whether your nameservers have changed it at all.

See Figure 9-11 to see how nameserver records are configured.

 ✔ **The name is, obviously, your domain name but it must have a period at the end of it.** Whether you need to physically put that period in depends on the system you're using to edit your DNS zone records. Some do it automatically for you; some do not.

 ✔ **The TTL is whatever you want it to be.** The convention has long been to keep it at around 86,400 seconds (24 hours), but many people are going for a shorter TTL now for NS records, often nearer 300 seconds (5 minutes). The advantage of a shorter time period is if your web server goes offline, you can bring a replacement server online and quickly change the IP addresses of the nameservers for your domain to the IP addresses of the new server. With a long TTL, the new IP addresses could take a day or more to replicate around the Internet.

 ✔ **The record type for nameservers is NS.** You must have a minimum of two nameservers for your domain, and it is recommended that you do not have more than seven.

 ✔ **By entering a record type of NS, you are required to give a hostname.** The hostname is, in effect, an FQDN, so it requires all three sections: the host followed by a period, followed by the domain name, a period, and then the TLD. If you're creating your own custom nameservers, the host can be anything you want it to be. The common convention is to use hosts such as NS1 and NS2 to make everything clean and easy to understand.

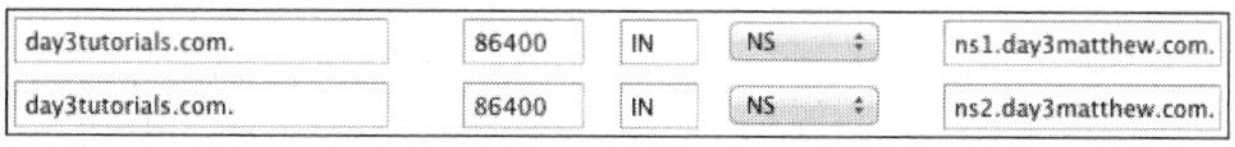

Figure 9-11:
Sample NS
records.

| day3tutorials.com. | 86400 | IN | NS | ns1.day3matthew.com. |
| day3tutorials.com. | 86400 | IN | NS | ns2.day3matthew.com. |

Although your nameservers may be numbered 1 to 34 and so on, that doesn't mean they will be queried in that order. The whole system is set up for speed, and it will query whichever nameserver responds fastest. Sometimes it will go in order. Other times it will pick a seemingly random nameserver. It is therefore important to make sure all your nameservers are kept up-to-date with the latest DNS zone file; otherwise, some of your visitors will be directed to the right place, and others won't.

CNAME records

Canonical Name (CNAME) records are crafty little records designed to make things quicker and easier for you in the future.

For example, you may want to set up a record for the www hostname, so that, if one of your visitors puts www at the beginning of the domain name, the server knows how to handle it. See Figure 9-12 for examples of CNAME records.

Figure 9-12: CNAME records.

| mail | | 14400 | IN | CNAME ⬍ | ghs.google.com. |
| www | | 14400 | IN | CNAME ⬍ | day3tutorials.com. |

So, you make a CNAME record for www which has the following details:

- ✔ Name: www
- ✔ Type: CNAME
- ✔ CNAME to use: `yourdomain.com`

Now, when someone's browser comes to the server, it will have a conversation like this:

Browser: Are you the Authoritative DNS server for yourdomain.com?

Server: Yes, I am. I'll send my SOA record to prove it.

Browser: Good. Now, can you tell me where to find www.yourdomain.com?

Server: Let's see . . . yes, I have a record for www — and it is directing you to yourdomain.com.

Browser: Okay . . . where do I find yourdomain.com?

Server: I have an A record for that, which says it's at 192.XXX.XXX.XXX.

Browser: Thank you!

Now, to be honest, the browser doesn't really say thank you; that would just add to the Internet traffic, but that's roughly how the conversation goes.

What you need to note is that the browser is ultimately looking for an IP address, something that the CNAME record doesn't include. This adds an extra step to the record — but it does so for a good reason:

You may have lots of hostnames that all need to point to the same server. Quite often you'll have records for `www`, `mail`, `webmail`, `pop`, `smtp`, and more, all of which go to the same IP address.

Using a CNAME record for them means you can point them all to the same CNAME, and you only need to make one record for that name with the IP address (which will be an A record).

If, in the future, you then change your IP address because you move from one server to another or you have to change the IP address for some other reason, you just have to change one record and all the CNAME records that point to it will automatically be pointing at the right place.

It may not seem like much now, but it can save a whole lot of time updating records later.

You have to find a balance between the ease of updating your DNS records and the added overhead that using CNAMES brings. When you use a CNAME, the browser has to do two DNS lookups. The first gives it the CNAME, and the second tells it what IP address the CNAME relates to. That may not be a problem for smaller sites, but when your server is being asked for IP addresses thousands or even tens of thousands of times a day, it can cause the whole server to slow down.

MX Records

Mail Exchange (MX) Records are slightly different from most other records in that they have a "priority" field. When the architecture of the Internet was created, it was decided that e-mail would be one of its very most important functions, and so a system was devised to try to ensure that e-mail would not get "lost" if there were problems with delivery.

One of the major ways to achieve this was to allow each domain name to have multiple post offices (mail servers), so if one was closed, a backup for it was already configured and open for business.

There is some debate over the real purpose of MX priorities, with very valid and good arguments on every side. However, I feel the simplest way to configure things is to have a primary mail server at the lowest MX and then backup (or secondary) servers at higher MX priorities, which are then configured to hold mail in a queue until the primary server is again ready to receive.

An MX record has five constituent parts (see Figure 9-13):

- ✔ **Domain:** This is always the domain name of the domain with the TLD and a trailing dot — for example, `yourdomain.com`. The trailing dot is *very* important.

- ✔ **TTL:** As with all TTLs, this can be set however you want it. The number 14,400 seems to be a fairly normal figure, though.

- ✔ **Record type:** The record type must always be MX for Mail Exchange records.

- ✔ **Priority:** The lowest number is the highest priority, so the system tries the servers in number order. Zero (0) is the highest possible priority.

- ✔ **Hostname:** This is the name of the server that the mail will be hosted on. A normal default setup points it to the same server as the domain name, but it can be changed to any other server that is configured to receive mail. Note that this is a name, not an IP address. A corresponding A record must be created in the zone file of the receiving server to resolve the name to an IP address.

day3tutorials.com.	14400	IN	MX	0	aspmx.l.google.com.
day3tutorials.com.	14400	IN	MX	5	alt1.aspmx.l.google.com.
day3tutorials.com.	14400	IN	MX	5	alt2.aspmx.l.google.com.
day3tutorials.com.	14400	IN	MX	10	aspmx2.googlemail.com.
day3tutorials.com.	14400	IN	MX	10	aspmx3.googlemail.com.
day3tutorials.com.	14400	IN	MX	25	day3tutorials.com.

Figure 9-13: A sample MX record.

CNAME records cannot be used in conjunction with MX records to direct the mail to the correct place. For example, if your MX record points to `mail.yourserver.com` as the mail server then `mail.yourserver.com` must be defined in `youserver.com`'s DNS zone record with an A record pointing to the correct IP address. You cannot use a CNAME record and attempt to pass the buck that way. The mail system will not allow it.

Some people recommend that if your mail is being delivered to another server — for example, to Google for use through Gmail — that your very lowest priority MX record should point back to your server. This would mean that if Google or whoever you are using for your mail service was to go down completely, there would still be a mail server configured to accept your mail as a last resort. (See Figure 9-14.)

Figure 9-14:
Google MX
record with
fallback
to origin
server.

day3tutorials.com.	14400	IN	MX	0	aspmx.l.google.com.
day3tutorials.com.	14400	IN	MX	5	alt1.aspmx.l.google.com.
day3tutorials.com.	14400	IN	MX	5	alt2.aspmx.l.google.com.
day3tutorials.com.	14400	IN	MX	10	aspmx2.googlemail.com.
day3tutorials.com.	14400	IN	MX	10	aspmx3.googlemail.com.
day3tutorials.com.	14400	IN	MX	25	day3tutorials.com.

Note fallback MX record points to main server

A Records

Last, but certainly not least, are A records. These records are the most commonly used and the simplest.

An A record must have a host, a TTL, and an IP address (see Figure 9-15):

- ✔ **Host:** The host can be a domain name or the host part of an FQDN. If it is a domain name, it must end with a trailing dot (.).
- ✔ **TTL:** The default time to live for A records is 14,400.
- ✔ **Record type:** This must be a single A.
- ✔ **IP address:** This must be a valid IP address.

Figure 9-15:
A sample A
record.

ftp	14400	IN	A	199.36.223.50
cpanel	14400	IN	A	199.36.223.50
whm	14400	IN	A	199.36.223.50
webmail	14400	IN	A	199.36.223.50
webdisk	14400	IN	A	199.36.223.50

There is also a record type of AAAA (pronounced *quad-a*), which is used for IPv6 addresses. Most sites still use version 4 addresses (IPv4), but the move to version 6 addresses has begun, and you may start seeing AAAA records instead of A records.

Chapter 10

Configuring Advanced Functions in cPanel

. . . .

In This Chapter

▶ Creating 404 pages

▶ Using automated functions

▶ Using FrontPage Extensions

. . . .

This chapter shows you some of the more advanced functions within your control panel. These functions don't have any particular natural grouping, so in different control panels they are put in different places. Wherever they are placed, though, these are some essential services that you may need at some point, and they are actually fairly easy to use when you know how.

Improving the User Experience with Error Pages

When a user requests a page from your website, one of the things that your website does is return a status code, which signals either a success or failure. As I explain in Chapter 6, the server logs each of these codes so that you can see how many pages are getting failures and how many are getting delivered as they should. Various status codes indicate errors; in addition to being logged, these codes are sent to your visitor's browser.

Depending on the setup in your web server and the particular browser the user is using, when the user receives error codes, quite often all she sees is a page saying, "File not found," "Webpage not found," or "Webpage not available." This doesn't really tell the user too much, and it doesn't help her in any way to find what she was looking for on your site.

You can set up custom error pages that the server will deliver to the browser in the event of an error. You can set up a different page for each error code, or you could use the same page no matter which error code is generated.

The most common error codes are 404 and 500. A 404 error code means that the page requested does not exist, so there is no page for the server to deliver to the browser. A 501 error means that the server has an error of some sort, and so it cannot deliver the website at this time.

Using cPanel as an example, this section describes how you can customize those error pages. The procedure is the same for all the different error codes. Table 10-1 shows some of the more common error codes, though there are many more than are shown in the table.

Table 10-1	Some of the Most Common Error Codes	
Error Code	*Meaning*	*Explanation*
4xx client error		
400	Bad Request	The request includes some bad syntax.
401	Unauthorized	You need to authenticate with the server first.
403	Forbidden	You are not allowed to view the resource you requested.
404	Not Found	The resource could not be found at this time.
410	Gone	The resource has been permanently deleted.
5xx server error		
500	Internal Server Error	Something went wrong with the server — but it's not sure what.
501	Not Implemented	The server is not configured to complete the request.
503	Unavailable	The server is currently unavailable due to service or maintenance.

To set up an error codes custom error message within cPanel, use the following steps:

1. **Log into cPanel using the login details provided by your host when you signed up.**

2. **Scroll to the Advanced section and click the Error Pages icon.**

3. **On the Error Page screen, select which error page you want to modify. (See Figure 10-1.)**

Figure 10-1:
The Error
Pages
screen in
cPanel.

Select which error code to make a page for

4. **The server displays a box with the current HTML code that is used to display the current error message. (See Figure 10-2.)**

This box may be blank if you haven't modified it previously. You can edit this information to display the page however you want. Above the Edit box are some tags you can insert. These place the appropriate data on your page wherever you insert them.

It is generally recommended that whatever page you generate for the error codes, or even if you forward users to a specific page when an error is generated, that you have some text prominently on the page to explain to the user that she was directed there because of an error. This then explains to her why she's not seeing exactly what she was expecting to see.

What many websites do is direct users to a page that has a search facility on it. This then gives the user the option of searching the website for the information that she was looking for.

Click these tags to insert into page

Enter code for the page here

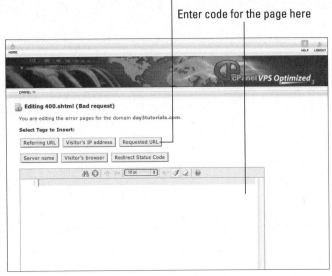

Figure 10-2:
Error page
editing
screen in
cPanel.

If you are creating one of the 5*xx* series error pages (that's 500, 501, 502, and so on), then the error page should be as small and simple as possible and inform the user that the website is down but you are working on bringing it back up as soon as possible. If you do not have a 500 series custom web error page, when users see a 5*xx* error, what they see in a browser may lead them to believe your website is no longer functioning permanently rather than it being a short-term problem. Having an error page that informs visitors that the error is just a temporary thing helps to keep them coming back. After all, you don't want them to just give up on your site.

You cannot anticipate in advance what errors your server or website might one day generate, so it is best to ensure that you have a custom error page for at least all of the common errors listed in Table 10-1.

You can create different custom error pages for each domain that you host.

The software you are using to create your website may also include the facility to make custom error pages. Software such as Joomla or WordPress may have error pages built into the themes or plug-ins you can install. You may find that these are more desirable than coding them manually in your control panel because the software enables you to create error pages that look like the other pages on your website.

Automating Functions with cron Jobs

There are times when you need to do various different things on a set schedule and the server can help you with that using what is known as the cron.

Think of *cron* as being short for *chronology,* and it will help you see that it is for jobs that are performed automatically on a fixed time schedule by the server's internal clock. It's like setting the timer to switch the heating on before you get up in the morning or setting your DVR to record the same show every week.

The command for a cron job basically has two parts:

- ✔ **The command that the server should run:** This means giving it the full path to the file that you need to run and any switches that are needed to perform the function. The software you run on your website should provide the correct switches to include.

- ✔ **The exact time and schedule on which the job should be executed:** There is huge flexibility built into this system, meaning you can schedule the task to run exactly when you want on whatever schedule you want.

cPanel provides an easy configuration screen for cron jobs. Here's how to use it:

1. **Open cPanel and log in using the details your host gave you when you signed up.**

2. **Scroll to the Advanced section and click Cron Jobs.**

3. **If you want to be e-mailed every time any cron job runs, enter your e-mail address in the first box and click Update Email.**

4. **Select the schedule on which you wish the command to run.**

   There are some common settings to select from, or you can create your own schedule.

   You must fill every box when setting the schedule; otherwise the cron job creation will fail.

5. **Enter the command you want the server to run into the Command box.**

   You must add the full server path to the file you want to run in the cron job. The server cannot guess which folder the file might be in!

6. **Click Add New Cron Job to create the job and add it to the cron.**

   (See Figure 10-3 for an example cron job.)

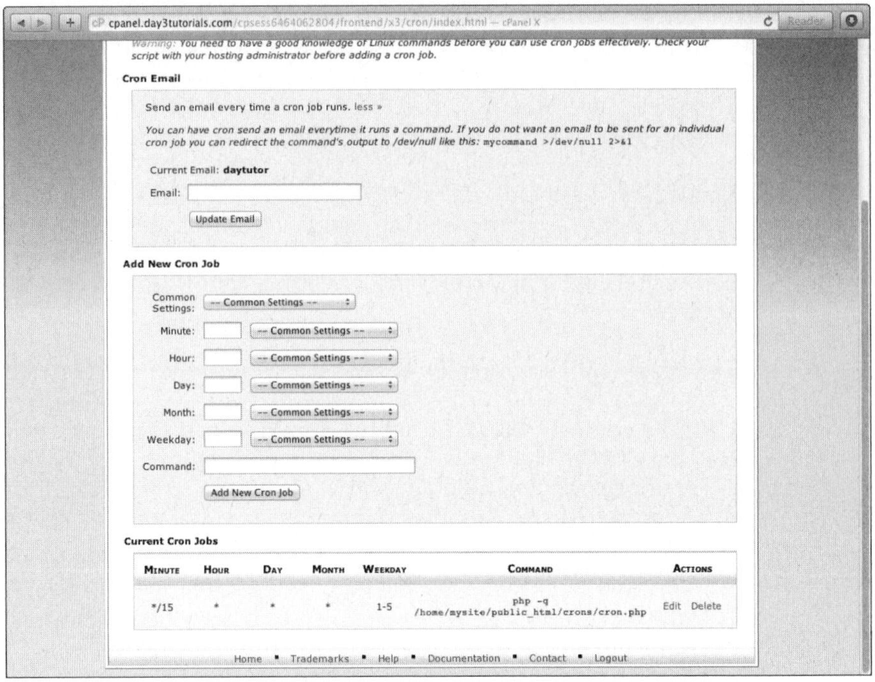

Figure 10-3:
Creating a
cron job in
cPanel.

It may take you a little while to get used to how cron jobs are scheduled because different characters do different things. Here is an explanation of them:

- ✔ **Numbers 0-59:** Which numbers you can use depends on whether you're setting the minute, hour, day, month, or weekday. Obviously, there are not 59 hours in a day, so you can't use 59 as an option for hours, but you can use any valid number for that time period. So if you want something to run at one minute past the hour, you put a **1** in the minute box. You can select for it to run at multiple different minutes by separating the minutes with a comma. For example, if you wanted it to run at 1, 5, 27, and 50 minutes past the hour for some reason, you would simply input **1,5,27,50** into the Minute box.

- ✔ **Asterisk (*):** An asterisk means "every," so putting an asterisk in the Hour box means the cron job runs every hour. Putting an asterisk in the Day box means the job runs every day, and so on.

- ✔ **Slash (/):** You can use a slash after an asterisk to divide that "every" by a number. A slash always has to have a number following it. For example, if you want the job to run every month, you simply put an asterisk in the Month box. If you want it to run every three months, though, you have to type ***/4** — which means every month divided by 4 (or 12/4), which equals every three months. It can be a little confusing, but the cron job screen has Common Settings drop-down boxes that help explain what to do.

✔ **Dash (-):** You can use a dash only in the Weekday field. The Weekday field is a special field that modifies the Day field. For instance, if you want to run the command only on the weekends, you type **(0, 6)** because 0 stands for Sunday and 6 stands for Saturday. You can use the dash to signify every day between two days, so for example, **1-5** signifies every day from one to five (Monday through Friday). Using **3-6** would mean Wednesday through Saturday.

You can edit or delete cron jobs at any time after you create them. Any change or deletion is immediate and stops the previously next scheduled run and replaces it with whatever you change the settings to.

You may find cron jobs extremely useful and their scheduling system is amazingly flexible, allowing you to schedule the server to run any job you want at pretty much any minute of the year you want it to.

Installing FrontPage Extensions

FrontPage is a piece of software, developed by Microsoft, that enables users to design websites on their own computers. FrontPage is a WYSIWYG editor, which stands for What You See Is What You Get. The name says it all — what you see on your screen as you are designing the site on your computer is what the users will see when they come to the site in the future. This is in stark contrast to the old system where you had to code everything by hand and then upload it to your website to see how your site looked. That's called manual coding, which is great if you're an expert and really know what you're doing. WYSIWYG, however, has made site design much easier for the masses and people not too versed in software development.

Microsoft actually discontinued support for the FrontPage product in 2006 and replaced it with a new product called Expressions Web, which could still take advantage of some of the FrontPage server features. Support for Expressions Web has now also been discontinued and no new versions will be made. Microsoft is instead pushing its Visual Studio product for web design.

FrontPage is, however, still used by many smaller site owners because they know how to use it and don't want to have to learn another program. This means that some hosts still offer FrontPage Extensions although many now don't.

FrontPage consisted of two separate parts. One was the software which the user had on his own computer to develop the site and get it looking the way he wanted it to look; the other was some software, called FrontPage Server Extensions, which needed to be on the servers. These extensions handled special requests from sites that were made using FrontPage, such as FrontPage–specific contact forms. The last version of the Extensions actually came out in 2002, but Microsoft continued to support them until July 2006, when all FrontPage support stopped.

Originally, any FrontPage website needed to be hosted on a Windows server. This was because Microsoft developed FrontPage for its own Windows software and thus developed the Extensions for its own Windows server software. Very quickly, though, the Extensions were ported over to Linux so that they could be run on UNIX/Linux boxes.

The major problem with Windows FrontPage Extensions is that they are so far out-of-date. Microsoft ceased to develop and support them in 2006, and server software has moved on a lot since then. Server administrators and users are increasingly finding that FrontPage Extensions are no longer compatible with the latest versions of Windows Server and have several security weaknesses, which will never be fixed.

The Extensions seem to be a little more stable on Linux servers, but many web hosts are now switching off the FrontPage Extensions facility altogether because it's more trouble than it's worth.

If your site requires FrontPage Extensions either because you developed it using FrontPage or because you developed it using Expressions Web and use some of the FrontPage features in it, you need to ensure that your web host allows FrontPage Extensions on its servers. If so, the Extensions may already be installed, or your host may have to install them for you. However, you may have the facility to install them yourself.

Hosts that still allow FrontPage Extensions often have an icon somewhere in the control panel that's helpfully labeled FrontPage Extensions. In cPanel, the icon is in the Advanced section (which is usually at the bottom of the page). (See Figure 10-4.)

Figure 10-4: Advanced section in cPanel.

If you do not see the install FrontPage Extensions icon (or text link), it probably means that your host does not allow them. In this case, contact your host because it may be willing to make exceptions for certain clients.

If you require FrontPage Extensions and the FrontPage Extensions installation icon is in your control panel, click it and follow the prompts to install them. It depends which control panel you are using exactly how the FrontPage Extension installation works. Some have more facilities than others. Normally, though, it tells you whether they are installed and gives you a button to install/uninstall them (see Figure 10-5).

Figure 10-5:
FrontPage installation screen.

Click to install extensions

Click to remove leftover extension files

Click Install Extensions and it either asks you to supply a FrontPage username and password or goes ahead and installs it directly. (See Figure 10-6.)

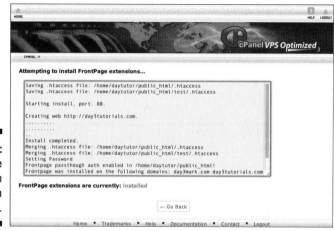

Figure 10-6:
FrontPage installation confirmation screen.

In some installations, after FrontPage Extensions are installed, you can use a facility to reinstall or manage those Extensions. This can sometimes be useful if you're having problems with an area of your site that requires the Extensions. Running the reinstall or cleanup rewrites all the Extensions files and most likely fixes any problems that have occurred. (See Figure 10-7.)

Figure 10-7:
FrontPage
manage-
ment
options.

After you install FrontPage Extensions, go back to FrontPage on your computer; if the server asked you to supply a username and password when you installed the Extensions, use the login details you created to upload your site to the web server. If it didn't ask for a username and password, then it either will have e-mailed them to you or will have used the same username/password combination you use to log in to cPanel.

FrontPage is old and buggy, and because it hasn't been updated for a long time it has many known security holes. Unless you really have to use FrontPage for your website, it is best to use one of the newer tools for website creation. Several free WYSIWYG site creation tools are available, as are several paid options. My favorite tool for building websites is WordPress.

If you don't absolutely need FrontPage Extensions, don't install them — and remove them if they are installed!

Chapter 11

Managing Your Control Panel from a Mobile Device

In This Chapter

▶ Modifying and repairing your server on the go

▶ Understanding different mobile operating systems' facilities

*T*he world of smartphones and tablets has created a situation in which people increasingly have the capability to be "online" even when they're not at their desks. When issues arise on your site or server or when you think of things you want to change, you want to make the changes immediately and have a mobile device to help you do it. You can make changes using your smartphone, although how easy it is to make changes with a mobile device depends on your web host and the control panel it uses. In this chapter, I show you briefly how to navigate inside your browser to your control panel's normal login screen and then look at some of the apps and facilities that are available for Android, BlackBerry, iOS, and Windows Phone.

Navigating Using a Mobile Browser

To get to your control panel using a mobile browser, you simply open the browser and type in the URL of your control panel as you would normally do. For instance, with cPanel the URL is normally `cPanel.`*`yourdomainname.`*`com`. For companies like DreamHost and GoDaddy, you can go the website and log in from the front page.

Depending on which control panel you use, making adjustments can get fiddly on a mobile browser screen because the screen is so small and the control panels are designed for much bigger computer monitors. However, some companies deliver a special mobile version of the control panel. cPanel, for example, does away with icons and instead uses a text-based interface. Compare Figure 11-1, which shows the cPanel interface in a normal browser, and Figure 11-2, which shows how it looks on a smartphone.

Figure 11-1:
The cPanel
front
screen in a
computer
browser.

There is no substitute to trying it yourself on your smartphone or tablet and seeing exactly how easy or difficult it is to use the control panel in the browser. That said, before you purchase any apps from the app store for your mobile device, try using the browser and see if you are able to do the things you need to do.

For the average user, using your control panel from your smartphone is not really essential because there are not that many things that go wrong or require changing that can't wait a few hours until you're next at your computer screen. However, if you're the server administrator for high-volume websites or for multiple websites, particularly if you have a Virtual Private Server (VPS) or dedicated server, you may find that being able to manage the control panel from your smartphone is very useful as well as convenient.

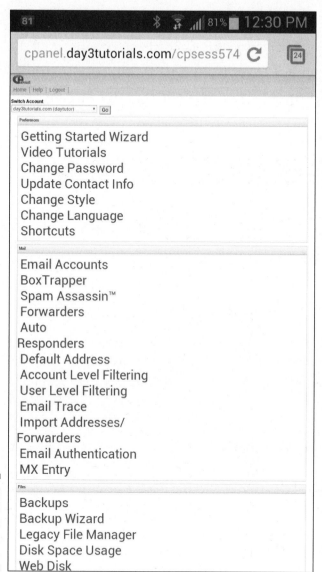

81

🔵 81% 12:30 PM

cpanel.day3tutorials.com/cpsess574

Home | Help | Logout |

Switch Account
day3tutorials.com (daytutor)   Go

Preferences

Getting Started Wizard
Video Tutorials
Change Password
Update Contact Info
Change Style
Change Language
Shortcuts

Mail

Email Accounts
BoxTrapper
Spam Assassin™
Forwarders
Auto
Responders
Default Address
Account Level Filtering
User Level Filtering
Email Trace
Import Addresses/
Forwarders
Email Authentication
MX Entry

Files

Backups
Backup Wizard
Legacy File Manager
Disk Space Usage
Web Disk

Figure 11-2:
The cPanel
front screen
on a
smartphone.

Some of the major hosting companies, such as DreamHost, GoDaddy, and 1&1, have smartphone apps available. Some are official and some are unofficial. There are always two schools of thought about the safety of unofficial apps; some people love them whereas others are a little wary of them. If you're uncertain about the trustworthiness of an app or its creator, it's always safer to not install it and use one of the official apps instead.

When installing apps for your smartphone or tablet, you first need to know what operating system your device uses. If you have an iPod or an iPad, which has an Apple symbol on it, then your device uses the Apple iOS. Please skip ahead to the "Installing and Using iOS Apps" section for details on how to find the installable apps on Apple devices. If your device is not running iOS, then there's a strong chance that it is running one of the versions of the Android operating system.

Installing and Using Android Apps

The Android operating system is written and developed by Google, which has its own store where you can purchase and download apps, some of which are free. The Android store is called the Play Store. There should be a Play Store icon like the one shown in the margin on one of the home screens on your smartphone or tablet.

Knowing where to find apps

The best place to find apps for your Android device is in the Play Store, where both free and premium apps are downloadable over Wi-Fi or a cellular data connection.

Some control panel apps are not available in the Google Play Store. These apps are written by third-party developers who do not want to use the Play Store system to distribute the apps they write. You can find these apps by doing an Internet search for Android apps for whatever control panel you use.

Generally, the sites with these apps give you a link to download the apps and normally give you installation instructions. The installation process often requires you to go into a special section within the Android settings called the Developer settings; there you have to disable the function that requires apps to be installed from the Play Store. Google provides this function so that you are not limited to acquiring apps from only the Play Store; at your own risk, you can add your choice of apps from anyone and anywhere.

Be cautious about installing apps from sources other than the Play Store. You will often find that developers who do not upload their apps to the Play Store have not done so for a reason. Some developers do naughty things with their apps, and those things may come as a shock to you after you install the app. For example, an app may access information that you would normally expect an application to access, such as e-mail addresses, phone numbers, or phone usage information, but the app then sends the information back to the developer. Some apps may plant viruses on your device, which enable the developer to steal information such as bank login details, Social Security numbers, and dates of birth. The viruses can also hide in the system and perform other functions for the developers, such as turning your device into a machine that runs attacks on websites, such as a distributed denial-of-service (DDOS) attack or sending out spam.

Scary, huh?

 That said, there are legitimate developers out there who write good applications that are trustworthy, and they might have legitimate reasons for not uploading their apps to the Google Play Store. Make it part of your search to look whether other people have experienced problems after installing third-party apps. If you read bad reviews, you may be warned away from malicious applications.

 It *is* possible for something untoward to sneak its way into the Play Store, although it's unlikely. It's always a good idea to read reviews of the apps you get from the Play Store to make sure other people haven't reported problems.

Installing apps with ease

You're probably already familiar with how to install applications through the Play Store, but here's a quick rundown of how to do it:

1. **Open the Google Play Store using the icon on your home page or in the settings.**

2. **Use the search box at the top of the screen to search for the app you're looking for and tap on the magnifying glass.**

   Google Play Store searches for the keywords that you typed and brings up a list of apps that match some or all of those keywords. Select your chosen app from the list to open it.

3. **Scroll down to get more information about how much the app costs and what it does.**

   If you want to install the app, look for an Install button (see Figure 11-3) at the top of the screen.

4. **Tap the Install button and the software downloads to and installs on your device.**

   The icon to access the app is placed either on one of your home screens or in your app list.

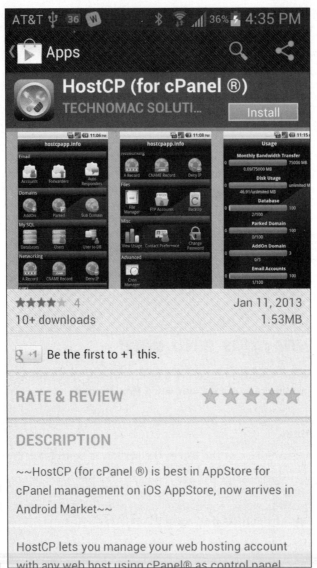

Figure 11-3:
Installing
an Android
app.

Finding the best apps

Apps are being developed all the time for various control panels — especially the major ones such as cPanel. It is always good to do a web search for something like *best cPanel Android app* to find what the newest and greatest recommended apps are. At the time of writing, two of the best Android apps available for cPanel are

- ✔ Control Panel for cPanel by 2312 Development
- ✔ HostCP by TechnoMac Solution

Of course, "best" is a subjective term, and what one person thinks is wonderful another person may find confusing and impossible to use. If an app has a free version, it is always a good idea to install the free version prior to buying the full version so you can test it out and find which works best on your particular device and for your needs.

Using apps to connect to your web host

Installing the app is only half of the process; you also must give the app permission to make changes to your server. Don't worry, though; it's easily done. All you need to do is type in the address of your website (`http://myweb site.com`) and your usual control panel login username and password.

It's really that easy!

Installing and Using iOS Apps

If you are using an Apple device, such as the iPhone, iPad, or iPod, your device is running an operating system called iOS. If you aren't using an Apple device, your device cannot run this software and you should instead refer to the section on installing and using apps for your operating system.

Knowing where to find apps

 Apps for iOS are found in the Apple App Store, for which you'll find an icon like the one shown in the margin on one of your home pages.

There may be some apps that are not available in the App Store, so to install these you first need to jail-break your phone or device. Jail-breaking can be risky, can damage your device, and will most likely void any warranty you have from Apple or the company you purchased the device from. I do not recommend jail-breaking Apple devices, but it is a matter of personal preference. If you choose to jail-break your device, you may be able to find apps for managing your web server that are not available within the App Store.

Be careful, though, because these programs have not been vetted by Apple and therefore have not been tested for malicious code. Jail-breaking your iPhone, iPad, or iPod and installing one of these apps opens you up to greater risk of viruses and malware.

Your smartphone or Internet device is your property. Although Apple or the developer of the operating system that runs on it may penalize you for jail-breaking your device, the prerogative is still yours to choose to do so. At this time, in most places, it is not illegal to jail-break your device, but the terms and conditions for most operating systems clearly state that the manufacturer will no longer support or update software on your phone in any way if your device is jail-broken. Essentially this leaves your device exposed and there is little or no liability on anybody who provides you with jail-breaking software or applications to install on jail-broken devices for any damage that may be caused.

Installing apps with ease

Installing apps on iOS devices is simple. You've probably already done it many times when you have installed games or applications.

Here's a quick rundown on how to do it:

1. **Tap the app store icon to open the App Store.**

2. **At the bottom of the App Store screen, tap the Search button. In the Search box, type the name of the app or control panel for which you are searching for an app and then tap Search.**

   The App Store displays a list of available apps based on the keywords you provided in the Search box.

3. **Pick the app you want to install and tap it.**

   The application's page opens to show you some screenshots and give you details of what the app can do for you.

4. **Click the Install button at the top of the screen.**

   Within a few minutes, the app should be installed on your device.

The app is installed as an icon on one of your home screens. Swipe through the screens to find it and tap the icon to run the app.

Finding the best apps

Apps are being developed all the time for different control panels, especially the major ones such as cPanel. It is always good to do a web search for something like *best cPanel iOS app* to find the newest and greatest recommended apps. At the time of writing, two of the best iOS apps available for cPanel are

- ✔ CP Control Panel by Dayana Networks Ltd.
- ✔ HostCP by Mihir Dhandha

Of course, "best" is a subjective term, and what one person thinks is wonderful another person may find confusing and impossible to use. If an app has a free version, it is always a good idea to install the free version prior to buying the full version so you can test it out and find which works best on your particular device and for your needs.

Using apps to connect to your web host

Installing an app is only half of the process because you need to give the app permission to make changes to your server. Don't worry, though; it's easily done. All you will need to do is type in the address of your website (`http://mywebsite.com`) and your usual control panel login username and password.

It's really that easy!

Apps for BlackBerry and Windows Devices

At the time of writing this book, there were no apps for any of the major control panels available on BlackBerry's BlackBerry World or the Windows Phone App Store.

Both stores are growing rapidly, though, so I expect some to be written for those devices soon.

In the meantime, both operating systems have good browsers built in, which enable you to use the mobile versions of the control panels, as I mention at the beginning of this chapter.

BlackBerry 10 also has the facility to use the browser as a normal browser instead of a mobile browser, thus displaying the full versions of the control panels.

To switch to the normal browser, do the following:

1. **Open your browser on your BlackBerry device.**
2. **Click the Settings icon at the bottom-right corner of the screen.**
3. **Select Settings.**
4. **Select Developer Tools.**
5. **Slide the switch next to Desktop Mode from Off to On. (See Figure 11-4.)**

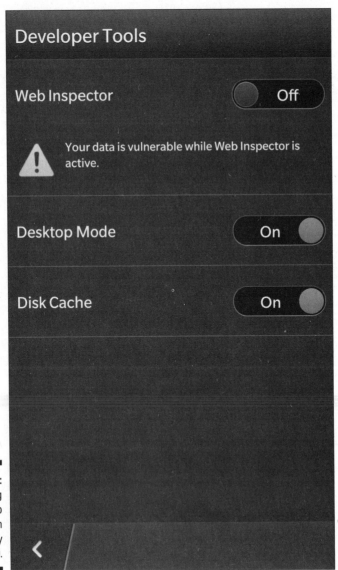

Figure 11-4:
Switching
to Desktop
Mode on
BlackBerry
10.

Part IV
Knowing What to Do When Things Go Wrong

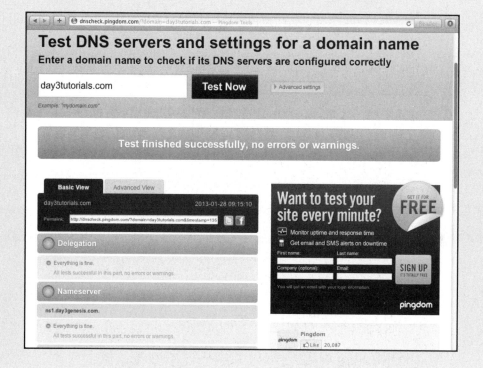

In this part . . .

- ✔ Fix issues with your hosted e-mail.
- ✔ Recover lost login details.
- ✔ Choose whether or not to switch hosts.
- ✔ Move from one host to another safely and easily.

Chapter 12

Troubleshooting and Resolving Issues

In This Chapter

▶ Understanding common issues

▶ Being your own knight in shining armor and fixing those issues

*T*he quality, quantity, and level of support you receive from your web host depends greatly on which host you choose and also on your own perception. I know of hosts that some people say provide terrible service, whereas others say the same hosts provide excellent service. Either way, your web host actually has little in the way of a mandate to support you with using the facilities it provides. As I explain in Chapter 1, your web host is more like a landlord who simply leases you space to use online. Problems with the bricks and mortar of that space are the host's responsibility to deal with, but anything related to the website you create or anything you put in that space (or even to difficulties using the facilities provided by your host) are your responsibility, not the host's.

You wouldn't ask your landlord for lessons on how to run a business or hang shelves on the wall, and many web hosts feel the same way about the basics of using your hosting account. And that's why I have written this book — to help you resolve issues on your own.

Some issues come up more than others. In this chapter, I explain what some of those are and what you can do to fix them if your host doesn't help. It's never a bad idea to ask for help. Some hosts help more than you might expect, whereas others refuse to help. Either way, you're no worse off for asking. (Sometimes getting an answer just depends on whom you speak to, how you ask the question, and how busy the person is when you ask.) However, if your host won't help, there are plenty of resource sites online where you can get answers to many of your questions, or your host may even offer to provide you training or fix the problem for a fee. This is normally an hourly rate, and you can expect it to be anywhere up to $100 per hour.

Recognizing Common E-mail Issues

The biggest and easiest way to spot that there is a problem with your e-mail is when you try and pick up your new mail and find you haven't received any for a long period of time. That's not a scientific method of detection, but not receiving e-mail, or getting reports from other people that they are not receiving e-mail from you, is a good indicator that something is wrong. Here are the top ways to tell there is something wrong with your e-mail:

- ✔ **No new e-mail is received for an extended time.** This may sound obvious, but just because you don't have new e-mail when you switch on your computer doesn't necessarily mean there is a problem. It may just be that nobody sent you an e-mail recently. If you have had your e-mail account for a while you'll know how regularly new mail comes in, and if you haven't had any for a period of time that would be unusual under normal circumstances then you know you should start checking into it.

- ✔ **You attempt to send an e-mail and your computer reports that it failed to send it.** Failing to send can occur as a result of a number of different issues, so read the error message carefully.

- ✔ **Sometimes after you have sent e-mail, an "e-mail undeliverable" message appears in your mailbox.** This message indicates that there is either a problem at your end or the recipient's end. The failure message can be hard to decipher but can tell you which end the problem is at.

- ✔ **Sometimes friends, contacts, or colleagues contact you some other way other than via e-mail and tell you their messages are not getting through to you.** The fault may be on their end, but you should ask them exactly what error message they are getting to ascertain which end the problem is at.

The main causes of error messages are the following:

- ✔ **Your site or server has been blacklisted.** The first thing to do when you find out there is a problem is to go to a security site such as mxtoolbox.com/blacklists.aspx, type your IP address into the box, and click Blacklist Check. The security site runs a scan on your site to see if it can find any issues, and it checks with the major spam blacklisting organizations to see whether your domain name or the IP address of your server has been blacklisted with them. (See Figure 12-1.)

- ✔ **Your mailbox is full.** On most web servers, you have to set a size for each mailbox. When your mailbox is full, new mail is rejected until you either clear some space or increase the size of the mailbox. To clear space, try emptying the trash folder or junk folder and go through and delete any mails you don't need. A good way to clear a lot of space quickly is to find any e-mails that have large attachments, download the attachments to your computer, and then delete the e-mail (and empty the trash folder).

🖊 **The mailbox does not exist.** Yes, I've done this myself . . . and felt stupid when I did. Sometimes you might want to create a special e-mail address for a particular project or event to help you collect all responses involving that project in one place. It's easy to overlook actually creating the mailbox in the rush of marketing and sharing the new address to use. Mailboxes also sometimes get deleted by accident. It's a good idea to check that the address actually exists! (See Figure 12-2.)

Check list for warnings

Click name of blacklist for contact information

Figure 12-1:
Sample
output from
MXtoolbox.
com.

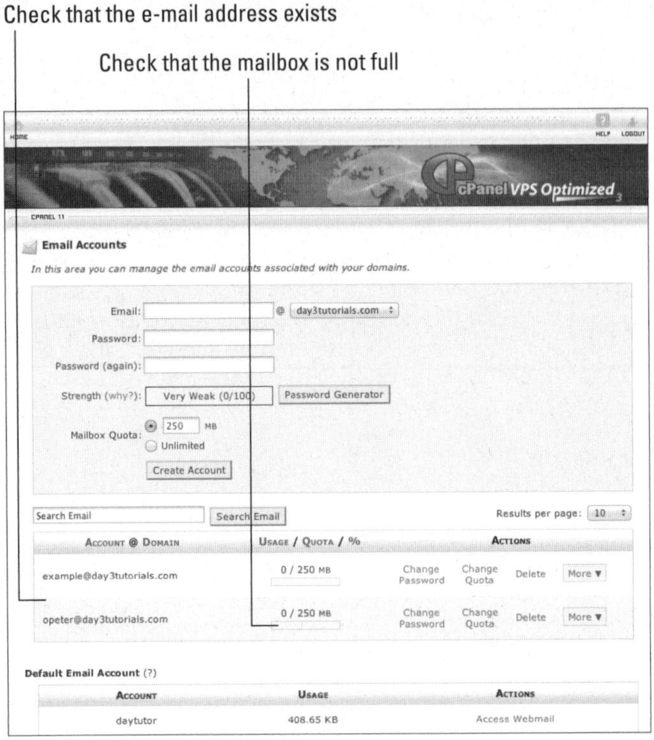

Check that the e-mail address exists

Check that the mailbox is not full

Figure 12-2:
Checking
that e-mail
accounts
exist in
cPanel.

✔ **Your mail server needs to be restarted.** You'd be amazed how many problems with computers can be fixed by simply shutting down and restarting. Your mail server is no exception to this rule, even though it's just some software running on your web server. If you have a Virtual Private Server (VPS) or dedicated server, you may find that you have access to a backend to the control panel or to additional services on the control panel that most shared hosting users are not privy to. For example, with cPanel, most VPS hosts and dedicated server hosts give you login details so you can use management software called WHM. The WHM software opens up a whole new array of facilities that normal cPanel users do not have access to. See Chapter 15 for details on how to use WHM.

There are a few commands in WHM that you can use to help solve e-mail issues if your site is not blacklisted and you are having messages bounce or are unable to send or receive. Do the following:

1. **Log into WHM using the details provided to you by your host.**

2. **Scroll down to the mail section near the bottom of the left-hand menu.**

3. **Select Repair Mailbox Permissions and click Proceed.**

   The command runs through all the associated file permissions related to your mailboxes and fixes any that are set wrong. Sometimes the permissions get themselves messed up for seemingly no reason.

4. **Click Mail Queue Manager.**

   You see a list of all the e-mail waiting to go in or out of the server. If there is a lot of mail in here, it may be that there is a spam mail script somewhere on your server being used to send e-mail without your permission.

5. **Scroll down to the Restart Services section and click Mail Server (exim). Click Yes.**

   This restarts the mail server. You could also try restarting the IMAP and POP services.

Removing Yourself from a Blacklist

Your domain name or IP address your domain is on is blacklisted when it has been found to send out spam e-mail.

If your site has been blacklisted, it may not be your fault — especially if you're on a shared server. It may be that another site on the server has been purposefully sending spam. It's also possible that your site, or another site on a shared server, has been hijacked and used for sending spam.

If you are on a shared server, inform your host that the server has been blacklisted and ask your host to investigate. Your host will normally be able to get your site unblacklisted within 24 hours. The host will first check to find out which site has been causing the blacklisting. If your site is the culprit, the host may take it offline until you can get a security expert to fix whatever is causing the problem.

If your server is a VPS or dedicated server, however, check with your web host. Your host may well say that cleaning the problem and repairing the damage done is your responsibility because it's your private server. In this case, the quickest and easiest way to fix the problem is to hire a security consultant to clean up your website and prevent the issues from happening again. The consultant is normally willing to contact the blacklisting agency and provide the details that are needed to unblock the site.

You can also contact the blacklisting agency yourself by going to its website and completing a form to remove a site from being blacklisted. Make sure that you have fixed any issue first because blacklisting agencies do not take kindly to whitelisting servers that are then very quickly blacklisted again because the issue still exists.

Fixing FTP Faults

Very few things can go wrong with File Transfer Protocol (FTP). Here's the list:

- ✔ **Your login details are incorrect.** Check that you're using the right login details, particularly if you have recently changed your password.

- ✔ **Your server uses a non-standard FTP port.** The standard port is 22. You need to specify in your FTP client if your server has been configured to use something different.

- ✔ **You're using Secure File Transfer Protocol (SFTP) and logging in using a username/password combination has been disabled.** Check that you don't need to use a private key to connect.

- ✔ **Your IP address has been banned from the server.** If you've tried multiple times to connect unsuccessfully, the server may have decided that you are a hacker and has banned you. Your web host probably needs to unlock your IP address if this is the case.

- ✔ **The FTP service is not working on the server.** If you have access to the backend then try restarting the service; otherwise, talk to your web host about getting the server restarted.

Losing Your Control Panel Login

It happens to everyone: From time to time, you forget your usernames or passwords. Generally, though, you don't need to contact your host to get a new password or retrieve your username.

Where you log in to your control panel, there is usually an option, often underneath the login box, to reset your password. (See Figure 12-3.)

Some control panels provide an option to retrieve your username as well. If that isn't the case, though, you should log in to your web host's billing dashboard (if it is separate from your control panel). There you should find either a link to the original e-mail the host sent you, which had all of your login details, or a page where you can view and change your server login details.

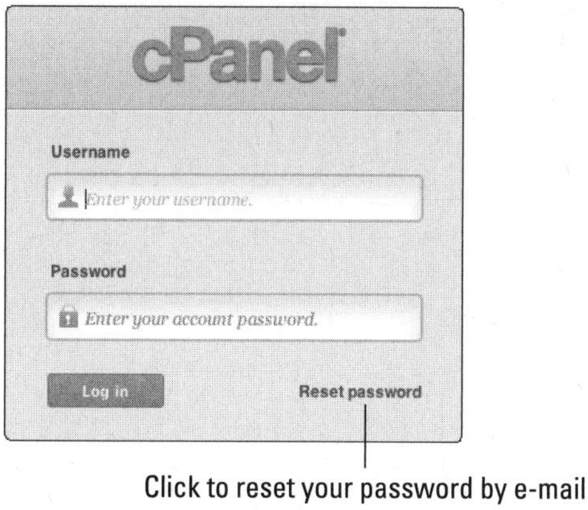

Figure 12-3:
Resetting
your pass-
word in
cPanel.

Click to reset your password by e-mail

It is unusual that you need to contact your host for help with usernames or passwords, but don't be afraid to ask if you need to. Your host's staff members will probably laugh about it in the break room, but don't be embarrassed. We've all done it at one time or another!

Finding DNS Problems

Domain Name System (DNS) problems are the bane of every web host's life. Most of the time, you won't have them, but they are likely to rear their ugly heads in the following circumstances:

- ✔ When you move your site from one server to another
- ✔ After a server crash
- ✔ When a user has been "playing" with subdomains, MX records, and other DNS-related things

If your domain name is not resolving or you're having other weird issues with errors appearing instead of web pages, check to see that your DNS records are set correctly.

The simple way to do that is to go to dnscheck.pingdom.com, put your domain name into the box at the top of the page, and click Test Now. (See Figure 12-4.)

Alternatively, go to intodns.com, type your domain name into the box, and click Report.

Type domain name here

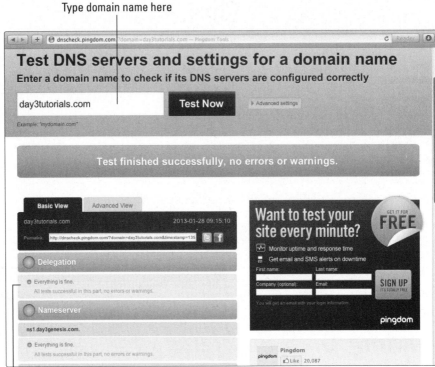

Figure 12-4:
Sample
output from
dns
check.
ping
dom.com.

Check for errors or warnings

Both sites check on your DNS configuration and report on any errors they find. This helps you know what the problem is and where to start looking for the solution.

Chapter 13

Moving to a New Host

- -

In This Chapter

▶ Knowing when it's time to change hosts

▶ Discovering the secrets to painlessly switching hosts

▶ Changing hosts with minimal or no downtime

- -

Moving to a new host is something that all of us encounter eventually for one reason or another. Sometimes moving to a new host can be for something as simple as a cheaper price or having a new designer who insists on using a different host. Sometimes you may be motivated by larger issues, such as problems with downtime or lack of service.

Whatever your reason for moving to a new host, there is a right way and a wrong way to go about it. In this chapter, I show you the right way to move and how to make it as quick and painless as possible.

Deciding Whether to Change Hosts

Are you happy with your current host?

I mean, really, are you *happy* with your current hosting company?

When asked that question, a lot of people initially say, "Um" and "Ah," before coming up with some kind of negative answer that isn't truly well thought out. When you really stop and think about it, though, often your host is fine. It's just that, put on the spot, your expectations are too high or you have been hearing things from other people that make you feel uneasy about your host even though you have not experienced the same issues.

Many times, people who change hosts because of bad press or unrealistic expectations end up regretting it.

The following are some of the valid reasons — in my opinion — to want to change hosts:

- ✔ **Cost:** Some hosts charge more than others. Some hosts charge even more than that. If you find that you are paying a lot more than other people who seem to be getting the same kind of service from their hosts that you're getting, then why stay with the more expensive host? Of course, you never know what you're getting yourself into when you move to a new host, so an argument can be made for staying with a host that seems good, even if it means paying a little more to stay there. You have to consider whether you're better off with the devil you know than the one you don't!

- ✔ **Poor service:** When I started my hosting business, customer service was the number-one reason for starting it. I had a bad experience with a web host, and one fateful day I said, "I can do better than this!" That set me on the journey to starting my own hosting company with the aim of providing a good level of customer service. It was only when I realized that I was failing to provide that good level of customer service that I realized the time had come for me to get out of the business and move on to other things. In other chapters, I cover what you can expect from your web host. Some do more than others and a lot of what customer service comes down to is the customer's perception of how well he is being served. That being said, the service that one person may feel is adequate or even good may, to another person, not feel the same way. I know of many hosts who are lauded by some and reviled by others simply because of personality clashes or different expectations.

- ✔ **Too much downtime:** Downtime in this context is time where your website is inaccessible to the world or does not load correctly due to problems with the server that are directly the host's fault. Downtime can also be a result of problems with the Internet connection at the data center. It would be unreasonable to expect your server to be online and working correctly 24 hours a day seven days a week every year. Servers are just computers being maintained by people, and, realistically, failures do happen. However, failures do not need to happen often. If you are seeing frequent server downtime that's not due to you or your specific website, it may be legitimate for you to feel that it is time to move to a different host.

- ✔ **Features available:** All kinds of things are possible with websites: different programming languages, different ways to create sites, different technologies, and different functionalities offered by the service. In fact, there are so many differences that I wrote a whole book on the subject. Some hosts restrict some features that they have the capability to provide or simply refuse to provide certain features at all, with or without extra charge. If you run into a situation you try to do something and your web host does not allow it, then maybe you can find another host who will allow you to do it. Be careful, though, because often the things that hosts do not allow are things that could weaken your website or create the most security holes. You may find that moving to a new host and implementing your ideas actually results in more downtime as a result of being hacked or from issues with the features you are trying to use.

✔ **Your designer or developer insists that you move:** Depending on how much work your designer does for you, there are times when a web designer or administrator will ask you to move a website to a different company's hosting. This can be for familiarity, because the designer is used to the control panel on a particular host, or it can be because the designer knows a new host provides certain things that your current host doesn't. It is up to you whether you choose to move, and your choice should probably hinge on how much you want to use that designer in the future.

Apart from the preceding five reasons, there are not many good reasons to change your web host. If you are suffering from one of these issues, then try contacting your host to explain how you're feeling so that your host has the opportunity to fix the problem or otherwise accommodate your needs. It is always easier to stay where you are, if your host is willing to help. The move can sometimes be a little tricky and can sometimes result in downtime, lost data, and lost visitors. With the help of this chapter and the help of hosting professionals, most of those issues can be eliminated. However, every move is different and you never quite know what can happen until it happens.

Getting Out of Your Contract

In reality, the majority of web hosts do not give refunds if you leave before your contract period has ended. In fact, if you got a cheap deal on your hosting, it may have come with terms and conditions that demand you either see out the term of the contract or pay for the privilege of breaking the contract early.

With most hosts, if you are paying the standard rates, there is either a one-month final fee (if you're paying monthly) or simply no refund for the remaining months if you are paying annually or semiannually.

If you decide you want to move hosts, check the terms and conditions of the contract you took out and maybe even ask your host what its reaction will be.

When I move sites for customers, I generally recommend that they keep (if possible) the old hosting plan running for at least a month, if not two, after they have moved. I suggest this for the following reasons:

✓ **The grass is not always greener on the other side.** Sometimes it's only when you get to the other side that you realize how good you had it before and you may want to switch straight back. Keeping your original hosting plan means you can do that quickly and easily — and keep the same original rate.

✓ **Sometimes you think you transferred over all your data and it is only later that you find that some is missing or got corrupted during the move.** If this happens, it is a great relief to know that your files are still at your old host and accessible so you can copy across what did not copy across correctly the first time. After a month or so, when you are sure that everything is copied across correctly and that things work the way you expect them to with the new host, you can close down your old hosting account so you no longer get charged for it. It's kind of like buying a new insurance policy. You don't want to let one lapse until the other is actually started; otherwise, you're sure to run into trouble right at the exact point where you have no insurance coverage.

Knowing What You Need for a Painless Move

Your website consists of various parts. For instance, your website might include the following:

✓ Website files (don't forget the hidden files!)

✓ A database or two (or more)

✓ Subdomains

✓ Add-on domains

✓ Parked domains

✓ E-mail accounts

✓ E-mails

✓ Mailing lists

✓ Multiple FTP accounts

✓ Password-protected areas

After you have decided to change hosts, you need to work out absolutely everything that your website and domain name use and figure out how to transfer those things. You can download site files using File Transfer Protocol

(FTP), and then you can upload those files to your new host by FTP. Likewise, you can download databases through phpMyAdmin and then upload them using the same facility on the new host. In most cases, however, things like e-mail addresses, password-protected areas, and FTP accounts cannot be copied across automatically. You must go through your control panel and re-create everything on the new host.

Take the time to think carefully about everything you do on your site and everything you use your hosting for. You don't want to miss something small that you rarely think about but which could really mess things up for you in the future if you overlook it.

Don't forget: This is a good time to clean out anything you no longer want or need, such as extra logins and superfluous e-mail accounts and old FTP accounts.

See the check list at the end of this chapter for a more comprehensive list covering what to check when you make your move. The things I just mentioned, though, are the main items and the ones that you must not ignore.

If you are moving to a server that uses the same control panel you are currently using, you may be able to save a lot of time and stress by using the built-in transfer facility to move everything over automatically. Your new host may also be willing to do the move for you.

Take out your new hosting contract prior to the move date so that you have time to set up and configure everything on the new server before you actually make the move.

Scheduling Your Move

When do you get the most visitors to your website? Most people do not know the answer to this question, or they think they know but are actually only guessing. Your website statistics show the busiest hours and days, so consult the stats to determine the best time to make the move. Schedule your move for a time and day when your website is naturally less busy so that you can minimize disruption to your visitors.

It is also a good idea to warn your visitors a few days (or even a week or two) in advance that things will be changing, so that they can be prepared and understand if they do find your site difficult to view during the changeover. On the day of the move, or the day before the move, put up a notice or blog post informing your customers that the site will be going down from time to time over the next couple of days to facilitate a move to a new server.

With the nature of the Domain Name System (DNS) and the possibility of having visitors to your site from all over the world, there can be disruption for some people for 48 hours or more, although most will see the change within a few hours.

The best time to schedule a move, apart from being a time where your statistics show you that you have fewer visitors, is in the evening or over the weekend. If you're making the move in the evening or on the weekend, then you need to ensure in advance that your designer and your web hosts both old and new will be working at the time that you do the move, just in case anything goes wrong and you need help.

Making a Foolproof Check List

Here are two check lists of just about everything you need to consider. One is for things to consider, collect, and do in advance; the other is for the day of the move.

A sample check list is available for download from `www.dummies.com/cheatsheet/webhosting`.

Creating a pre-move check list

The following sections list everything you need to do in advance.

Domain name

✔ **Is your domain name provided free with your current hosting?** If so, transfer it somewhere where you can continue to own and manage it.

✔ **Do you have forwarders or redirects set up on the domain?** If so, list them all.

✔ **Do you have parked domains?** If so, list them so they can be configured on your new hosting. (This configuration may be possible to do in advance.)

✔ **Do any of your parked domains have forwarding or redirects?** List them all.

✔ **Do you have add-on domains?**

✔ **Are there any forwarders or redirects on your add-on domains?**

✔ **Do you have subdomains?** Subdomains must be configured correctly prior to moving the data.

✔ **Do you know how to change the nameservers on your domain(s)?**

Website

✔ **In advance of the move, make a backup to your own computer of all your website files using FTP.**

✔ **Check whether you have any hidden files or .htaccess files and ensure that they are copied across.** You also need to check that any file paths in those files remain correct; paths can sometimes be slightly different from server to server.

✔ **Find out how to connect to your new server via FTP before you change the nameservers**. You need this info to be able to upload your files on move day.

✔ **Notify your visitors in advance that there may be some disruption on move day.**

✔ **Are there any password-protected folders?** List them all with their usernames and passwords.

✔ **Do you use any caching plugins with your website?** Caching needs to be switched off before the move and switched on again afterward.

✔ **Do you use databases?** If so, make a backup in advance. List all the databases and the usernames and respective passwords.

✔ **Is the database name/username format the same on the new server you're moving to?** If not, you need to create a new database name and username and update the configuration file within your website.

✔ **Find out which file holds the database username and password info within your site so you can edit it if necessary on move day.**

✔ **SSL certificates.** If you use a Secure Socket Layer (SSL) certificate, you need to find out in advance how to change it over to the new hosting.

✔ **Dedicated IP addresses.** Most sites do not have dedicated IP addresses, but some, particularly ones with SSL certificates, do. Check if you have one because you will need to get a new one from your new host. Shared hosting plans do not normally come with dedicated IP addresses.

E-mail

✔ **Which e-mail addresses need to be transferred over?** List them all.

✔ **Does the new host allow for transfer of e-mail history?** Unless you are doing a server-to-server copy of the hosting plan, most do not allow for transfer of e-mails already received.

✔ **Make sure all e-mail users back up or download any e-mails they need to keep in advance, even if their history is being copied across.**

✔ **Warn people you regularly correspond with via e-mail that e-mails might get lost or undelivered during the move.** Until the domain propagation is complete, some e-mails could be delivered to your old server that you might not be able to access.

✔ **Do you have mailing lists?** If so, how do you copy those mailing lists across? Some may have to be copied manually.

✔ **Do you use an external mail service?** If so, you need to copy the MX records across to the new server. You can do this in advance.

✔ **Do you have any mail aliases?** List these to ensure that you re-create them correctly.

✔ **Do you have any mail forwarders or group forwarders?** List all of these.

✔ **Do you use server-based spam filtering?** If so, check that no legitimate e-mails have been caught in the spam filter.

✔ **Do you have spam filter rules set up?** List these so they can be re-created on the new server.

✔ **Do you have auto-responders on any mail accounts?** Note what these are so you can re-create them.

Miscellaneous

✔ **Do you have any extra FTP accounts set up?** List them and re-create them in advance on the new server.

✔ **Do you use cron jobs?** If so, list them so you can re-create them on move day.

✔ **Do you use the server's built-in backup facility?** If so, does the new server have the same facility available?

✔ **If you use your server's built-in stats system, check with your host to find out how to transfer the stat history to your new server.**

✔ **Do you regularly use Secure SHell (SSH)?** If so, talk to your new host about how to configure SSH access.

✔ **Do you use FrontPage Extensions?** If so, check that your new host allows them.

Creating a move day check list

You also need a check list for move day. You should mark out these headings on a piece of paper or a file on your computer and have two columns next to them. Mark one column when you have copied those things from the old server; mark the other column when you have restored or uploaded those things to the new server. You should also go through and, line by line, mark through any items that do not apply to your site — for instance, mailing lists, parked domains, or add-on domains.

Domain name

✔ Parked domains

✔ Add-on domains

✔ Forwarders and redirects

✔ Subdomains

   Subdomains need to be configured correctly prior to moving the data.

✔ Change the nameservers on your domain(s) after the data is all moved.

Website

✔ Download all files via FTP and upload them to your new server.

✔ Put a notice on your site saying that there will be some disruption for up to 48 hours. Alternatively, put up a "We are moving" front page.

✔ Re-create password protection on appropriate folders and inform users if the details have changed.

✔ Use phpMyAdmin to download all databases and then re-create them on the new server and upload the data into them.

✔ If the database names, usernames, or passwords have changed, update the configuration files in your website.

✔ If you use an external database manager such as MySQL Workbench, update your logins with the new details.

✔ Reconfigure SSL certificates with new server details.

E-mail

✔ Re-create all e-mail addresses.

✔ Transfer e-mail history, if possible.

✔ Copy across or re-create mailing lists.

✔ Check that MX records are the same as on the old server.

✔ Re-create mail aliases.

✔ Re-create forwarders.

✔ Switch on server spam filtering and configure it, if necessary.

✔ Re-create auto-responders.

Miscellaneous

- ✔ Re-create all FTP accounts and notify users if details have changed.
- ✔ Re-create all cron jobs.
- ✔ Set up server-based backup facility, if necessary.
- ✔ Check that SSH access works correctly.
- ✔ Reinstall FrontPage extensions, if needed.

Every site is different. I may have missed something in these lists that is relevant to your site, so ensure in advance that your check list covers absolutely everything for your specific site!

Part V
Increasing Control with a Virtual Private Server or Dedicated Server

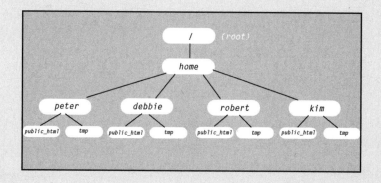

In this part . . .

✔ Step up to a more personal server with a VPS or dedicated server.

✔ Learn how to manage the backend of a web server.

✔ Set up your own hosting accounts and set your own limits.

✔ Learn how to access the command line and enter basic commands.

Chapter 14

Making the Right Technology Choices

In This Chapter

▶ Picking the right server

▶ Being realistic about your abilities

There are so many choices out there that even I get confused by it all sometimes. With many different control panels, many types of servers, and many hosting plans, the range of options seems endless.

In this chapter, I help you wade through the choices and decide what's right for you individually.

Weighing the Differences between Virtual Private Servers and Dedicated Servers

Most of us start out on a shared server, which is one web server housing multiple websites, potentially from dozens or even hundreds of different clients. Shared servers are a good place to start but, at times, can be poor in terms of service, depending on the particular host, the sites that happen to be on that machine, and the number of sites that the host allows on the machine. All resources on the server, such as memory, hard drive space, processor speed, and so on, are shared between all the websites on the machine. This means that if one site gets too busy or starts using large amounts of the server's resources, all the other sites on the server suffer.

You can avoid this by using a Virtual Private Server (VPS) or dedicated server for your site instead.

I've given shared servers a bit of a bad rap here because I want to try to high-light all their possible shortcomings. However, there are many hosts who do an admirable job of balancing the need for lots of sites to be on the server to keep costs down with ensuring that the servers perform well. Don't be afraid to use a shared server until your site gets too big for it.

The major difference between a VPS and dedicated server comes down to the *V* (for virtual) in VPS. A VPS gives you your own server with its own resources, but only a virtual one — meaning some software is running on a physical server that splits it up into a number of theoretical pieces and assigns an amount of resources to each of those pieces. It's like cutting a pie into slices; when someone comes to take a slice, he just takes the piece you've cut for him without disturbing the rest of the pie. A common way to do this is for a server that has, say, 8GB of memory in it to be split into four VPSs, each of which is given 2GB. The virtualization process works fairly well, and for the most part you have your own small, self-contained server. In theory, each VPS can access only the resources allocated to it, but in practice, many are set up to allow some overflow — that is, to steal resources from other VPSs on the same dedi-cated box. This means that although in theory you are guaranteed to have, for instance, 2GB of RAM, if another VPS on your server gets really busy it might steal some of your memory and processor time.

Although a VPS is a much cheaper option than a dedicated server, if you expect to significantly grow your site, it may be a false economy. The nature of a VPS as a virtual server created by partitioning off a physical server means your upgrade options are limited. Servers can only have so much in them physically to start with, and, if your needs expand, a VPS might not have the resources available for you to expand into, which means that a scary, time-consuming move to a dedicated server might be necessary.

Dedicated servers, on the other hand, are servers you purchase (or lease) for yourself that give you a guaranteed amount of resources with nobody else able to use the server or able to "share" any of your resources. A dedicated server is a physical box in a rack in a data center somewhere; it is physically, individually yours. Obviously, it is considerably more expensive to have your own personal server than shared or VPS hosting, so there are three main fac-tors to consider when choosing between the types of server:

✔ **Cost:** Shared hosting is by far the cheapest. VPS is considerably more expensive (five to ten times the cost). Dedicated servers are normally at least three or four times as expensive again.

✔ **Mission criticality:** Deciding how important it is to have your website always available and always running at the fastest possible speeds is important. If you have a blog about the fluff and other things you find between your toes and you're making no money from it, it isn't so important that your site is always available or is always running extremely fast. However, if you're running an Internet-based business, every second your website is down or running sluggishly could mean reduced sales and lost revenue.

✔ **Website traffic:** If your website's traffic consists of your mother coming by once a week to find out what you're up to and some guy you met in an Arkansas bar checking it out because he thinks you're his best friend then you're safe to use a shared server. The more visitors you get, however, the higher up the server scale you need to go. A shared server is a good start but if your traffic is increasing rapidly and you expect it to continue to do so, a VPS or dedicated server may be what you require.

Selecting an Operating System

Go for Linux, either the CentOS or FreeBSD variety.

There, that was easy, right?

Seriously, though, if you know you absolutely need a Windows server then go for a Windows server. Otherwise, Linux is what you want, and CentOS certainly seems to be the most popular and stable system.

Ask your host what it recommends because you will want your host to support you when necessary. Using the operating system that your host knows best is a good idea.

Choosing Your Control Panel

My personal preference of control panel is cPanel because of its balance between flexibility and ease of use. It's what I use on my servers, but choice of control panel is a matter of personal preference.

Other options include:

✔ Parallels Plesk, which is available for both Windows and Linux servers. Plesk is a panel I have used extensively, and I can see why many people like it a lot. Running a hosting business, I found cPanel to be a little more flexible and easy to use, but as an individual, I don't see much difference between the two.

✔ Parallels Helm for Windows servers is a friendly, comfortable piece of software. I used it for my Windows servers for the first few years of my time as a web host. It's actually my favorite control panel for Windows.

✔ DotNetPanel has become WebSitePanel and is now an open-source Windows panel. Open source means it's free, which can be a big plus, but I personally find it a little restrictive and hard to navigate. The fact that it's free makes up for some of those issues, and I know that it is still being refined and developed. I hope it will become a more usable product than I have previously found it to be.

Deciding Whether to Use Managed Services

In the hosting industry, *managed services* means an additional level of support and assistance over and above what you would normally get with a VPS or dedicated server.

Every company has its own version of managed services, with different levels of support and assistance from company to company.

In essence, though, using managed services means that the hosting company takes over many of the technical, backend aspects of the hosting. The result is that you have an experience more like you would have with a shared server, but you still have the speed and power benefits of a VPS or dedicated server.

It's a little like maintaining a car. If you don't mind getting your hands dirty and sometimes spending a few frustrating hours (or days) fixing a problem yourself, it's cheaper to maintain your own car. If you want some assurance the job has been done right by someone who actually knows what he's doing, though, taking your car into a service center is often worth the cost.

If you don't mind tinkering with your server, you don't need managed services. You can find the answers to everything if you search the Internet. However, using managed services can give you peace of mind. It just comes at a price.

The decision, therefore, comes down to how much you want to do yourself — and how much it's worth to you to have someone else do it for you.

Check with your host before you opt for managed services, though, to find out what its managed service contract includes. Otherwise, you could be in for a shock when you find that the managed services don't provide everything you hoped or expected them to do.

Chapter 15

Keeping the Lid on Pandora's Box with WebHost Manager

*I*f you are using a Virtual Private Server (VPS) or dedicated server, you most likely have access to a whole range of facilities that people on shared servers do not have access to. The reason you have access to these services is that the server you are on (or the part of it, with a VPS) is all yours. Because you aren't sharing it with anyone, you can have access to some behind-the-scenes functions that normally wouldn't be open to you because they give you the capability to affect other people's websites.

In this chapter, I explain a few of these features and how to use them. I focus on a piece of software called Web Host Manager (WHM), which is part of the cPanel installation. Other panels have their own backend areas for dedicated servers and VPSs, but this chapter gives you an idea of what you can and can't do with WHM.

Creating a Hosting Package or Plan

When you sign up for shared hosting, your host decides what facilities will be available to you. It does this by creating a hosting plan or package on the server that is then applied to your domain name. When creating this package, the host defines the facilities and resources that are available to users of that plan. Understanding how plans are defined helps you better understand how shared hosting plans work, and what choices a host is given. Effectively, when you are on a VPS or dedicated server, you are your own host. On one level, the people you lease your server from are your hosts, but on another level, you have control over a bunch of things that previously only your web host could change.

You can create a range of different hosting packages for yourself, if you want to, depending on what you're going to use your server for. I have a number of different websites on my own personal server, and I have a couple of different hosting packages set up to help me organize them. I use some domains purely for e-mail, some are for full websites, and some of them are smaller sites (landing page websites). Because the server belongs to me, it would make no difference if I gave myself unlimited resources in every package, but it makes it easier for me to group them together in my control panel if I have them set up under different packages that have logical, self-explanatory names. So I have one package called "e-mail only," another package called "full hosting," and yet another package called "Landing Pages." These are simply names I made up for my own use so I can easily see what's what.

When your server was set up, you most likely had to have a primary domain name to set it up under — and this may be the only domain name you use. The primary domain is always set up with a default package that normally gives you unlimited use of all the hosting facilities.

If you are using only one domain, you don't need to worry about setting up other packages or accounts, but most people whose site is big enough to require its own server generally have more than one domain.

Although you can set different functions to give you "unlimited" access in your hosting package, you are still limited by what your host physically allows you to use. So, for instance, if your host only allows you 20GB of disk space then setting the allowed disk space on your server to unlimited grants you an unlimited amount *up to* the 20GB limit set by your host. Your setting does not override your host's limits.

Before you can set up any domains on your server, you need to set up hosting packages. Your host may well have set up some default packages that may cover everything you require. However, your host may not have set them up, or the plans may not be set the way you would like.

The following steps describe setting up a new hosting package using WHM. Other tools should operate similarly.

1. **Log in to your WHM using the details that your host provided when you signed up for a VPS or dedicated server.**

   The address for your web host manager is normally `whm.yourdomainname.com`.

TIP

WHM is somewhat different from cPanel. cPanel and WHM don't have many facilities in common. This is because facilities don't need to be in both and each dashboard has its own specific use and purpose. If you scroll down through the menu on the left, you will see a dazzling array of options, the very names of which may scare you.

2. **Scroll down to the Packages section and click Add a Package.**

3. **Give your package a name.**

   This name can't be changed at a later date, but don't worry about getting it perfect the first time; you can create as many packages as you want and delete any you no longer need. Type the name in the box at the top of the page.

4. **Scroll through the list and pick which facilities are and aren't available in this package and how many of each are available. (See Figure 15-1.)**

   In general, if this is your own server and you aren't sharing it with other people, you can select Unlimited for all of these options. The advantage with giving yourself limits is that you will be notified by e-mail when you're reaching those limits and will thus find it easier to manage how much bandwidth and disk space you're using. The options are fairly self-explanatory. The amount of disk space you can select is up to that available under the hosting plan you have purchased. You can also select the amount of bandwidth available and many other options, such as the number of FTP accounts and a number of e-mail accounts that can be created.

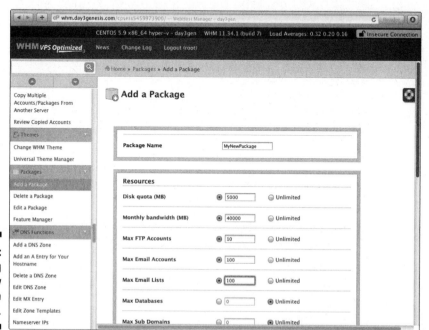

Figure 15-1: Creating a new package in WHM.

5. **When you have selected your chosen limits, click Add at the bottom of the page.**

   Your package is saved. You can go back in and edit the limits at any time.

That's all there is to creating a hosting plan. You now have a package that you can use for any domains on your server.

Use the following steps to edit a package in WHM:

1. **Log in to WHM.**

2. **Scroll down to Packages in the left-hand menu.**

3. **Click Edit a Package.**

4. **Select your package from the list and click Edit.**

5. **Make any changes you need to make.**

6. **Click Save Changes.**

Setting Up Your Accounts

With a VPS or dedicated server, you can set up separate user accounts, each with its own domain (or domains). If you are the only one using the server, this may not be necessary, but if you are sharing the server with friends or family, then it can be useful to set up separate accounts for each person so each has his own cPanel login and can manage his own accounts. Do the following to set up a new account:

1. **Log in to WHM.**

2. **Scroll to the Account Information section and click Create a New Account.**

3. **Enter the primary domain name and an account user ID.**

   Each new account requires a primary domain name and an account user ID. You can give it any ID you wish, but in WHM you are limited to eight characters for the ID. It is easier if you select an ID that has some relevance to the person using it, such as her name or the first eight characters of the domain name. (See Figure 15-2.)

4. **Create a password for the user and enter his e-mail address. Click OK.**

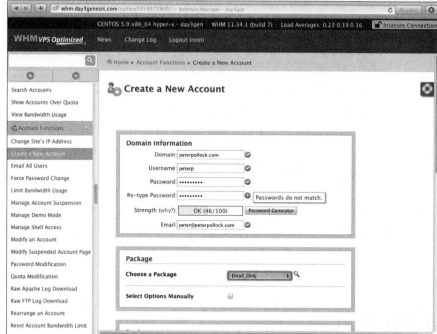

Figure 15-2:
Creating
a new
account in
WHM.

5. **Select the hosting package this account will be under and make any necessary changes to the Reseller, DNS, and Mail Routing settings.**

It is not normally necessary to make changes to the Reseller, DNS, and Mail Routing settings.

6. **Click Create.**

You have now set up the user account and given it a hosting package. The nameservers for the domain must point to the server you are on for this hosting package to become live. If they do, you can now go to cPanel. *thedomainname.com* and you will be able to log in with the username and password you just set up.

Managing Users

Each account has its own folder tree on the server where its files are kept.

As the owner of the server, you have superuser access to the whole server, meaning you can see all of the other account holders' files. All account files are kept in folders inside a folder called home, which is a subfolder of the root of the drive.

Each account has a folder within the home folder, the name of which corresponds with the account name.

Imagine my server has four different accounts on it: one for me (Peter), one for my wife Debbie, and one each for my friends Robert and Kim.

The folder structure would be like this: In the root of the drive (the root is symbolized by a /) would be a folder named home and within the home folder there would be four subfolders: peter, debbie, robert, and kim. See Figure 15-3 for a graphic representation of the structure.

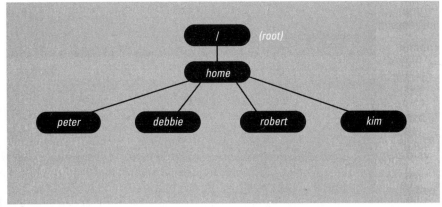

Figure 15-3:
Folder tree
for WHM
home
folders.

Each of those folders then has a number of folders inside it including a folder named public_html.

The public_html folder is very important because it is what is known as the *document root* for that account (and the primary domain name associated with it). The document root is the top-level folder that users on the Internet can see for that domain. This means that anything above the document root in the folder tree is not accessible by anyone using the Internet. All of your website files must go inside the document root. I illustrate this in Figure 15-4 by making the folders that are accessible to the Internet white. Any subfolders and files within them would also be accessible to the Internet. Black folders and any files within them can't be viewed through the Internet.

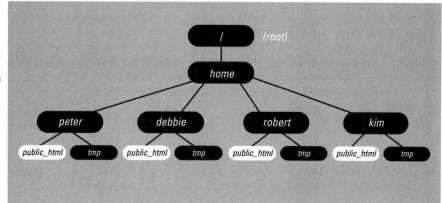

Figure 15-4:
public_html
folders
are the
document
roots for
their user.

Other control panels use different folders for the document root, but every control panel has one. It may be called `public_html`, `wwwroot`, or something different. Your host will be able to tell you which folder is the document root for the domain.

When a user logs in through cPanel or through FTP, the highest folder she can see is the folder in the `home` folder named with her username. She can't see the `home` folder or the other usernames within it.

Only the superuser can see all the folders, which means you can safely give other people their own accounts, and they won't be able to view, delete, copy, or mess with anyone else's files.

Securing Your Server

Security is a big deal online and there are no magic solutions to make your server absolutely secure, no matter what anyone else may tell you. Famously in the past, the secure networks of banks, international corporations, government departments, the CIA, the Department of Defense — even Microsoft, Google, and Apple — have been hacked.

The only truly secure way to protect your site and files is to switch the server off, unplug it, crush it into dust, and sprinkle the dust particles over a thousand square miles of the Pacific Ocean . . . and even then someone might find a backup of your data.

There are different levels of hackers, though, and there *is* plenty you can do to keep out any but the most persistent of hackers. The following steps outline a good way to get started:

1. **Keep all your software up-to-date on your personal computer and on your server, including using the EasyApache facility under Software in WHM to update to the latest versions of PHP and MySQL.**

2. **Go to the cPanel section of the WHM menu (near the bottom of the menu options on the left of WHM) and click Manage Plugins.**

3. **Select and install the ClamAV and ConfigServer Security & Firewall (CSF) plugins, if they are not already installed.**

   See Chapter 8 for details on configuring CSF.

4. **At the bottom of the left-hand menu in WHM, confirm that Mod Security is installed (see Figure 15-5).**

   If Mod Security is not installed, install it by running the EasyApache facility under the Software menu.

Figure 15-5:
WHM
Plugins
section.

When Mod_Security is installed, you need to also install some security rules for Mod Security. These differ depending on how your website is built so it's best to get some expert advice on which rules are right for you. Your web host would be a good place to start when looking for advice on Mod_Security rules.

5. **Scroll up in the WHM menu to the Security Center and click on cPHulk Brute Force Protection to check that it is enabled.**

   This facility watches for people trying to log in to your server multiple times without success. If there are too many failed login attempts, the facility decides the person doesn't know your password and locks him out.

6. **In the Security Center, click Shell Fork Bomb Protection and check that it is enabled.**

   This prevents any one user from overloading the server if she gets in via Secure SHell, or SSH.

7. **Click SMTP Restrictions in the Security Center and check that they are enabled.**

   SMTP stands for Simple Mail Transport Protocol and is the system that the server uses for sending e-mail. Enabling this blocks some of the tricks spammers use to hijack your server to send spam.

8. **Select the Apache Mod_userdir Tweak option in the Security Center and enable it.**

   It is highly unlikely that you'll ever need `mod_userdir` — it's something only web hosts really need to use. If you do ever need it, it's simple enough to go back in and disable it or just disable it for a specific domain.

9. **Scroll down to the Account Functions section and click Manage Shell Access.**

   Only users who specifically require shell access should have it enabled, so select Disabled Shell for all other users.

10. **Check with a service such as `sucuri.net` that your site/server has not already been compromised.**

    You may want to consider signing up for a yearly protection and monitoring plan. Your host may also supply a service like this.

Managing Your Mail Queue

With access to the backend of your server, you also gain access to some mail functions that were previously unavailable to you. Scroll down the left-hand menu of WHM to find the section called Mail that's near the bottom. In this section, there are a few options that may be useful to you if you have problems with your mail or if you want to monitor the mail that goes through your server. I briefly explain how to use two of the main functions, although there are other functions that you may use at other times.

Repair mailbox permissions

Sometimes, if your mail is not working correctly it is simply because the folder permissions where your mail is stored have become messed up. I'd love to give you an intelligent reason why this happens, but I honestly just don't know. It's something that just happens. It doesn't hurt to click Repair Mailbox Permissions and then Proceed every now and then and allow the server to check that everything is in order. This may even solve certain problems you didn't know you had.

Occasionally users on my server complain they cannot access the e-mail or cannot access certain folders. Running the repair command often solves that problem for them. It should take five minutes or less to run, depending on how many domains you have on your server and how many e-mail addresses are set up under each domain.

Mail queue manager

In theory, when you click Mail Queue Manager there shouldn't be any mail shown. However, the way the mail system works, the mail queue manager handles the sending and receiving of all mail. It is like a mailroom at your local post office: It sorts the mail and directs it to the correct location. There are a couple of reasons why mail gets caught up in the mail queue.

✔ You are trying to send too many e-mails at one time. This can happen if you have a large e-mail list and your server is set up to limit the number of e-mails per hour. You can set this limit by doing the following:

1. Scrolling up to the Server Configuration section at the top of the left-hand menu in WHM and clicking Tweak Settings.

2. Clicking the Mail tab in the screen that opens.

3. Scrolling down to the Max Hourly Emails per Domain item and changing the number in the box (see Figure 15-6).

4. Scrolling to the bottom and clicking Save.

✔ Items also get trapped in the mail queue manager if they are being sent to servers that have blacklisted you and will not accept your e-mails. This happens if your server or website has been hacked and someone is using it to send spam e-mail. If people are reporting that they are not getting e-mails from you, it can be a good idea just to check your mail queue manager to make sure your e-mails are not held up.

There are two main options within the mail queue manager. One is to deliver the mail now; the other is to delete it permanently. You should check your mail queue manager periodically, delete mail that is stuck if it is not needed, and force it to deliver any that you need delivered. If the mail queue manager is still unable to deliver your mail, it adds the mail back into the queue, and you can look at the error message to see the reason why it didn't go.

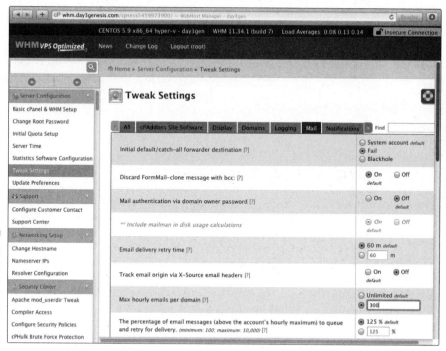

Figure 15-6: Configuring Max Hourly Emails per Domain in WHM.

If you are having mail issues, try restarting the three mail services (IMAP, Mail Server, and POP3 Server) and sending/receiving mail again. See the "Restarting Services" section for details on how to restart those services.

Restarting Services

The beauty of a web server is that each of its major functions has its own "service." A service is a piece of software — a program that runs on the server handling a particular function. If one of the services stops functioning correctly, you do not necessarily have to reboot the entire server to get it working again. In most cases, you can simply restart the service that has broken.

To view the current status of services on your server, scroll down to the Service Status section of WHM and click on Service Status. You see a screen something like Figure 15-7, which lists each service with a green check mark next to it if it is running correctly or a red cross if it has a problem.

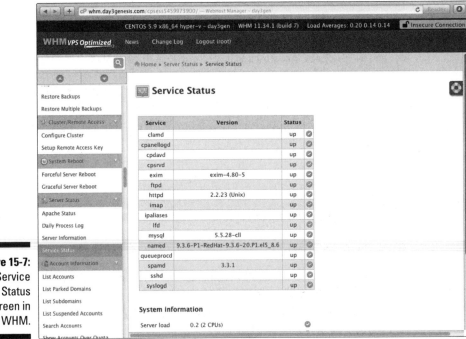

Figure 15-7: Service Status screen in WHM.

If one or more of your services has a problem, the first thing to try is simply restarting it, as described in the following steps:

1. **Scroll down to the Restart Services section.**

2. **Find the service that currently has a problem and click it.**

3. **Click Yes to confirm that you want to restart the service.**

4. **Watch for the status message that tells you that the service is being restarted and then reports whether it was successful.**

5. **If the restart is reported as successful, scroll back up to the Service Status section and check the service status again.**

6. **If the restart was not successful, contact your host for support.**

You need to do the same process for each service that is not running.

Sometimes a service may say that it is running correctly but may have an issue anyway. I have found this happens repeatedly with some of the mail services. Restarting a running service to try to clear errors is not a problem unless you are in the middle of running another command in WHM that expressly forbids you from doing so.

Updating Your Server Software

There is no single place for ensuring that all server software is up-to-date. There are simply too many different pieces of software and different options to make that feasible.

You can, however, make some server updates automatic or do them manually using the following methods:

Automatic updates

To configure your server to do automatic updates (recommended):

1. **Go to the Server Configuration section at the top of the left-hand menu in WHM and click Update Preferences.**

   This will set your update preferences for cPanel/WHM specific software.

2. **Select the Release Tier you want to have installed.**

The options are LTS, Stable, Release, Current, and Edge. They are listed in order of reliability, with LTS being the oldest and the most tested version currently supported, and Edge being the newest, just-in-the-process-of-being-tested version. You should not use Edge on a "production" server (one that hosts your live website). I normally recommend using the Release tier version because it gives a good balance between the latest and greatest updates and innovations and testing and stability.

3. **Scroll down the screen and select how the server should update individual products and services.**

I recommend Automatic/Inherit for every option unless you have a specific reason to change it for any one or more.

4. **Click Save.**

Those are all of the automatic updates you can configure. There are other updates, which you should run manually regularly.

Manual updates

There are some updates that cannot be automated. The following is a list of those updates and how to manually update them:

1. **Scroll down to the Software section of the WHM left-hand menu and select EasyApache (Apache Update).**

   This should only be done by an expert, but it is where you select your version of Apache and PHP. You can follow through the prompts if you want to try it yourself, but do not change any options you are unsure about. Consult your host and web designer before making any changes.

2. **In the Software section, select MySQL Upgrade.**

   The next screen will have selected your current version of MySQL and if there is a newer version, consult with your host and web designer about whether or not you should upgrade. Upgrades are one-way. After you go up a level, you cannot go down again.

3. **Click Update Server Software in the Software section and click Proceed.**

   This manually forces an update on some of the software that should have been automatically updated through your automatic update settings. Occasionally, one update or another will not work right and this will force the system to rerun it.

4. **Click Update System Software and then Proceed.**

   This updates certain software files that are not done automatically but that rarely need updating.

5. **Scroll down to the cPanel section of the WHM left-hand menu and click Upgrade to Latest Version.**

   This gives you the option to manually force the upgrade to the latest version, based on your preferred version set in the automatic upgrades section. This is useful if your server is having problems, and you know that cPanel has just released fixes for them. It forces an upgrade now rather than waiting for the next scheduled upgrade.

Rebooting Your Server

Sometimes your entire server needs to be rebooted. This doesn't happen often, and many cPanel web servers run for months — or even years — without needing a reboot. If your server does need to be rebooted, though, there are three ways to do it:

- **Gracefully reboot the server.** Scroll down to the System Reboot section in the left-hand menu of WHM and click Graceful Server Reboot. This reboots the server, allowing all the services to shut down correctly before doing so. This is the best way to do a reboot, if you can.

- **Force the server to reboot.** Scroll down to the System Reboot section in the left-hand menu of WHM and click Forceful Server Reboot. If your server is having big problems, there may be services that are locked up and cannot be shut down. In this instance, a graceful reboot will fail because it will wait for those services to close. A forceful reboot doesn't wait for anything; it just goes ahead and reboots regardless of whether services shut down or not.

- **Log in via SSH and run the command** `reboot`. This does a graceful reboot of the system. You can also do a forceful reboot by using the command `echo 1 > /proc/sys/kernel/sysrq` followed by the command `echo b > /proc/sysrq-trigger`.

Chapter 16

Getting Down to the Command Line with Secure SHell

Secure SHell (SSH) is the system you use to connect to your server from a remote location (like your home or office) and type commands in as if you are standing in front of it.

SSH is, all at the same time, useful, powerful, and potentially dangerous.

If you don't know what you're doing, using SSH can be like letting a sumo wrestler loose in a china shop. On the other hand, if you exercise caution, it can be as graceful and powerful as a prima ballerina.

To use SSH, you need an SSH client such as PuTTY or, on a Mac computer, the built-in Terminal application.

Most shared hosting servers do not give access to SSH, and if you are on a shared server you should ask your host if it can provide you with access if you need it.

If you are using a Virtual Private Server (VPS) or dedicated server, however, you should be able to connect using SSH unless you have paid for managed services from your host. Some hosts do not allow their managed services clients access through SSH because it gives the clients access to areas that the host is being paid to manage.

Installing an SSH Client on Your Computer

Before being able to open a command line on your server, you need to install the correct software for your operating system. On Windows, the best choice is PuTTY. On Mac and Linux machines, you can use the built-in Terminal program, which does the same job PuTTY does on Windows.

PuTTY

PuTTY, which is available only for Windows, is a powerful tool that enables you to connect to devices online, using a system called telnet, providing you have the correct login details. It is something that may be used by hackers to gain backend access to servers.

Consequently, PuTTY comes with dire warnings. You must not use it anywhere where it is illegal to do so. The research I've done suggests that it is legal to use it within the U.S., the U.K., and most of Europe, providing you're using it to connect to a device that you own or have the right to connect to.

PuTTY is very useful to website owners, especially those with a VPS or dedicated server, because it enables you to open a command-line prompt on your server from a remote location by logging in via SSH so that you can run commands as needed.

You do not need to install PuTTY on your computer if don't intend to connect by SSH and don't need to use the command line on your server. You should only open your server to allow SSH connections if you know there is a good reason for using them. Otherwise, keep SSH closed to help prevent intruders from gaining access.

You can download PuTTY from `www.chiark.greenend.org.uk/~sgtatham/putty/download.html`. (See Figure 16-1.)

After you have downloaded PuTTY, you simply double-click it to run it. There is no Install facility; it is a single file called `Putty.exe`.

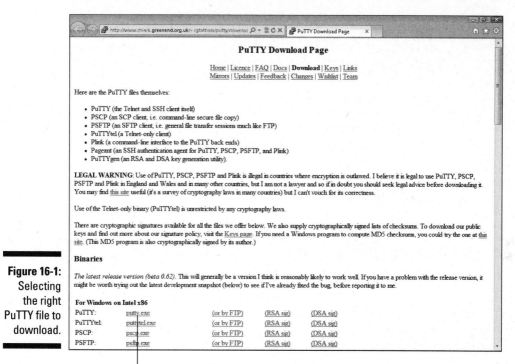

Figure 16-1:
Selecting
the right
PuTTY file to
download.

The first file is
usually the best.

Terminal

Mac computers and Linux-based computers come with a program called
Terminal, so you do not need to install PuTTY or any other SSH software.

To find Terminal on a Mac, go to the Launcher and open the utilities
folder.

To find Terminal in Linux, go to Applications⇨System Tools⇨Terminal.

Connecting to Your Server

The first thing you need to do to be able to connect your server is to set your
server up to allow SSH connections.

See Chapter 8 for details on how to allow SSH connections.

How you log in depends on whether you are using a username/password combination or a username/key system. It also depends on which operating system you are using on your computer.

Connecting with Windows

If you are using a username/password combination, connect like this:

1. **Double-click on the** `Putty.exe` **file you downloaded.**

2. **Type the hostname of your server (normally your primary domain name) or its IP address into the first box.**

3. **Click Open (see Figure 16-2).**

4. **Type your username and press Enter.**

5. **Type your password and press Enter.**

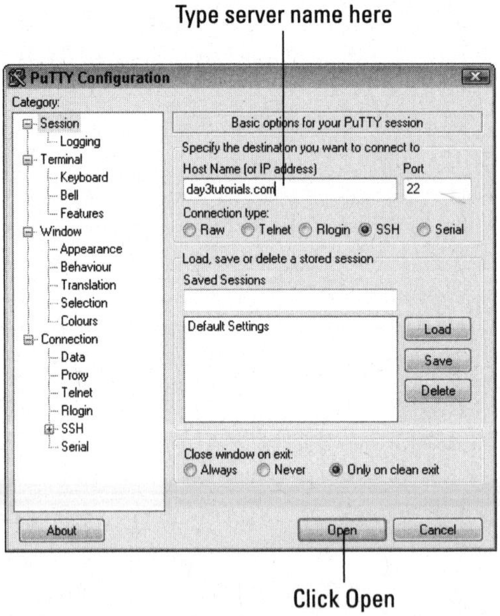

Type server name here

Figure 16-2:
Opening
an SSH
connection
in PuTTY.

Click Open

If you have configured your server correctly and entered the correct user-name and password, you should be logged in and have a command prompt with your username, your server name, and a # sign. (See Figure 16-3.)

Successful login results
in command prompt.

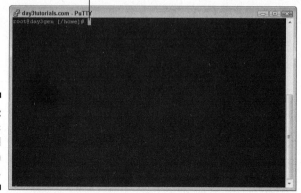

Figure 16-3:
Basic
command
prompt in
PuTTY.

During the login process, the server may give you warnings about not logging in if you're not allowed to do so and might even tell you that it has notified the administrator that you've tried. You don't need to worry about this unless you're trying to break into someone else's server!

If you are using a username/key combination, you first have to save the key in PuTTY. This is a little complicated, but it's easy enough if you follow these steps carefully:

1. **Create a public/private key on your server as described in Chapter 8 and download the private part as a ppk key.**

2. **Double-click on the** `Putty.exe` **file.**

3. **Type the hostname of your server (usually your primary domain name) or its IP address into the first box.**

4. **In the Saved Sessions box, type a name for this connection and then click Save (see Figure 16-4).**

5. **In the category menu at the left of PuTTY, click SSH and then Auth (see Figure 16-5).**

6. **Click Browse and then browse to and select the ppk file you downloaded from your server.**

7. **Click Connection in the Category list and then click Data.**

8. **Type your username in the Auto-login username box.**

9. **Click Session and save the session again.**

10. **Click Open and PuTTY opens a connection to the server and attempts to log in using the username and key you provided.**

Type session name   Click Save

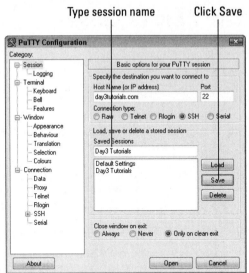

Figure 16-4:
Saving a new connection in PuTTY.

Browse to location of file and select it

Figure 16-5:
Connecting a PPK key to a connection in PuTTY.

Every time you want to log in, you simply have to open PuTTY, select your saved session, and click Load. Click Open and PuTTY logs you back in.

Connecting with Mac or Linux

1. **Open the Terminal program.**

2. **Type** ssh *username@Server IP Address*.

   Make sure to use your actual username and the IP address of your server.

3. **Terminal attempts to connect to the server and, if it is successful, prompts you for the password for the account.**

You can also connect using the command ***username:password@Server IP Address*** (replace *username*, *password*, and *Server IP Address* with your actual details) and Terminal sends both pieces of data to the server automatically. Either way should be secure because the secure session is created before any login details are sent. I prefer not to do it this way, but that's probably just paranoia on my part.

Make sure you type your password correctly because too many incorrect attempts cause your server to lock you out!

Using the Command Line

You may be familiar with the old Windows/DOS command line (which is still available although underused these days). Using the UNIX/Linux command line is similar. There are some basic commands that allow you to navigate around the files on the server, view lists of files in folders, create new files and folders, and edit or delete files.

This is where the danger comes in: It is difficult if not impossible to recover files once they have been deleted, so you must always take a lot of care when entering commands not to delete files you really need to keep.

Each command also has modifiers, or switches, allowing you to dramatically expand what the command does and what information it returns. I do not have space here to go into every command and every possible switch for those commands. There are resources available online that give you this information, or you could buy the excellent *Linux For Dummies* by Richard Blum (John Wiley & Sons, Inc.).

Here is a list of some of the basic commands you may need to use:

- ✔ `ls`: Lists files in a folder
- ✔ `mkdir`: Creates a new folder/directory
- ✔ `cd`: Enables you to change your current directory
- ✔ `vi`: Enables you to view the contents of a file and then quickly and easily edit it

Inputting Some Basic Commands

This section shows you how to use some commands and just a few of the switches that you need to modify them. These commands can do far more than this basic information I am explaining here, and there are many more commands that you can use.

Commands and their switches are case sensitive, as are filenames and folder names. The command `ls` is not valid if typed in capitals (`LS`), and with some commands the capitalized version actually means something different entirely.

Changing directory with cd

As I mention earlier in the book, I use the words *directory* and *folder* fairly interchangeably. The word *folder* was not really widely used until Microsoft introduced Windows, which had a folder icon that showed when something was a directory. The terminology of *folders* then became normal because it matched the visual image, which was also used in the Mac operating system. There are many applications and operating systems that hark back to the good old days when everything was on the command line and the term *directory* was used instead of *folder*. Do not be confused. A folder and a directory are the same thing.

Linux was written in the 1980s, way before the term *folder* was commonplace. The different folders were called directories at the time, so logically, if you want to change the directory that you're looking at on the server, you use the change directory command, which is written as `cd`.

Directories are created in a tree format. Any number of directories can be created within the main directory and are classed as *subdirectories* of the directory. Picture the organization as branches of a weeping willow tree with directories coming off the trunk and subdirectories being the small branches hanging from those directories. You can go up and up and up through the different levels of the branches until you reach the trunk (the main directory), which is known as the `root` and is referenced with a slash (`/`). See Figure 16-6 for a graphical illustration of the directory tree.

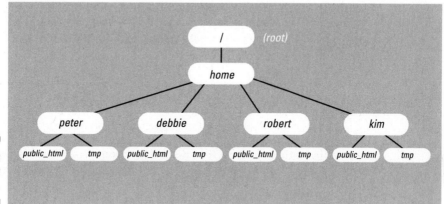

Figure 16-6:
A directory
tree.

When you have connected via SSH, on the command line you see a command prompt (normally ending in # or @). This shows you two important pieces of information:

✔ The username you are logged in as and the system you are on (*username@ system name*)

✔ The directory you are currently in (see Figure 16-7).

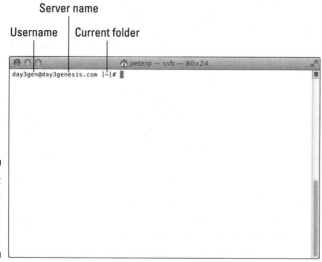

Figure 16-7:
Information
shown in a
command
prompt.

You can go up one directory by typing **cd ..** (cd then a space then two periods).

To make that a little easier to understand, the directory you are currently in is thought of by the computer as the dot directory, so two dots refers to the next directory up the tree (the directory containing this directory).

You can also navigate to any point in the directory tree by typing the full path to the directory you want to view.

The root (the beginning of the drive/the top level) is always called slash (/). So you can always get straight back to the root by typing **cd /**.

The full path of a directory starts with a slash to show that you are starting with the root of the drive; it then has all of the names of the subdirectories you have to go through to get to the one you want. These names are separated by slashes, but those slashes are just punctuation and do not refer to the root.

For instance, on a standard Linux installation there is a directory that comes off of the root of the drive called var. In the var directory is a subdirectory called log, where you will find many server log files. You can navigate directly to that directory from anywhere on the drive by typing **cd /var/log**. This command is saying, "Change to the directory that starts at the root of the drive (/) and then goes into the var directory (var/) and is called log (log)."

If the path you type is incorrect, it comes back with an error message saying, "No such file or directory" (see Figure 16-8). There is no limit to how long a folder path can be, and likewise there is no limit to how deep in a folder path you can jump using the cd command.

On my server, for instance, there is a folder at /usr/lib/ruby/gems/1.8/ doc/rubygems-1.3.7/rdoc/files/lib/rubygems/commands, and I can go directly to that folder from anywhere simply by using the cd command (if I can remember the whole path off the top of my head). See Figure 16-9.

The interface shows the error that occured.

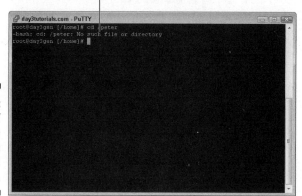

Figure 16-8:
PuTTY
showing an
error in
the cd
command.

Change directory using cd
and the full directory path.

Figure 16-9:
Long folder
tree in
Linux.

Full path to current folder shows
between square brackets.

Viewing a list of files with ls

It's all fine and dandy being able to navigate to whichever folder you want to go to, but how do you find out which files and subdirectories are in that directory?

The answer is to ask the server to give you a *list* of files, which is shortened to the command ls.

Simply type **ls** and press Enter for a list of all the files in that folder. If there are a large number, it keeps scrolling until it has shown you all the files. There are times when this can be useful just to get an overview of the folder or if you are looking for a particular file and you want to see if it's there. Most of the time, though, it is better to use **ls** with a modifier, like this:

```
ls | less
```

This command does what's called *piping,* which means rerouting the output to another program. The other program is called less and enables you to scroll forward and backward through whatever was piped to it.

The basic controls you need to know for less are the following:

- ✔ space: Go forward a page
- ✔ b: Go back a page
- ✔ up arrow: Go up a line
- ✔ down arrow: Go down a line
- ✔ q: Gets you out of the less program back to the command line

You can also use switches to modify what information is shown by the ls command. By default, ls simply lists all the files with spaces between their names. Sometimes you want more information than that, so you might use, for example, the -l switch, which also lists file permissions, owner, file size, and last modified date, as shown in Figure 16-10.

There are more than 20 different switches you can use for the ls command, and people tend to develop their own preferred set of switches. You can use multiple switches at the same time; for example, you can use the -l, -a, and -x switches like this:

```
ls -lax
```

Owner   Date last modified

Group   Filename

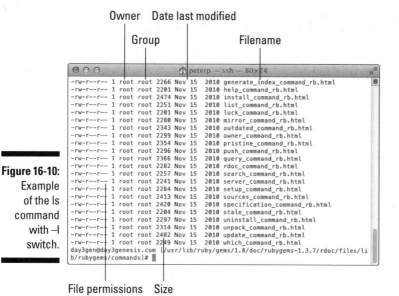

Figure 16-10:
Example
of the ls
command
with –l
switch.

File permissions   Size

This shows all the files, including the hidden ones, in a single column format with all the extra details included.

You can also list files in another folder than the one you're in by simply adding the full path to the file at the end of the command — for example, `ls -l /var/log/`.

Making new directories with mkdir

When you want to create a new directory or folder using a graphical interface such as Windows, you probably right-click in the directory you want and choose New Folder from the contextual menu. When using a command line, you don't have a right-click option; instead you have to type the command manually.

If you want to create a new folder, you have to use the make folder command, or, more precisely the make directory command, which is written as `mkdir`.

To use the command correctly, simply type **mkdir *directory*** (replace the word *directory* with the name you want to create). For example, typing **mkdir tmp** creates a folder named `tmp` within the current folder.

You may, however, want to create a subdirectory of a subdirectory, and you can do so without navigating there first.

For example, in Figure 16-11, I have created a subdirectory called `peter`, and I know that within it I need another directory called `tmp`. To do this from within the current directory, I would type **mkdir peter/tmp**.

mkdir peter creates a subdirectory called peter.

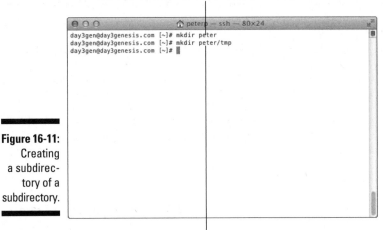

mkdir peter/tmp creates a subdirectory within peter.

You can create a directory anywhere on the drive by giving it the correct folder path.

You cannot create a subdirectory of a directory that doesn't currently exist. The computer will not create the entire directory tree in one step; you have to create it one directory at a time.

Editing Files Using vi

Linux has a couple of very useful built-in file editors. vi is my favorite.

vi originated as a mode of a file editor called ex, which was a line editor that grew over the years with the changes in technology until it had a visual mode that users activated with the command `vi`. vi then became an editor itself, and you can call it directly from the command line.

vi works in two distinct modes:

✔ Normal mode is where you navigate around the file you are editing using typed commands.

✔ Insert mode is where anything you type becomes a part of the file.

For example, in Normal mode, a typed letter **i** is regarded as a command that puts vi into Insert mode. After vi is in Insert mode, though, a typed letter **i** (or any letter, for that matter) is not seen as a command; it is a request to make *i* the next letter in the file.

You have to press the Esc key to switch from Insert mode to Normal mode.

There are dozens of different commands you can use in Normal mode, so the following is a quick example of how to edit a file. In this example, I have a file called index.php that I've noticed is displaying my name as Peter Pollack when it should really be Peter Pollock (*ock*, not *ack*). I'm going to edit the file, move to the offending text, go into Insert mode, delete the bad text, type the correct letters, and then save and quit the file.

Here are the steps:

1. **Select the file for editing by typing** vi index.php **at the command line. (See Figure 16-12.)**

Type command and press Enter.

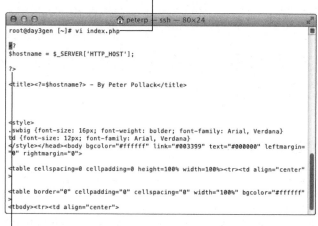

Figure 16-12:
Opening a file for editing with vi.

vi opens the file.

2. **Use the arrow keys to move the cursor to the part of the file you want to change.**

3. **Use the i command to enter Insert mode, which is shown in Figure 16-13.**

Gray block is cursor — move it with the arrow keys.

Figure 16-13:
vi in Insert
mode.

After pressing ; , --INSERT-- appears to
show you are in Insert mode.

4. **Use the Delete key and the letters on the keyboard to make the correction.**

Figure 16-14 shows the file after I've made the change.

Edits made show live on screen.

Figure 16-14:
Corrections
made in vi.

5. Press the Esc key to get back to Normal mode.

6. Type a colon (:) to move the cursor to the bottom of the screen, where final commands can be made (see Figure 16-15).

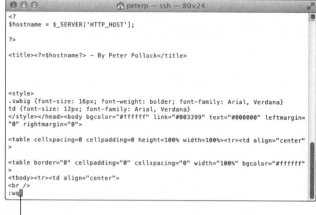

Figure 16-15:
Using a colon to enter commands in vi.

Press : and cursor
moves to command area.

7. Type wq.

wq is two individual commands: w for Write (or Save) and q for Quit. This command combination returns you to the command line.

Part VI
The Part of Tens

the part of tens

See my Top Ten Tips for Getting More from Your Hosting Plan at www.dummies. com/extras/webhosting.

In this part . . .

- ✔ Find programs and apps to help you master your hosting.
- ✔ Learn what your host *won't* help with.
- ✔ Discover online resources to teach you more about your hosting.
- ✔ Get help with beautifying your website.

Chapter 17

Ten Invaluable Free Apps

In This Chapter

▶ Finding free FTP apps

▶ Downloading the editors the professionals use

▶ Shrinking your images to make your site faster

*N*obody wants to pay for something if he doesn't have to, and there are hundreds of useful, free applications out there that are designed to make your life easier.

Don't just do a Google search for free FTP apps and install what comes up without knowing anything about an app's reputation. There are a number of FTP apps out there which are wolves in sheep's clothing and will steal your data and credentials.

Here are ten apps that I use regularly when I'm dealing with web hosting stuff:

MySQL Workbench

MySQL Workbench is an app that I cannot live without. In some ways, it is slightly trickier to use than phpMyAdmin. However, it's located on your PC, and it gives you the power to do backups and repairs on your databases and enables you to make changes in a slightly different environment from phpMyAdmin through your browser. Try it; it's a tool I prefer to use.

You can download MySQL Workbench for Windows, Linux, or Mac OS X at `http://dev.mysql.com/downloads/workbench/`.

FileZilla

FileZilla is one of the best — if not the best — free File Transfer Protocol (FTP) clients available. There are other free ones and there are many that you can pay for, but FileZilla is my go-to FTP client. It's fast; it's efficient; it can do Secure File Transfer Protocol (SFTP, which you really should be using) or basic FTP; and it lays everything out in a simple, easy-to-use window.

One warning with FileZilla is that it stores your passwords in a non-protected file, which means virus and malware writers, if they write stuff which gets onto your computer, could theoretically read that file and get your FTP login details, including your password. Of course, that means the attack must specifically look for your password file — and it has to make it past the virus checker, which I'm sure you have installed on your PC — but it is a consideration to note, and you should remember to not store your passwords within FileZilla.

You can download it for Windows, Linux, or Mac OS X at `http:// filezilla-project.org`.

Notepad++

Notepad++ is a wonderful editor for editing any kind of files: text files, PHP files, HTML files, CSS files. You name it, Notepad++ can read it. One of things I like most about it is that, with PHP files, it includes color coding to delineate different types of elements and helps you see where you are in the file and identify where the code elements you are working on close.

Notepad++ is free. I've seen no other free applications that come even close to the facilities Notepad++ offers. (Some people use paid applications that they say are better.) The speed, the ease of use, and the integration with FileZilla are all excellent. You can edit a file on your server by simply logging on using FileZilla, right-clicking on the file you want to edit, and clicking View/Edit. The file downloads and opens in Notepad++ so you can make the changes you need. When you save it again, FileZilla automatically prompts you that the file has changed and asks if you want to re-upload it. You simply click Yes or No.

Notepad++ is available for Windows only. You can download it at `http:// notepad-plus-plus.org`.

CoffeeCup FTP

CoffeeCup makes a range of utilities, some of which are free, some of which aren't. CoffeeCup FTP is free and is a very good alternative to FileZilla. It all comes down to personal preference, and I prefer FileZilla. That said, CoffeeCup FTP is well worth checking out.

CoffeeCup has a premium version called Direct FTP that has some cool additional features. If you're looking for CoffeeCup FTP, don't accidentally download Direct FTP and have to pay for it by mistake. Oh, and you can expect CoffeeCup to periodically try to tempt you into buying the premium version. That's one of the things that put me off.

CoffeeCup FTP is available for Windows only. You can download it at `http://coffeecup.com/free-ftp/`.

PuTTY

PuTTY is a powerful tool that enables you to connect to devices online, using a system called telnet, providing you have the correct login details. It is very useful to website owners, especially those with a Virtual Private Server (VPS) or dedicated server, because it enables you to open a command-line prompt on your server by logging in via Secure SHell (SSH), so that you can run commands as needed.

PuTTY comes with dire warnings that you must not use it anywhere where it's illegal to use. The research I've done suggests that it is legal to use it within the U.S., providing you're using it for connection to a device that you own or have the right to connect to.

You do not need to install PuTTY if you don't intend to connect by SSH and do not need to use the command line on your server. You should only open up your server to allow SSH connections if you know there is a good reason for using them. Otherwise, keep SSH closed to help prevent intruders from gaining access.

PuTTY is available for Windows only. You can download it at `http://www.chiark.greenend.org.uk/~sgtatham/putty/download.html`.

Transmit

Hailed (by its own company) as the number-one FTP client for Mac OS X, Transmit is a popular free FTP client for the Mac.

Transmit has a host of features and boasts super speeds especially for smaller files. I haven't used it extensively, but it does appear to be faster than FileZilla, although I still prefer the layout of the FileZilla screen to that on Transmit.

Transmit is available for Mac OS X at `http://panic.com/transmit`.

Cyberduck

Another FTP client? I know, I know . . . . Here's the deal: FileZilla and CoffeeCup are the best options for Windows PCs. Transmit and Cyberduck are the best options for Mac OS X, even though there is now some crossover apps that are available for each OS.

Cyberduck has to get a mention, if nothing else, for its name. I just LOVE the name Cyberduck. It's also an incredibly full-featured piece of software that I am more than happy to recommend.

The great thing about all the free FTP client software is that you can download it, install it, test it out, and, if you don't like it, you haven't lost anything except perhaps a little time! Personal taste plays into which piece of software you prefer to use, so why not download them all and try them out?

Cyberduck is available for Mac OS X or Windows. You can download it at `http://cyberduck.ch`.

Komodo Edit

ActiveState produces two code editors in the Komodo range: Komodo Edit, which is free, and Komodo IDE, which is a premium version but adds lots of valuable features for more advanced designers.

What I like about Komodo Edit is that there is a Linux version available, so if you have eschewed Windows and Mac for the joy of Linux, you can get a full-featured code editor that is designed to run on your system.

Komodo Edit is available for Mac, Windows, or Linux. You can download it from `www.activestate.com/komodo-edit`.

Terminal

Terminal is built into all versions of Mac OS X and is a native telnet command-line interface that is similar to PuTTY for the PC.

You can use Terminal to connect to your server, providing you enable SSH connections and have the valid login details.

I've never heard anyone suggest you need to look any further than Terminal for telnet connections from a Mac; it simply does its job efficiently and easily.

Caesium

One of the easiest ways to make your website faster is to compress your images — and Caesium makes that easy to do.

Data compression is hard to understand, and even harder to explain, but Caesium basically uses some technical magic to make the file size of your pictures smaller without losing any visual quality (for viewing on a screen, at least).

You don't need to know how the magic works; all you need to know is that this application can make your images up to 90% smaller and thus 90% faster to load, so opening your website isn't like watching paint dry.

Caesium is available for Windows from `http://caesium.source forge.net/`.

Chapter 18

Ten Things Your Host Won't Help with (for Free)

··

In This Chapter

▶ Learning the limits of your host's responsibility

▶ Discovering if what your host won't help you with is "normal" or just poor service

··

As awesome as your host is, there are limitations to what it will do to help you as you design, build, and run your website. It all comes down to money.

Your host will be more than happy to help with some things as long as you're happy to pay, but don't expect the world for your $50-a-year hosting fee! The ten things in this chapter are all requests I have been asked to help with in my time as a web host. Some of them I was able to help with, and some . . .

Each host is different. Some hosts will help with some of these ten things, whereas others will not. If you find one who will, stick with it! Your tenacity will probably be worth it in the long run.

Website Design

As I mention in Chapter 1, your host is like your landlord. It is not your landlord's responsibility to decide what color you want to paint the bathroom or to help you do it. Likewise, your host will generally not give you free advice on how to design your site, what your site should look like, or how to implement your ideas. Many hosts will, however, be more than willing to do this for a fee.

Writer's Block

Of course, because I do my own hosting, for years I have been out of luck when asking my host to help with writer's block. You'll probably find the same thing with your host, too. Your host's job is to keep the servers running, not to help you with writer's block. If you can't think what to write in your blog, then I'm sorry, but your host isn't going to provide much help.

Some things that I find to help with writer's block include Swiss chocolates, strong coffee, classical music, and having kids. Go into a room with some screaming kids for a while and you will be eager to get out of there and hunker down to the business of coming up with lots of words that flow onto the paper. What's more, the words probably won't stop flowing as long as you don't go back in that noisy room again!

Spam

Spam is pretty much your problem, I'm afraid.

Spam is awesome when it is a processed meat product (especially if it's deep-fried in batter . . . *yum!*). It's not so awesome, though, when it refers to unwanted e-mails begging you to buy everything from nutritional supplements to get-rich-quick schemes.

Your host will probably have some kind of spam filtering on the server, but probably not anything too strong because it doesn't want to accidentally reject an e-mail you need. It's your job to switch a spam filter on and set it to a level that works for you.

Malware

Malware and viruses are the bane of the Internet, and I doubt we'll ever rid ourselves of them.

If your site gets infected, your host might be kind enough to help you out by suspending or deleting your account, but it isn't going to do too much more than that.

Think of your hosting like a rented building: If you leave the door unlocked one night, it's hardly the landlord's fault if you get robbed of everything you own, and your landlord is not going to pay for the replacements or spend any time helping you to fix up the place.

Increasing Traffic

People pay professionals hundreds of dollars to help them get their sites to the top of the search rankings through search engine optimization (SEO).

Essentially, SEO is marketing — and it isn't your host's job to do your marketing for you.

Moving to a New Host

"Hi. I don't want to pay you for your services anymore, so I'm going to move my site somewhere else. I'm not sure how to do that, though, so could you help me?"

Yes, someone asked me that in real life. I know, right?

A host will probably happily help you move *to* its server, but if you're trying to leave, don't expect your current host to drop everything and help you out the door.

Web Application Problems

This is a big one, and a tricky one.

Depending on how busy it is, your host *might* be willing to help you when your WordPress installation doesn't seem to be working, or you can't get Joomla running on the server, or something along those lines. Such things are not your host's job, though. It's like asking an electrician to change all the light bulbs in your house, "While you're here, would you . . . ." It can be done, but it's time-consuming and not part of your contract, so don't be surprised if your host says you have to pay for its assistance.

Uploading Files

This *is* a service I offered in my hosting business. If my clients didn't know how to use FTP, I'd do it for them, if they asked.

That isn't how most hosts work, though. They provide you with the facilities to upload files and might even be willing to give you a little training, but uploading and downloading are totally your responsibility.

Installing Some Software

Software installations on servers can cause problems . . . to the *entire* server.

Sometimes you hear about some facility or another online and you want to include it in your site, but some essential software is missing from the server.

Contact your host. It sometimes may be willing to add the software for you, but if it's buggy or could potentially disrupt other sites on the server, then you're probably out of luck.

Remember, unless you are on a dedicated server, you aren't alone on the server, and so you have to share nicely and responsibly.

Problems with Your Computer

I ended up buying a Mac computer once just so I could see the problem the client was having and try to fix it.

It was a crazy thing to do, really. Spending hundreds of dollars to try to fix a problem with a machine she wasn't even paying me to maintain just didn't make any kind of good business sense.

Most web hosts have better sense than I do, so it's probably not even worth asking. If the fault is with something that belongs to you, it isn't your host's responsibility, and your host likely doesn't have the time or resources to make it so.

Chapter 19

Ten Essential Online Resources

Books are great, and I would love it if this book becomes dog-eared from all the times you use it for reference. There are also some (nearly as good) resources available online to give you extra information. These are just some of the ones that I love to use.

TentBlogger.com

TentBlogger.com is owned and written by John Saddington (who just happens to be the technical editor of this book). It is probably the best online resource for virtually everything with regard to blogging. There are articles explaining how to use different parts of your web hosting service, how to succeed as a blogger, how to use programs such as WordPress, and how to do a whole bunch of stuff you haven't even thought of yet.

I personally reference TentBlogger.com regularly for some of the step-by-step guides for things that I can't remember. I simply search TentBlogger.com for the information I need and there's always an easy, well-written guide for it. (See Figure 19-1.)

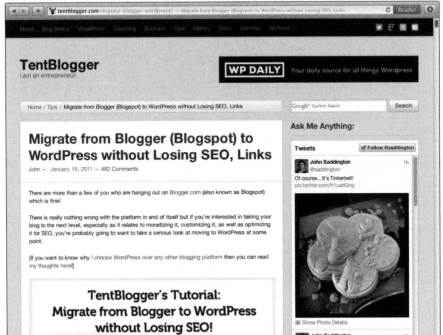

Figure 19-1:
Sample
tutorial on
Tent
Blogger.
com.

cPanel.net

cPanel has a fairly extensive guide to using cPanel and Web Host Manager (WHM), which covers different versions of the software so that, even if you aren't using the very latest version of the software, you can often find information on how to use the version you have.

There are also FAQs (frequently asked questions) and forums on the cPanel website where you can find the answer to just about everything you could ever want to ask. Just go to `cpanel.net/help/` and start a search for what you want to know. (See Figure 19-2.)

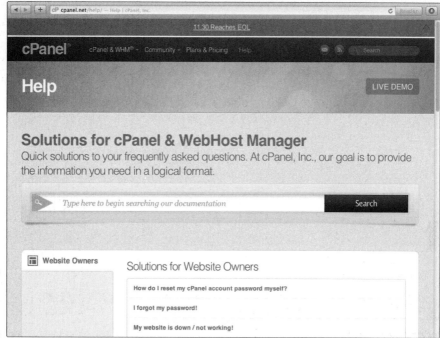

Figure 19-2:
cPanel's
Help page.

w3schools.com/hosting

As its name suggests, w3schools.com is an extensive website that is there to educate you on using the Internet and its related technologies. It has an entire section dedicated to hosting (w3schools.com/hosting), which has some useful tutorials and information. It may be worth you dropping by there just to familiarize yourself with what the site has for future reference. (See Figure 19-3.)

Figure 19-3:
The
w3schools.
com Hosting
section.

WebhostingTutorial.com

What can I say about this that isn't already in the name of the website (webhostingtutorial.com)? To state the obvious, this website is dedicated to teaching all about web hosting. The number of articles it has at the moment is fairly limited, but the ones that are there offer great advice and information, and there is a forum where you can get answers to your questions, if you have any. (See Figure 19-4.)

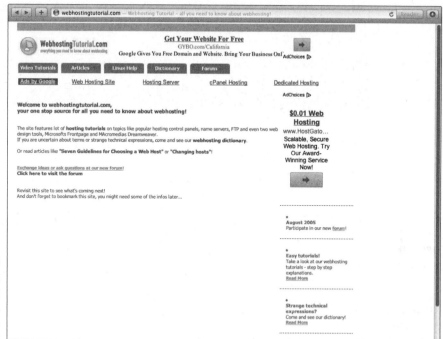

Figure 19-4:
Webhosting
Tutorial.
com.

kb.parallels.com

KB is an Internet term for *knowledge base,* so this is the knowledge base at `parallels.com`. Parallels is the manufacturer of the Plesk hosting software.

The knowledge base at `kb.parallels.com` is fairly extensive, just like cPanel's, and covers all of the products from Parallels so it should be your first port of call if you have questions on how to use facilities in Plesk or any other Parallels software. (See Figure 19-5.)

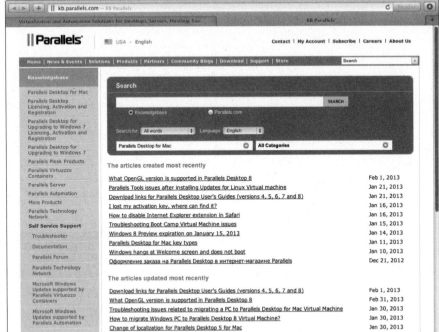

Figure 19-5:
Parallels.
com
searchable
knowledge
base.

w3schools.com/CSS

I mention the hosting section of the `w3schools.com` website earlier in this chapter. CSS isn't directly related to hosting, but if you have website hosting, you probably have a website, and if you have a website, you probably are (or at least, should be) using CSS on that site. The W3 schools information on how to use CSS (`w3schools.com/CSS`) is some of the best I've ever found and is invaluable in guiding you on how to make your site pretty. (See Figure 19-6.)

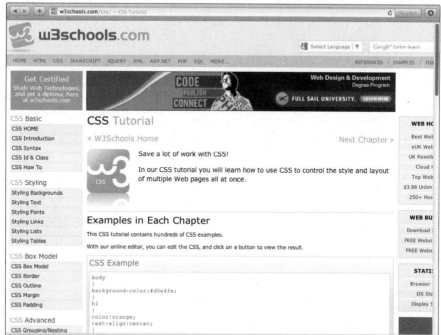

Figure 19-6:
The
w3schools.
com CSS
section.

Your Host's FAQ Page

With a little bit of luck, your host has an FAQ page, knowledge base, or some forum of its own. These resources can be extremely useful if you come across problems, particularly when using a host like GoDaddy, which wrote its own control panel. Even with other hosts, common control panels can be configured differently, and you'll often find that they provide information within forums, a knowledge base, or a Wiki/FAQ page on how to use specific areas within the control panel. (See Figure 19-7.)

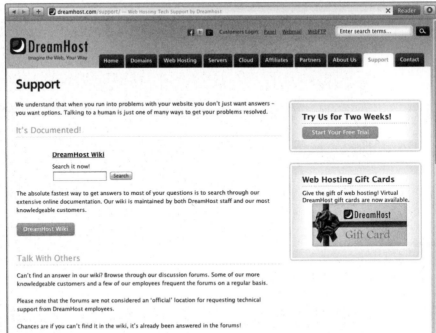

Figure 19-7:
DreamHost's
Wiki search
page.

PeterPollock.com/webhosting

At my site, `peterpollock.com/webhosting`, I will be putting up a number of tutorials, including video tutorials, in addition to the ones available at the `www.dummies.com/extras/webhosting` site to show you how to use some of the functions of your hosting and to walk you through it visually. I also have a contact form on my site in case you need to ask me any questions about how different functions work. Feel free to use the contact form at any time. I'll get back to you as soon as possible. (See Figure 19-8.)

Figure 19-8:
The Peter
Pollock.com
hosting tuto-
rials page.

Dummies.com/extras/webhosting

You can check out www.dummies.com/extras/webhosting for bonus
content available for free when you buy this book. You can find videos,
screen casts, and downloadable check lists, plus all kinds of other good stuff.
Feel free to visit www.dummies.com/extras/webhosting as often as you
need to access the bonus content.

WebHostMagazine

WebHostMagazine has been around in one form or another since the 1990s and is an excellent and trustworthy resource to find information, tutorials, and web host reviews. When considering a new host, it's always worth stopping by the WebHostMagazine site at www.webhostmagazine.com to see what it says. Their reviews always seem objective and fair.

Part VII
Appendixes

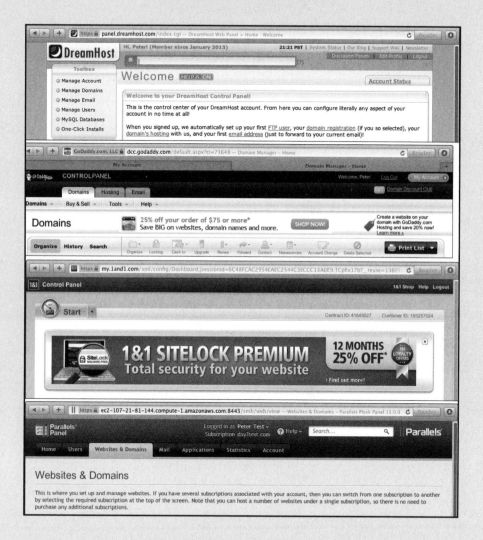

Watch a video comparing some of the major control panels at www.dummies.com/extras/webhosting.

In this part . . .

- ✔ Find your way around your dashboard.
- ✔ See the dashboards before you choose which host to use.
- ✔ Learn to speak like a techie.
- ✔ Discover what all this Internet jargon really means.

Appendix A

Navigating Your Control Panel

In This Appendix

▶ Finding functions in your control panel

▶ Comparing your control panel to the cPanel screens described in the book

*N*ot all control panels are the same. In fact, no two control panels seem to be the slightest bit the same. Each company thinks it has the perfect solution to making its control panel simple and easy to navigate. Each program has a different layout, menu order, command groupings, and even titles.

It would be impossible to write a book that included details on how to do things in every different control panel, so for this book I use cPanel for the examples because it is the most popular control panel.

In this appendix, I have taken some screenshots from some of the other major control panels to show you where to find the different functions and facilities in your control panel.

DreamHost

DreamHost's control panel is almost entirely text-based with little in the way of icons or graphics to beautify it — but then, why do you need graphics when text will do?

The DreamHost control panel is also one of the most powerful and versatile, as Figures A-1 through A-11 show you.

There are three main sections to the DreamHost control panel front page: the toolbox in the top left, the main menu at the bottom left, and the Let's Get Started area in the middle of the screen.

You will probably find you mostly use the two menus on the left. A little secret that not too many people know is that you can drag your most commonly used menu items into the Toolbox for easy access. See Figure A-1.

Clicking Manage Account takes you to the account overview page where you can see and manage almost everything in your account. This page is so long and comprehensive that I had to split it into Figures A-2 and A-3.

Items you can use regularly from the menu can be dragged into the toolbox.

...Or the buttons.

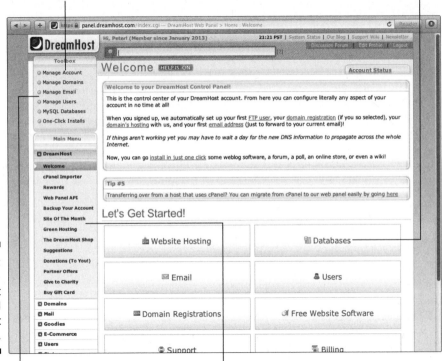

Figure A-1:
The
DreamHost
control
panel front
page.

Navigate using the toolbox...   ...Or the menus...

Anything underlined or small in blue can be clicked on.

Figure A-2:
The DreamHost Manage Account page gives an overview of everything in your account. This is part 1.

You can add mailboxes and other things right from this page.

Figure A-3:
Part 2 of the DreamHost Manage Account page.

The Manage Domains page is where you can see all of the domains you have hosted in the account and access their DNS settings, FTP settings, and online file manager (called WebFTP). (See Figure A-4.)

Your domains appear in a list.

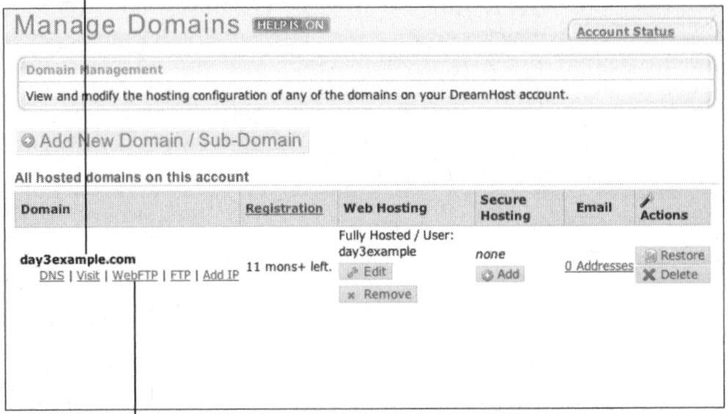

Figure A-4:
The
DreamHost
Manage
Domains
page.

Use the links below each domain to edit / manage / use it.

Click the Manage Email tab in the Toolbox at the top of the left column to go to the Email Accounts page. Click Create or click the name of an already-created e-mail account to edit one. (See Figures A-5 and A-6.)

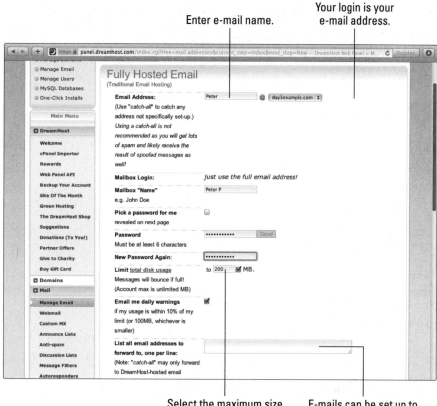

Enter e-mail name.

Your login is your e-mail address.

Figure A-5:
Part 1 of the DreamHost e-mail setup/edit page.

Select the maximum size for the mailbox.

E-mails can be set up to forward to one or more addresses.

DreamHost enables you to set up additional users for your account. Each user is given a folder within your site and cannot see any other users' files. (See Figure A-7.)

There is no way to set up a second master-user who can see all the files under the account.

If you want to set up an address to only
forward mail, not store it, put the name here.

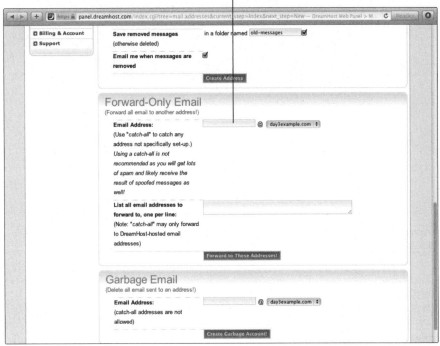

Figure A-6:
Part 2 of the
DreamHost
e-mail
setup/edit
page.

Click to add a new user.

Figure A-7:
The
DreamHost
Manage
Users page.

Users can connect via
FTP, but can only see
their own files.

To manage your databases, click MySQL Database in the Toolbox. This gives
you access to phpMyAdmin for all the databases on the account and to quick
links for each database to perform common actions. (See Figure A-8.)

Manage all databases by
clicking here.

All databases are
listed here.

Make changes to an
individual database.

Clicking Mail in the Main Menu takes you to the e-mail management page and
opens up the full mail menu where you can modify MX records, configure
antispam protection, and create lists and auto-responders. See Figure A-9.

The Goodies menu, situated half way down the Main Menu on the left of the
screen, is where you find advanced functions for defining cron jobs, along
with a range of other useful tools such as Chartbeat Analytics, which gives
real-time reporting on who is using your website. (See Figure A-10.)

The Status menu in the Main Menu shows you site statistics and usage figures for bandwidth, disk space, and MySQL database sizes. (See Figure A-11.)

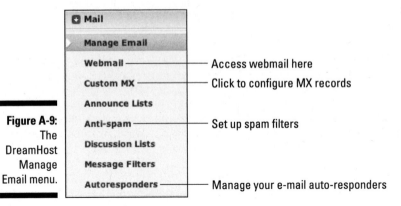

Figure A-9:
The
DreamHost
Manage
Email menu.

Access webmail here

Click to configure MX records

Set up spam filters

Manage your e-mail auto-responders

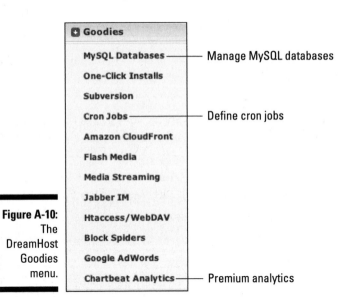

Figure A-10:
The
DreamHost
Goodies
menu.

Manage MySQL databases

Define cron jobs

Premium analytics

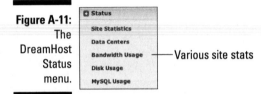

Figure A-11:
The
DreamHost
Status
menu.

Various site stats

GoDaddy

GoDaddy is reportedly the world's largest domain name registrar and web hosting provider, and it seems to be constantly changing, refining, and improving its control panel.

The GoDaddy control panel has two sections, the front of which lists the various product groups from which you may have purchased products. You can see the products on that page by clicking on a product group.

Clicking on a product launches the second section of the control panel, where you use tabs across the top to access the three main groups — Domains, Hosting, and Email.

Figure A-12 shows the front page of the control panel with the Domains section expanded.

GoDaddy runs auctions for popular domain names.

Click to hide your details from the Internet.

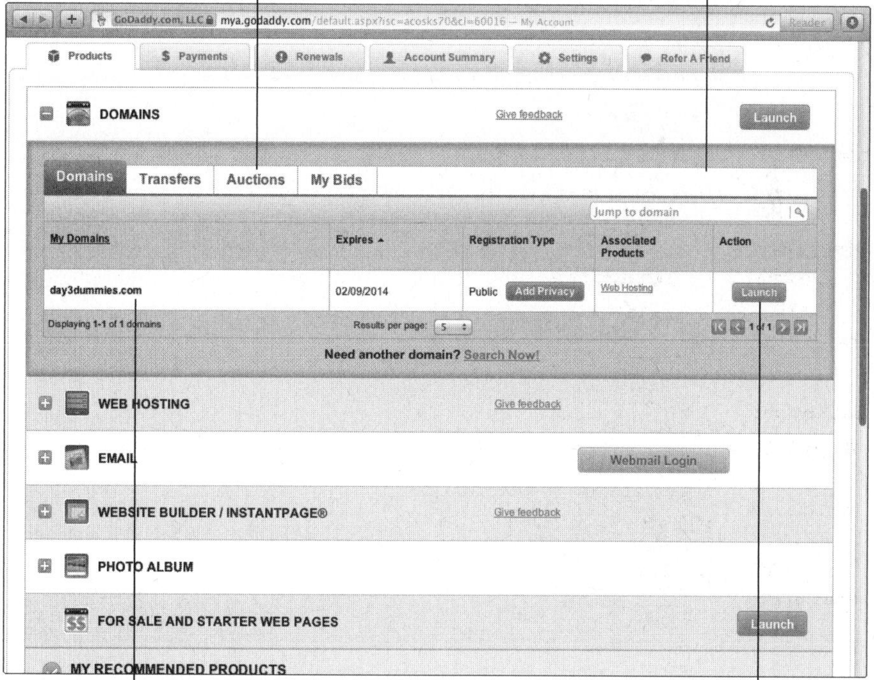

Figure A-12: The Domains section of the front page of the GoDaddy control panel.

Current domains are listed here.

Click to launch Domain Manager.

The second section of the control panel front page is the Web Hosting section, which lists all of your hosting plans. From here, you can launch the control panel for each individual plan. (See Figure A-13.)

The Email section (see Figure A-14) is the next section of the front page. E-mail is not always switched on for a domain by default, so sometimes you have to click the Set Up button to enable e-mail. Each domain has a separate e-mail control panel.

Clicking the Launch button for a domain's control panel (refer to Figure A-12) brings up a list of your domain names as shown in Figure A-15. If you check the box next to your domain name, the icons above it become live, enabling you to make changes to its properties, such as DNS, nameservers, contact details, and so on.

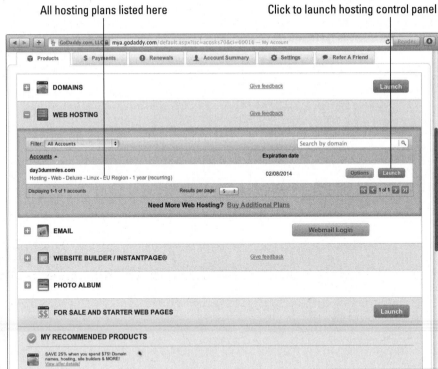

Figure A-13: The Web Hosting section of the front page of the GoDaddy control panel.

Click to set up e-mail for your domain

Click to log in to webmail

Click to manage e-mail addresses

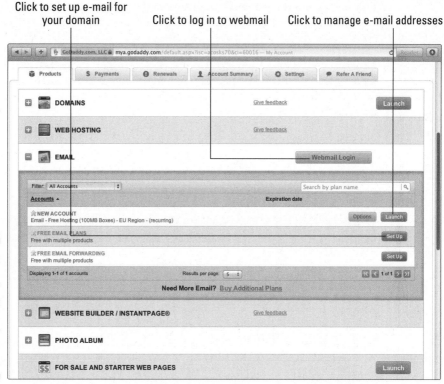

Figure A-14:
The Email section of the front page of the GoDaddy control panel.

Options to switch to hosting/e-mail control panels

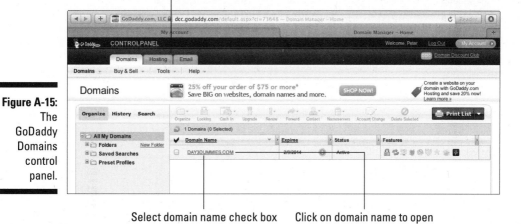

Figure A-15:
The GoDaddy Domains control panel.

Select domain name check box to make icons above live

Click on domain name to open admin panel

Clicking one of the domain names opens its page where you can see many of the details associated with the domain and can make changes as necessary. (See Figure A-16.)

You can go back to the front page or click on the Hosting tab at the top of the Domains or Email screens to access the hosting control panel. On the Hosting Details page (see Figure A-17) you find options relating specifically to the hosting of your website.

Lock/Unlock domain for transfer

Set EPP (transfer auth code) for transferring domain

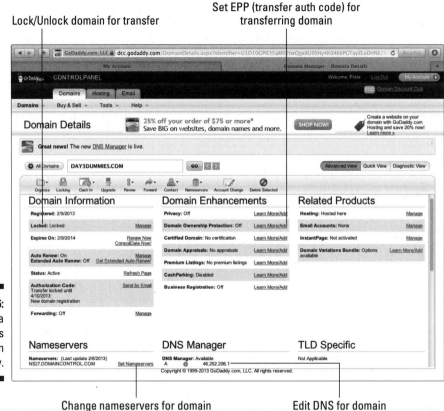

Figure A-16:
Editing a domain's details in GoDaddy.

Change nameservers for domain

Edit DNS for domain

Details of your hosting

Menu for editing files/databases   Snapshot of your home page

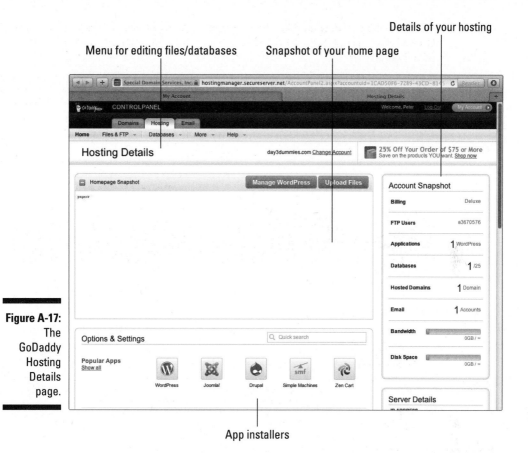

Figure A-17:
The
GoDaddy
Hosting
Details
page.

App installers

The drop-down menus on the hosting page enable you to access many different facilities. For example, the More menu (see Figure A-18) enables you to access some site stats, error logs, Secure SHell (SSH) setup, and much more.

Get usage stats and other advanced options

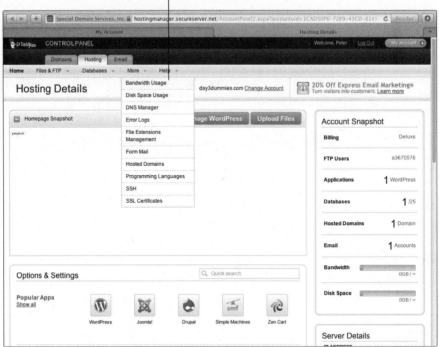

Figure A-18:
The More
drop-down
menu in the
GoDaddy
hosting con-
trol panel.

Click on the Email tab (or click Launch in the Email section of the front page) to see all of the e-mail accounts you have set up, edit them, and access web-mail for them. (See Figure A-19.)

Edit details for addresses   Log in to webmail

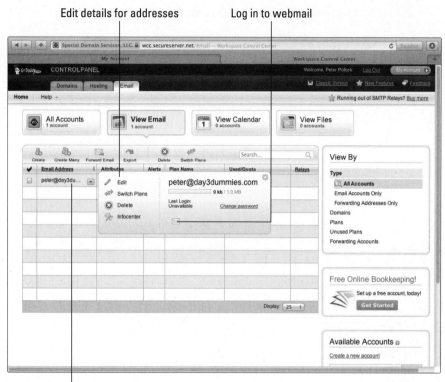

Figure A-19:
The Email
control
Panel for
GoDaddy.

E-mail addresses listed here

Creating new e-mail addresses is simple. Clicking the create icon brings up the Create Account page (see Figure A-20), where you can also opt to create calendars and file storage for the e-mail user.

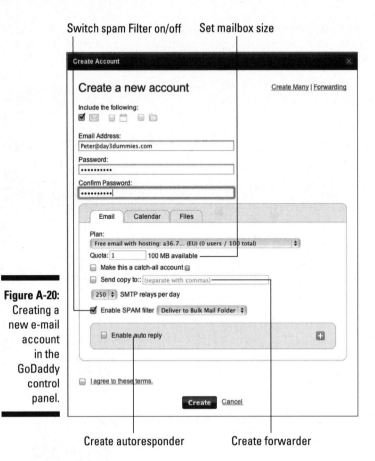

Switch spam Filter on/off   Set mailbox size

Create autoresponder   Create forwarder

Figure A-20: Creating a new e-mail account in the GoDaddy control panel.

1&1

The control panel designed by 1&1 is strangely complicated but yet is quite usable once you find your way around.

When you log in, you go to the Start page, which, if you have more than one site hosted with 1&1, lets you select your package from a drop-down menu and gives you a plethora of options of what to do with that package.

There are so many options, in fact, that I had to split them into two images, Figures A-21 and A-22.

Modify domain details   Click to select your package   Manage your 1&1 account

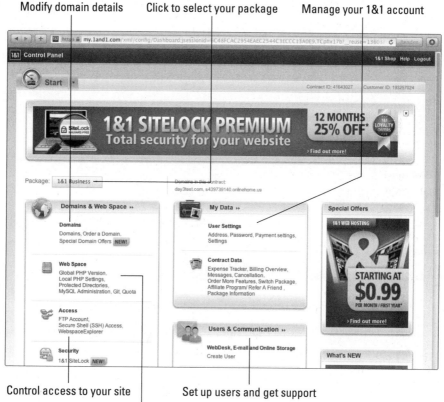

Figure A-21:
Part 1 of the
1&1 Start
page.

Control access to your site   Set up users and get support

Site-specific utilities

Site stats   Easy website builders   Create e-mail accounts and access them

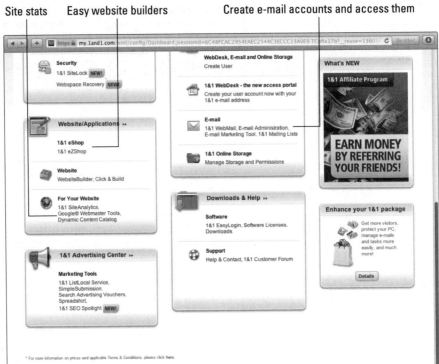

Figure A-22:
Part 2 of the
1&1 Start
page.

If you click the Domains option on the Start page, you can manage your
domain names (providing they are registered through 1&1).

Figure A-23 shows the Domain Overview page. Click the domain name you
want to manage and then use the drop-down menus to make alterations.

Use the drop-down menus to make
changes to your domain

Check the box for the
domain you wish to manage

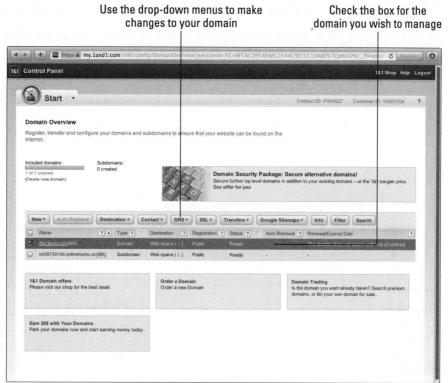

Figure A-23:
The 1&1
Domain
manage-
ment panel.

Clicking MySQL Administration on the start page (refer to the Web Space
area of Figure A-21) brings up the MySQL Database Set Up and Configuration
page shown in Figure A-24. Here you can see and administer all of your databases, including seeing how much web space they are taking up.

Create new database   Open phpMyAdmin

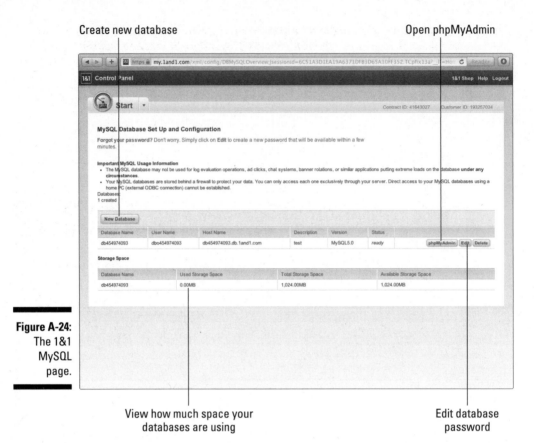

View how much space your   Edit database
databases are using   password

Plesk

Parallels, the makers of the Plesk Panel, claim that Plesk is "the most widely used hosting and control panel solution" worldwide. My experience, in the U.S. at least, is that you're more likely to have cPanel installed on your server than Plesk, but it's a big world out there and Parallels may well be right when the worldwide audience is considered.

There have been many different versions of the Plesk Panel (at the time of writing, the current version is Plesk 11), and what you see on your screen varies depending on what version your host is running and what facilities are available to you.

The front page should look a little like Figure A-25.

Use tabs for more options

An overview of your hosting plan usage

Install apps such as WordPress

Figure A-25:
The Plesk
front page.

Create and navigate
e-mail addresses

Manage domains and
their hosting

Online site builder

Plesk enables you to create additional users and give them roles that limit the facilities they can access. (See Figure A-26.) This is handy if you have other people helping to manage your website.

Modify user roles and
their capabilities

Add or remove
users

Set the appropriate role
for each user

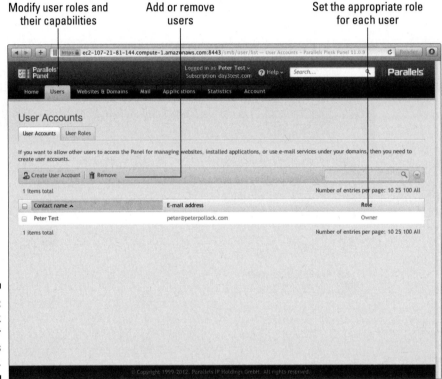

Figure A-26:
The Plesk
User
Accounts
page.

The Websites & Domains page gives a whole plethora of options, where you can do everything from using an online website builder to managing databases, creating FTP accounts, and even managing DNS settings (see Figure A-27).

Install apps, such as WordPress

Manage files online   Edit DNS settings   Web statistics   Use SSL certificates

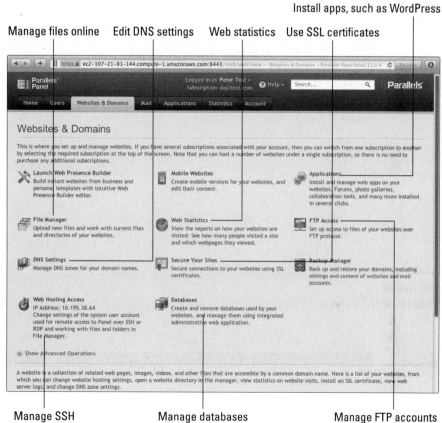

Figure A-27:
The Plesk
Websites
& Domains
page.

Manage SSH   Manage databases   Manage FTP accounts

Plesk handles databases in two phases. From the Websites & Domains page, you select the Databases option. The first database screen enables you to add and remove databases (see Figure A-28).

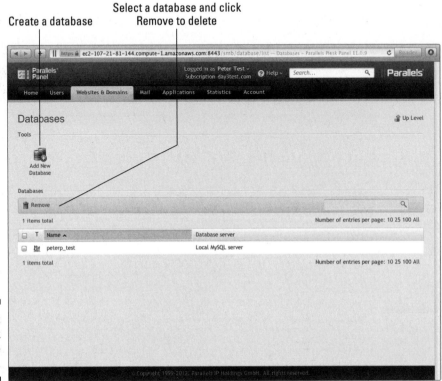

Create a database

Select a database and click
Remove to delete

Figure A-28:
The Plesk
Database
page.

You then click on the database name to go to the second screen, where you can access phpMyAdmin (called Webadmin in Plesk), add and remove users, and make copies of the database. (See Figure A-29.)

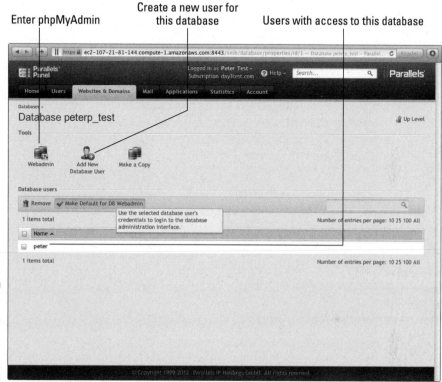

Figure A-29:
The Plesk Database users and admin page.

The Create E-mail Address page (see Figure A-30) enables you to create e-mail addresses, forwarders, aliases, and auto-responders. You have to create the address and then you can click the other tabs to dictate what the address is used for.

Set forwarding settings   Specify the size for the mailbox

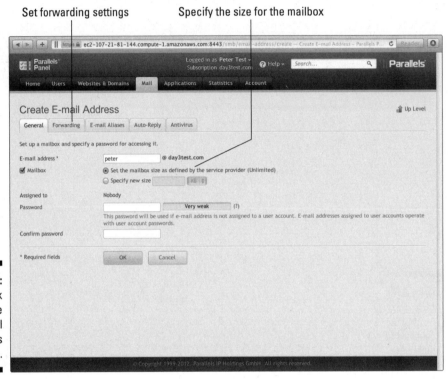

Figure A-30:
The Plesk
Create
E-mail
Address
page.

The Statistics page (see Figure A-31) gives you some basic information about how much space and bandwidth you are using but also has links to see more detailed information about where and how the data is being used.

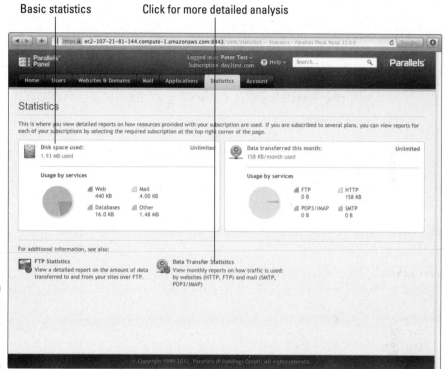

Basic statistics   Click for more detailed analysis

Figure A-31:
The Plesk
Statistics
page.

Appendix B

Glossary

AIX (Advanced Interactive eXecutive): A series of operating systems based on UNIX sold by IBM. See also *UNIX.*

Apache: Software that provided the necessary framework for Linux servers to deliver websites to the Internet. See also *NGINX* and *IIS*.

App: See *script*.

ASP.Net: A programming language used to create websites on servers running the Windows operating system.

bandwidth: The amount of data used by a hosting plan in a month. The term is also sometimes used to describe how much data can be sent at one time, but rarely in web hosting.

blog: A web-based journal or writing outlet. Short for web log.

botnet: A virus that infects multiple computers and enables its creator to use them as a network of virtual "robots" that the creator can give commands to. These networks are often used to launch massive attacks on websites or servers, known as DDOS attacks. A single botnet can control millions of computers at one time. See also *DDOS*.

BSD (Berkeley Software Distribution): A version of the UNIX operating system, also known as Berkeley Unix. See also *UNIX.*

ccTLD (Country-Code Top-Level Domains): The top-level domain is also known as the extension, for example .com or .org. A ccTLD is an extension that has an additional code for the country it is associated with. For example, .org.uk has .uk at the end to indicate it is a ccTLD for the United Kingdom.

CNAME (Canonical Name): A type of DNS Zone Record.

cPanel: A commonly used web hosting control panel. cPanel is both the brand name and the name of the front-end software, which is backed up by the administrator panel, WHM. See also *WHM.*

CSF (ConfigServer Security & Firewall): A security system for use with the cPanel control panel.

CSR (Certificate Signing Request): Part of the process of registering and installing an SSL certificate. See also *SSL*.

DDOS (Distributed Denial of Service): A DDOS is a type of attack on a server where a botnet launches a simultaneous attempt to overload an individual server from all of the members of the network. See also *botnet*.

dedicated server: A server that is entirely owned by one person or organization and is therefore dedicated to serving that individual or organization.

directory: See *folder.*

DNS (Domain Name System): The system that controls where the various parts and services of a website are physically located.

DNS Zone Record: A DNS record connected to a domain name that holds the details of where that part of the website can be found.

document root: Refers to the point in the file system that is designated as the top level of the website, or the root of the website. This is not physically the root of the drive, but rather is a folder defined as the root for a given website.

download: A request that a file or files be sent from another computer.

DSA (Digital Signature Algorithm): A DSA is an encryption/decryption format used to create secure login keys for computers. Keys are split into two components: a public key and a private key. Both the host and client computers must have opposite halves of the key for authentication to take place.

e-mail (electronic mail): E-mail is a popular system for sending communications online and can include text, pictures, and other files.

EV (Extended Validation): A system for verifying that the purchasers of SSL certificates are legitimate. See also *SSL.*

folder: A container for files and/or other folders on a server. Also known as a directory, folders are part of a tree. All folders are subfolders of the root. See also *document root.*

forwarding: Automatically directing something to another location. This can be either a web page forwarding the user to another page or an e-mail address automatically redirecting or copying e-mails to another address.

FQDN (Fully Qualified Domain Name): A Fully Qualified Domain Name is one made up of all three requisite parts: The TLD (for example, .com), the domain name (for example, dummies), and the host (for example, www) which together are formatted as www.dummies.com.

FTP (File Transfer Protocol): A protocol to enable computers to transfer entire files between each other. The computer initiating the request is described as uploading files when it sends them and downloading files when it receives them. FTP is inherently insecure as information is sent in plain text. See also *download* and *upload*.

GNU Project: A project to create an operating system and other programs that would be inherently and permanently free for anyone to use, modify, and distribute.

gTLD (Generic Top-Level Domains): The term Generic Top-Level Domain covers all domain extensions which do *not* include a country code — for example, .com or .org. See also *TLD* and *ccTLD*.

hosted e-mail: E-mail at your domain name that is delivered through a mail server running on your server. You literally "host" the mail server yourself. See also *hosting*.

hosting: Providing server space on which people can hold websites and e-mail.

HTTP (HyperText Transfer Protocol): The protocol understood by browsers and web servers to mean you are requesting to view how a file is designed to be seen, including executing all markup. See also *markup.*

IDN TLD (Internationalized Top-Level Domains): IDN TLDs are domain names that appear in the specific character set of the language they are used for. Examples are Arabic or Greek character sets.

IIS (Internet Information Services): IIS runs on Windows servers and provides the framework needed for those servers to serve websites to the Internet.

ISO (International Organization for Standardization): The ISO is the world's largest developer of voluntary international standards.

Linux: A free version of UNIX developed originally by the GNU Project and now available from a variety of developers. Each different version is known as a *flavor* of Linux. See also *GNU Project* and *UNIX.*

mail alias: Another e-mail name by which an e-mail address can be known. This can be useful when you want to make a special e-mail address such as info@*yourdomain*.com but don't want to have to visit another mailbox to check the mail. A mail alias tells the server to automatically route all mail to that address to your usual address. See also *forwarding.*

markup: A way of notating a document to indicate how text and other elements should be displayed.

NGINX: Web server software that can enable Linux-based systems to serve websites to the Internet. It is the biggest rival of Apache. See also *Apache* and *Linux.*

ORDBMS (Object-Relational Database Management System): ORDBMS is a technology designed to bring together the best of two different database technologies, object-oriented and relational databases. ORDBMS is used in database systems such as Oracle and Microsoft SQL.

platform: The software used to develop your website, such as WordPress or Joomla. It is also sometimes used to describe the setup of the server, although the more normal usage there is "server platform."

protocol: A protocol is an established code of procedure. In computer terms, this means it is a procedure known and understood by multiple devices online to enable those devices to communicate with each other.

RDBMS (Relational Database Management System): An RDBMS is a form of database technology that follows a specific logic known as the relational model. It is used by MySQL, the database technology that is most commonly used wherever websites require a database.

root: The beginning of a file system. File systems (trees) are measured top-down with root being the top level (or highest level). The root is normally signified with a slash (/). See also *tree.*

script: A piece of code containing one file or a number of files, designed to do a specific job. Also called a web app or app, a script can cover anything from a single process to creating an entire website.

SEO (Search Engine Optimization): The process of modifying a web page or site to get optimal results when indexed by a search engine. The objective of SEO is to have your site or page show at or near the top of the search results when a user searches for a specific term or string.

SFTP (Secure File Transfer Protocol): A protocol designed to enable encrypted communication between computers to allow files to be securely exchanged between them. See also *FTP.*

shared server: When a web host places more than one client site on a single server, that server is classified as a shared server because its resources are shared on a first-come, first-served basis to all the sites on it.

site: See *website.*

SOA (Start of Authority) records: Special records that are part of the DNS system and verify that this DNS Zone Record is the authoritative file for a given domain name. See also *DNS* and *DNS Zone Record.*

SQL (Structured Query Language): A way of storing large amounts of data and quickly retrieving, searching, and storing that data.

SSH (Secure SHell): A method of securely accessing a server from a remote location.

SSL (Secure Socket Layer): Provides secured communication for sending data through online forms.

subdirectory: See *subfolder.*

subfolder: Also known as a subdirectory. Any folder located within another. The only folder that is truly not a subfolder is the root (/), but in practice, for ease of explanation, any folder can be called a folder and the folders within it called subfolders. See also *folder* and *root.*

TLD (Top-Level Domain): A Top-Level Domain is what is commonly referred to as the domain extension and is comprised of the characters that come immediately after the period (.) after the domain name in a Fully Qualified Domain Name. Examples include com and org.

TLS (Transport Layer Security): TLS is a form of communication encryption that enables data to be transferred securely between devices online. It is the successor to the *SSL* encryption protocol.

tree: Relationship of the paths between each folder and subfolder on a drive. Each folder (except the root) must have a folder above it which it is a subfolder of. Thus the paths show visually which folder is inside which other folder to form the branches of the tree. See also *folder* and *subfolder.*

TTL (time to live): The amount of time (in seconds) a DNS Zone Record is to be considered valid. After the TTL has expired, the client computer should check again with the DNS record that the zone record is still correct and has not been changed. See also *DNS Zone Record.*

UNIX: An operating system designed to be easily accessible by multiple users simultaneously.

upload: To send files to another computer.

VPS (Virtual Private Server): A step up from a shared server in terms of speed and reliability but a step below a dedicated server. Each VPS is a virtual machine created in a server that is allocated a percentage of the resources of that server. See also *dedicated server* and *shared server.*

web script: See *script.*

website: A website is a series of pages that are contained on a computer connected to the Internet.

WHM (Web Host Manager): A piece of software that is part of the cPanel web hosting control panel installation. It provides back-end services that most users don't see, behind cPanel. See also *cPanel.*

Index

• F •

• I •

• *Y* •

• *Z* •

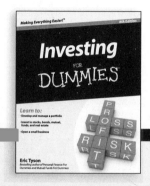
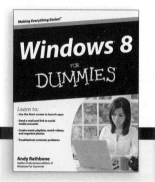

Math & Science

Algebra I For Dummies,
2nd Edition
978-0-470-55964-2

Anatomy and Physiology
For Dummies,
2nd Edition
978-0-470-92326-9

Astronomy For Dummies,
3rd Edition
978-1-118-37697-3

Biology For Dummies,
2nd Edition
978-0-470-59875-7

Chemistry For Dummies,
2nd Edition
978-1-1180-0730-3

Pre-Algebra Essentials
For Dummies
978-0-470-61838-7

Microsoft Office

Excel 2013 For Dummies
978-1-118-51012-4

Office 2013 All-in-One
For Dummies
978-1-118-51636-2

PowerPoint 2013
For Dummies
978-1-118-50253-2

Word 2013 For Dummies
978-1-118-49123-2

Music

Blues Harmonica
For Dummies
978-1-118-25269-7

Guitar For Dummies,
3rd Edition
978-1-118-11554-1

iPod & iTunes
For Dummies,
10th Edition
978-1-118-50864-0

Programming

Android Application
Development For
Dummies, 2nd Edition
978-1-118-38710-8

iOS 6 Application
Development For Dummies
978-1-118-50880-0

Java For Dummies,
5th Edition
978-0-470-37173-2

Religion & Inspiration

The Bible For Dummies
978-0-7645-5296-0

Buddhism For Dummies,
2nd Edition
978-1-118-02379-2

Catholicism For Dummies,
2nd Edition
978-1-118-07778-8

Self-Help & Relationships

Bipolar Disorder
For Dummies,
2nd Edition
978-1-118-33882-7

Meditation For Dummies,
3rd Edition
978-1-118-29144-3

Seniors

Computers For Seniors
For Dummies,
3rd Edition
978-1-118-11553-4

iPad For Seniors
For Dummies,
5th Edition
978-1-118-49708-1

Social Security
For Dummies
978-1-118-20573-0

Smartphones & Tablets

Android Phones
For Dummies
978-1-118-16952-0

Kindle Fire HD
For Dummies
978-1-118-42223-6

NOOK HD For Dummies,
Portable Edition
978-1-118-39498-4

Surface For Dummies
978-1-118-49634-3

Test Prep

ACT For Dummies,
5th Edition
978-1-118-01259-8

ASVAB For Dummies,
3rd Edition
978-0-470-63760-9

GRE For Dummies,
7th Edition
978-0-470-88921-3

Officer Candidate Tests,
For Dummies
978-0-470-59876-4

Physician's Assistant Exam
For Dummies
978-1-118-11556-5

Series 7 Exam
For Dummies
978-0-470-09932-2

Windows 8

Windows 8 For Dummies
978-1-118-13461-0

Windows 8 For Dummies,
Book + DVD Bundle
978-1-118-27167-4

Windows 8 All-in-One
For Dummies
978-1-118-11920-4

Available in print and e-book formats.

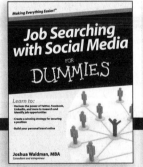

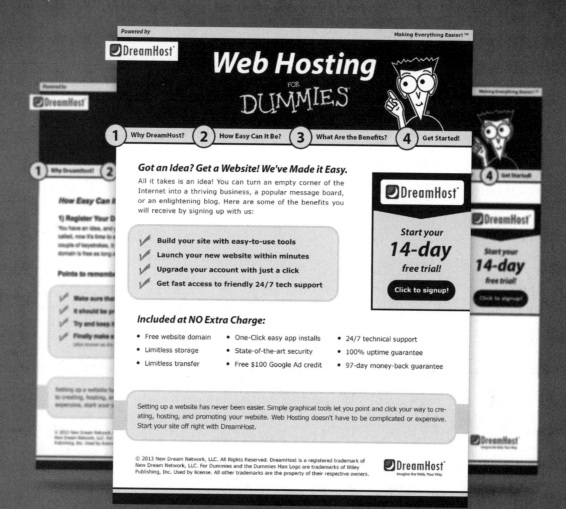